Third Edition

Leading and Managing People in Education

Tony Bush and David Middlewood

Los Angeles | London | New Delhi
Singapore | Washington DC

Los Angeles | London | New Delhi
Singapore | Washington DC

SAGE Publications Ltd
1 Oliver's Yard
55 City Road
London EC1Y 1SP

SAGE Publications Inc.
2455 Teller Road
Thousand Oaks, California 91320

SAGE Publications India Pvt Ltd
B 1/I 1 Mohan Cooperative Industrial Area
Mathura Road
New Delhi 110 044

SAGE Publications Asia-Pacific Pte Ltd
3 Church Street
#10-04 Samsung Hub
Singapore 049483

Editor: Marianne Lagrange
Assistant editor: Kathryn Bromwich
Project manager: Bill Antrobus
Production editor: Nicola Marshall
Copyeditor: Phebe Kynaston
Proofreader: Caroline Stock
Marketing manager: Lorna Patkai
Cover design: Wendy Scott
Typeset by Kestrel Data, Exeter, Devon
Printed in Great Britain by:
CPI Group (UK) Ltd, Croydon, CR0 4YY

© Tony Bush and David Middlewood, 2013

First published in 1997; second edition published in 2005,
and reprinted in 2006, 2010, 2011
Third edition published 2013

Library of Congress Control Number: 2012949776

British Library Cataloguing in Publication data

A catalogue record for this book is available from
the British Library

ISBN 978-1-4462-5651-0
ISBN 978-1-4462-5652-7 (pbk)

Contents

List of tables and figures

Preface

This is the third edition of this highly successful book. Since it was first published in 1997, there have been many changes in education and, specifically, in the leadership and management of people. These changes include new research and literature, and developments in policy and practice in many countries. This new volume gives much more attention to international research and practice, as educational leadership has become a field of global significance since the second edition was published in 2005.

People are the most important resource in any organisation. They provide the knowledge, skill and energy which are essential ingredients of success. Even given the contemporary importance of information and communications technology, what differentiates effective and less effective organisations is the quality and commitment of the people employed there. In countries where even basic resources are barely adequate, the opportunities for an effective education may depend even more upon the attitude and commitment of the people in them.

Education provides a unique leadership and management challenge because it is geared to the development of human potential. Schools and colleges should be 'people centred' because children and young people are at the heart of their 'business'. Just as good teachers value the children and students for whom they are responsible, so institutional leaders should value all staff who work in the school or college. Consideration for adults is just as important as care for children if schools are to be genuine learning organisations.

Like the previous edition, this book comprises chapters prepared specifically for this volume and thus includes the most recent research and literature on each theme.

The first part of the book, 'Setting the Scene', comprises three overview chapters. The opening chapter, 'The context for leadership and management', defines educational leadership and management and distinguishes between these twin concepts. It examines the international trend towards decentralisation in education and notes that this has considerable implications for the leadership and management of people. The chapter assesses the impact of globalisation and the paradoxical parallel emphasis on culture and context. It concludes with a brief discussion of leadership development in education.

In Chapter 2, 'Models of educational leadership', we examine the main approaches to educational leadership, and consider the strengths and limitations of the various models discussed and advocated in the literature. The chapter assesses the significance of instructional leadership, which focuses on the main purpose of schools and colleges, and presents an overview of the other main leadership models.

Chapter 3 considers the way in which staff in schools and colleges who are not teachers or lecturers have come to be considered a crucial and integral part of ensuring effectiveness in learning, whatever their individual roles. This is particularly true in certain countries, and this chapter examines this development and its impact on the organisations and the other people who work in them.

Part II, 'Key Concepts', examines some of the main factors influencing the leadership and management of people. Chapter 4, 'Organisational cultures', explains the contemporary interest in culture and its significance for educational leaders and managers. It distinguishes between national, or societal, culture, which provides a context for school leaders, and organisational culture, which may be susceptible to change. A case study of South African schools illustrates the difficulty of re-establishing a culture of teaching and learning following systemic trauma and the chapter concludes by stressing the importance of attitudinal change to educational success.

In Chapter 5, 'Organisational structures and roles', the focus is on the framework for educational leadership and management. The chapter examines the nature and purpose of structure, links it to the concept of hierarchy and assesses the various ways in which organisational theory portrays structure. The chapter also addresses role theory and its applicability to school and college leadership. A central issue is the extent to which people simply take on roles prescribed by managers or use their specific talents and experience to design and develop their own approach. The chapter concludes by examining the links between structure and roles, and by stressing the need for flexibility in interpreting both concepts.

Chapter 6 focuses on 'Leading and managing for diversity'. Issues of diversity and inclusion permeate all chapters of this book, sometimes implicitly. This chapter traces the development in education – and society generally – from a focus on equal opportunities to a focus on the way in which the values underpinning diversity and inclusion are central to effective leadership and management.

In Chapter 7, 'Motivation and job satisfaction', the need for leaders and managers to enable all employees to find fulfilment in their work is examined and discussed. The recognition of the individuality of personal motivation is made clear and how this is affected by key factors which the leaders can influence.

Chapter 8, 'Leading and managing through teams', explains the rationale for team work and considers the composition of leadership and management teams in several countries. It notes how teamwork can be developed and examines the notion of team learning within a learning organisation. It gives case examples of teamwork in New Zealand, South Africa and England and notes that, despite the pervasive nature of teams, they do have limitations when applied to education, not least because teaching tends to be a solitary activity.

The final part, 'Key Processes', addresses five central aspects of the leadership and management of people in education. Chapter 9 deals with the essential starting point, 'Recruitment and selection'. This is an under-researched area in education but much practice in business, for example, has been adapted for schools and colleges. The recognition of fallibility and subjectivity in selectors needs to be acknowledged but the attempt to make the process as objective as possible remains important for leaders for both moral and legal reasons. As the nature of staffing in education is undergoing change in many countries, the need for effective recruitment and selection processes becomes even more important.

Chapter 10, 'Induction and retention', focuses on the stage following appointment, that of staff induction, and on an increasingly important issue for school and college leaders, that of retention. An effective start to an individual's employment is shown to increase the chances of that person remaining longer in the organisation. The chapter stresses that induction is a process not a programme and that socialisation is a key element. In a climate of enhanced staff mobility in some countries, the need to retain part-time and temporary colleagues, as well as those considering retirement, is equally important, and the chapter also examines how best to support such staff.

In Chapter 11, 'Mentoring and coaching', the focus is on these important processes for supporting and developing staff. It begins by defining these terms and distinguishing between them. It examines mentoring practice in Hong Kong, Singapore, England, South Africa and the USA. The chapter notes the benefits of mentoring, for mentors and the educational system as well as mentees, and it concludes by proposing a model for effective mentoring.

'Leading and managing for performance' is the focus of Chapter 12, which includes a discussion of the ways in which performance can be appraised. Two dimensions of performance management, professional development and accountability, are explored and schemes which reconcile the two are described. The chapter considers different schemes to manage performance in various countries, for example performance related pay, but concludes that the main factor in successful schemes continues to be the relationship between the appraisees and their leaders and managers, and that mutual trust remains the crucial component of this relationship.

Chapter 13, 'Organisational learning and professional development', examines the ways in which schools and colleges focus on their core purpose, learning, through becoming learning organisations. In such contexts, staff as well as students are regarded as learners and the chapter considers how organisational learning can be integrated into leaders' plans for the development of learning. The chapter concludes by stressing the need for training for all staff and by encouraging positive attitudes to learning for everyone. The leader's task includes being a role model, by prioritising personal learning.

The final chapter, 'Succession planning and leadership development', considers a topic of great contemporary significance: how to ensure a steady supply of high quality leaders at a time when demographic changes and concerns about the pressures of senior leadership, are leading to shortages in several countries. The chapter also examines ways in which leaders are prepared to be principals, an essential part of a succession planning strategy.

The authors wish to thank Chabala Bush for producing the index for this book, and both Cha and Jacqui Middlewood for their support and understanding.

Tony Bush and David Middlewood
University of Warwick

About the Authors

Tony Bush is Professor of Educational Leadership at the University of Warwick, UK, and previously held similar posts at the universities of Leicester, Reading and Lincoln. He is also visiting professor of education at the University of the Witwatersrand, Johannesburg, South Africa. He has written or edited 33 books, including the fourth edition of *Theories of Educational Leadership and Management* (Sage 2011). His recent research includes directing the evaluation of the National College for School Leadership's (NCSL's) succession planning programme and leading the NCSL-funded research on high performing leadership teams. He is Vice-President of the British Educational Leadership, Management and Administration Society (BELMAS) and editor of the Society's leading ISI-listed international journal, *Educational Management, Administration and Leadership (EMAL)*.

David Middlewood is a Research Fellow in the Institute of Education at the University of Warwick, UK, having previously been Deputy Director of the Centre for Educational Leadership and Management at the University of Leicester and then a Research Associate for the University of Lincoln. Prior to working in higher education, David taught in schools in England for more than 20 years, culminating in his being head of a secondary comprehensive school for nine years. He was editor of two practitioner journals for school leaders from 1999 to 2005. David has taught and researched in various countries and been a visiting professor in New Zealand and South Africa. David's research has included projects on support staff, diversity in further education, new school leaders, effective leadership teams and school improvement strategies.

Part I

Setting the Scene

1

The context for leadership and management

Introduction

The first edition of this volume, published in 1997, was titled *Managing People in Education*. The addition of 'leading' to the title in the second and third editions illustrates the growing significance of this concept, notably in England, where a National College for School *Leadership* (our emphasis) was opened in November 2000. The inclusion of both terms in the title of this third edition signals the authors' recognition of this trend but also their view that effective 'management' is just as important as visionary leadership if educational organisations are to be successful. Bush (2008, p. 276) asks whether the shift from leadership to management is purely semantic, or whether it represents a genuine change in the ways in which schools and colleges are organised?

Gunter (2004) shows that the labels used to define this field have changed from 'educational administration' to 'educational management' and, more recently, to 'educational leadership'. Bolam (1999, p. 194) defines educational management as 'an executive function for carrying out agreed policy'. He differentiates management from educational leadership which has 'at its core the responsibility for policy formulation and, where appropriate, organisational transformation' (p. 194). Bush (2011) argues that educational management should be centrally concerned with the purpose or aims of education. These purposes or goals provide the crucial sense of direction which should underpin the management of educational institutions. Management is directed at the achievement of certain educational objectives. Unless this link between purpose and management is clear and close, there is a danger of 'managerialism', 'a stress on procedures at the expense of educational purpose and values' (Bush 1999, p. 240). The emphasis is on managerial efficiency rather than the aims and purposes of education (Gunter 1997). This appears to have been the case in further education in both England (Elliott and Crossley 1997) and Scotland (McTavish 2003). The latter refers to the 'dominance' of business managerialism and points to the prioritisation of managerial rather than educational concerns at one of his case study colleges in Glasgow. (See Chapter Two for an extended discussion of managerialism.)

There are many conceptualisations of leadership and Yukl (2002, pp. 4–5) argues that 'the definition of leadership is arbitrary and very subjective. Some definitions are more useful than others, but there is no "correct" definition'. Three dimensions of leadership may be identified as a basis for developing a working definition:

1   Leadership involves a process of influence 'exerted by one person (or group) over other people (or groups) to structure the activities and relationships in a group or organisation' (Yukl 2002, p. 3). Yukl's use of 'person' or 'group' serves to emphasise that leadership may be exercised by teams as well as individuals. Influence is independent of formal authority, vested in positional leaders such as principals, and is intended to lead to certain outcomes or purposes.

2   Leadership is often grounded in firm personal and professional values. Day, Harris and Hadfield's (2001) research in 12 'effective' schools concluded that good leaders are informed by personal and educational values. However, Bush (2008, p. 277) argues that the dominant values are those of government and that they are imposed on school leaders. Teachers and leaders are more likely to be enthusiastic about change when they 'own' it rather than having it imposed on them. Hargreaves (2004), drawing on research in Canadian schools, notes that teachers report largely positive emotional experiences of self-initiated change, but predominantly negative ones concerning mandated change.

3   Leadership involves developing and articulating a vision for the organisation. The vision needs to be specific to the school or college, and be embedded in the organisation, if leadership is to be successful. However, Bottery (1998) and Bush (2011) are among the

authors who question whether it is possible for leaders to develop school-focused visions within a centralised policy framework supported by a national inspection regime. Hoyle and Wallace (2005, p. 11) are critical of visionary rhetoric; 'any vision you like as long as it's central government's'.

Cuban (1988) provides one of the clearest distinctions between leadership and management. He links leadership with change while management is seen as a maintenance activity. He also stresses the importance of both dimensions of organisational activity. 'I prize both managing and leading and attach no special value to either since different settings and times call for varied responses'. Day et al. (2001) add that management is linked to systems and 'paper', while leadership is about the development of people, an important emphasis, given the focus of this volume.

Leadership and management need to be given equal prominence if schools and colleges are to operate effectively and achieve their objectives. While a clear vision is essential to establish the nature and direction of change, it is equally important to ensure that innovations are implemented efficiently and that the school's residual functions are carried out effectively while certain elements are undergoing change. Hallinger (2003) argues that a leadership perspective on the role of the principal does not diminish the principal's managerial roles. In any case, the differences cannot easily be observed in the day-to-day practices of leaders (Leithwood 1994). Briggs's (2003, p. 434) study of middle managers in English further education colleges suggests that these two dimensions have a symbiotic relationship and need to be kept in balance.

Decentralisation and self-management

Educational institutions operate within a legislative framework set down by national, provincial or state parliaments. One of the key aspects of such a framework is the degree of decentralisation in the educational system. Highly centralised systems tend to be bureaucratic and to allow little discretion to schools and local communities. Decentralised systems devolve significant powers to subordinate levels. Where such powers are devolved to the institutional level, there is 'self-management'.

Lauglo (1997, p. 3) links centralisation to bureaucracy. 'Bureaucratic centralism implies concentrating in a central ('top') authority decision-making on a wide range of matters, leaving only tightly programmed routine implementation to lower levels in the organisation'. Such centralised controls often include curricula, books and teaching materials, staff recruitment and appointments, budgets, and management of real resources such as staff, buildings and equipment.

Leaders operating in such controlled systems experience particular problems in developing a distinctive vision for their schools and in responding effectively to school needs. When heads and principals are reduced to implementing directives from national, provincial or local government, they lack the scope to articulate school goals. They also cannot lead and manage staff effectively because all the major decisions about staff appointments, promotions and development are made by government officials. This approach is evident in China (Bush et al. 1998), the largest educational system in the world, and also in the Seychelles, one of the smallest (Bush et al. 2008). It is also evident in Greece, where principals are unable to function effectively as instructional leaders (Kaparou 2013).

Decentralisation involves a process of reducing the role of central government in planning and providing education. It can take many different forms, several of which simply devolve power to lower levels in the bureaucracy. Self-management occurs where decentralisation is to the institutional level, as Caldwell and Spinks (1992, p. 4) suggest: 'A self-managing school is a school in a system of education where there has been significant and consistent *decentralisation* to the school level of authority to make decisions related to the allocation of resources'.

Self-managing schools and colleges may be regarded as potentially more efficient and effective but much depends on the nature and quality of internal management if these potential benefits are to be realised. Caldwell (2008, p. 249) argues that 'those at the school level are best placed to determine the particular mix of all the resources available to achieve optimal outcomes'. This view has led governments in many countries, including Australia, England, Hong Kong, New Zealand and South Africa, to locate enhanced powers with school governing boards and principals. Certainly, the scope for leading and managing staff effectively is much greater when the major educational decisions are located within schools and colleges, and not reserved for action outside the school.

Culture and context

Many of the major themes of educational leadership and management have global significance. Notions of bureaucracy, autonomy and control, accountability and quality, for example, are evident in many different countries. However, it is vital to be aware of the powerful differences between countries and not to overestimate their similarities. Some of the problems may be the same but their solutions often depend more on local circumstances than on importing ready-made answers from very different contexts. 'It is easy to become over-impressed by apparent similarities between "reforms" in various countries and to neglect deep differences at the level of implementation and practice' (Glatter 2002, p. 225).

Some of the differences between educational systems can be attributed to economics. Many developing countries do not have the resources to ensure universal education, even at primary level, or to provide buildings, equipment or staffing of the quality which is taken for granted in the developed world. These countries are caught in a vicious circle. They lack the resources to develop all their children to their full potential. This contributes to a continuing economic weakness because they do not have the skills to compete effectively with fully developed economies. As a result, the tax base is too weak to fund a really effective educational system (Bell and Bush 2002).

Although the economic issues should not be underestimated, the main differences between countries may be cultural. Dimmock and Walker (2002) explain and compare organisational and societal culture:

> Societal cultures differ mostly at the level of basic values, while organisational cultures differ mostly at the level of more superficial practices, as reflected in the recognition of particular symbols, heroes, and rituals. This allows organisational cultures to be deliberately managed and changed, whereas societal or national cultures are more enduring and change only gradually over longer time periods. (p. 71)

Cultural differences play an important part in explaining the varied approaches to apparently similar issues in many different countries. One example relates to attitudes to bureaucracy. As we noted earlier, it is the preferred approach to management in many countries, including very large and complex systems, for example in China, and smaller states such as the Seychelles. It is also the dominant model in South America (Newland 1995). In some Western countries, however, it is associated with inefficiency and excessive centralisation. The differences may be explained by alternative perspectives on the nature of authority with those favouring bureaucracy more willing to defer to those holding positional power than people who feel constrained by it (Bell and Bush 2002).

Differences within countries

It is also unwise to assume that educational problems are the same *within* countries let alone between them. In developing countries, there are often considerable differences between urban and rural schools (Bush et al. 1998; Bush et al. 2010). In both developed and developing nations, socio-economic variables inevitably influence the educational context. South Africa, for example, is still coming to terms with the institutionalised differences in its schools arising from the apartheid era. Comparing the best schools in the major cities with those in remote rural areas provides as sharp a contrast as the differences between developed and developing countries (Bush 2007).

There are also significant differences among schools within developed nations. Harris (2002) reports on the particular issues faced by the leaders of schools in challenging circumstances in England. She paints a picture of schools with multiple indicators of difficulty:

- low levels of achievement in public examinations

- high proportions of children eligible for free school meals

- categorised as requiring 'special measures' or having 'serious weaknesses' by the Office for Standards in Education (Ofsted)

- located in urban areas with low socio-economic status.

She conducted research with ten such schools that were showing evidence of school improvement. Her findings provide valuable evidence about the nature of successful leadership in such schools. The main features of such leadership were:

- 'an alignment to a shared set of values' (Harris 2002, p. 18) and a vision, built around these core values, that was communicated to staff and students

- distributing leadership: a shift from autocratic styles of leadership to a greater focus on teams and distributed leadership as the schools improved

- investing in staff development as a means of maintaining staff morale and motivation as well as improving their capability

- the heads 'placing an emphasis on *people not systems* and inviting others to lead' (p. 22) (present authors' emphasis)

- the heads emphasising the need to establish the interconnectedness of home, school and community, and being aware that forces within the community impeded learning.

Harris (2002: 24) concludes that these successful leaders displayed people-centred qualities and skills: 'The context in which people work and learn together is where they construct and refine meaning leading to a shared purpose or set of goals.'

These dimensions of successful leadership could arguably be applied to schools in any situation. The distinguishing feature is the recognition that leaders' approaches have to be tailored to the specific needs of the school and the context in which it operates. A 'one size fits all' approach is unlikely to be effective, as we argue in Chapter 2.

Leading and managing people

There is ample evidence that high-quality leadership is vital in achieving successful schools and colleges. The Commonwealth Secretariat (1996), for example, states that 'the head . . . plays the most crucial role in ensuring school effectiveness'. Leithwood et al.'s (2006) study of successful school leadership reinforces previous research which stresses that leaders improve teaching and learning *indirectly*. This means developing and sustaining good relationships with teachers, who work *directly* with students. Effective processes are required to enhance classroom practice but they must be supported by an approach which recognises, values and celebrates the achievements of staff and students. This book examines many of these core processes.

There is convincing evidence that successful leaders focus most strongly on motivating and developing people rather than establishing and maintaining systems and structures. The latter is important but should always be a second-order priority. In education, as in many other settings, people are most likely to show commitment if they are valued by those who have responsibility for them. This applies to teachers just as much as to the children and students. It also applies to the many support staff who work in schools and colleges. An inclusive approach, involving all categories of staff, is most likely to produce the teamwork which is also a feature of successful organisations (Bush and Glover 2012).

Conclusion: developing people

There is considerable international interest in teacher and leadership development, evidenced, for example, in the opening of the English NCSL. Bush and Jackson's (2002) review of provision in seven developed countries shows that there are diverse approaches to leadership development but policy-makers in all these systems recognise its vital importance. Such major initiatives suggest that this is a national policy issue in many countries (see Chapter 14), but the purpose of this section is to argue that principals and headteachers also have a role in teacher and leadership development.

The increasing range and complexity of leadership and management responsibilities in schools and colleges means that it is no longer possible, if it ever was, for the principal to be the sole leader. Deputy and assistant heads, and middle-level leaders such as heads of department or subject leaders, are increasingly important for effective management in schools (Woods et al. 2004) and colleges (Briggs 2003). This emphasis requires specific and sustained attention to leadership and management development as a central part of the wider staff development agenda.

Developing middle and senior managers has two main advantages. First, it increases the likelihood that they will perform effectively in their present role. Secondly, it provides a cadre of trained people for advancement to more senior posts as they become available. It is a mode of succession planning, a 'grow your own' model of securing a successful future for the school or college (see Chapter 14).

The development of future leaders may take several forms but it is underpinned by an approach which is 'people' orientated. It begins with the needs of the individual and might involve a formal staff development or appraisal process. It should provide a means of meeting the aspirations of the person while also anticipating the needs of the institution. When it works well, the requirements of the individual and the organisation are harmonised to promote learning for all who work or study in the school or college.

References

Bell, L. and Bush, T. (2002) 'The policy context', in Bush, T. and Bell, L. (eds), *The Principles and Practice of Educational Management*, London, Paul Chapman Publishing.

Bolam, R. (1999) 'Educational administration, leadership and management: towards a research agenda', in Bush, T., Bell, L., Bolam, R., Glatter, R. and Ribbins, P. (eds), *Educational Management: Redefining Theory, Policy and Practice*, London, Paul Chapman Publishing.

Bottery, M. (1998) *Professionals and Policy*, London, Cassell.

Briggs, A. (2003) 'Finding the balance: exploring the organic and mechanical dimensions of middle manager roles in English further education colleges', *Educational Management and Administration*, 31 (4), 421–436.

Bush, T. (1999) 'Crisis or crossroads? The discipline of educational management in the late 1990s', *Educational Management and Administration*, 27 (3), 239–252.

Bush, T. (2007) 'Educational leadership and management: theory, policy and practice', *South African Journal of Education*, 27 (3), 391–406.

Bush, T. (2008) 'From management to leadership: semantic or meaningful change', *Educational Management, Administration and Leadership*, 36 (2), 271–288.

Bush, T. (2011) *Theories of Educational Leadership and Management, Fourth Edition*, London, Sage.

Bush, T. and Jackson, D. (2002) 'Preparation for school leadership: international perspectives', *Educational Management and Administration*, 30 (4), 417–429.

Bush, T. and Glover, D. (2012) 'Distributed leadership in action: Leading high-performing leadership teams in English schools', *School Leadership and Management*, 32 (1), 21–36.

Bush, T., Coleman, M. and Si, X. (1998) 'Managing secondary schools in China', *Compare*, 33 (2), 127–138.

Bush, T., Purvis, M.-T. and Barallon, L. (2008) 'Leadership development in small-island states', in Lumby, J., Crow, G. and Pashiardis, P. (eds), *International Handbook on the Preparation and Development of Leaders*, New York, Routledge.

Bush, T., Joubert, R., Kiggundu, E. and Van Rooyen, J. (2010) 'Managing teaching and learning in South African schools', *International Journal of Educational Development*, 30 (2), 162–168.

Caldwell, B. (2008) 'Reconceptualising the self-managing school', *Educational Management, Administration and Leadership*, 36 (2), 235–252.

Caldwell, B. and Spinks, J. (1992) *Leading the Self-Managing School*, London, Falmer Press.

Commonwealth Secretariat (1996) *Better Schools: Resource Materials for Heads: Introductory Module*, London, Commonwealth Secretariat.

Cuban, L. (1988) *The Managerial Imperative and the Practice of Leadership in Schools*, Albany, NY, State University of New York Press.

Day, C., Harris, A. and Hadfield, M. (2001) 'Challenging the orthodoxy of effective school leadership', *International Journal of Leadership in Education*, 4 (1), 39–56.

Dimmock, C. and Walker, A. (2002) 'School leadership in context – societal and organisational cultures', in Bush, T. and Bell, L. (eds), *The Principles and Practice of Educational Management*, London, Paul Chapman Publishing.

Elliott, G. and Crossley, M. (1997) 'Contested values in further education: findings from a case study of the management of change', *Educational Management and Administration*, 27 (3), 253–266.

Glatter, R. (2002) 'Governance, autonomy and accountability in education', in Bush, T. and Bell, L. (eds), *The Principles and Practice of Educational Management*, London, Paul Chapman Publishing.

Gunter, H. (1997) *Rethinking Education: The Consequences of Jurassic Management*, London, Cassell.

Gunter, H. (2004) 'Labels and labelling in the field of educational leadership', *Discourse – Studies in the Cultural Politics of Education*, 25 (1), 21–41.

Hallinger, P. (2003) *Reshaping the Landscape of School Leadership: A Global Perspective*, Lisse, Swets and Zeitlinger.

Hargreaves, A. (2004) 'Inclusive and exclusive educational change: emotional responses of teachers and implications for leadership', *School Leadership and Management*, 24 (3), 287–306.

Harris, A. (2002) 'Effective leadership in schools facing challenging circumstances', *School Leadership and Management*, 22 (1), 15–26.

Hoyle, E. and Wallace, M. (2005) *Educational Leadership: Ambiguity, Professionals and Managerialism*, London, Sage.

Kaparou, M. (2013) 'Instructional leadership in England and Greece: a cross-country comparative approach', unpublished Ph.D thesis, Coventry, University of Warwick.

Lauglo, J. (1997) 'Assessing the present importance of different forms of decentralisation in education', in Watson, K., Modgil, C. and Modgil, S. (eds), *Power and Responsibility in Education*, London, Cassell.

Leithwood, K. (1994) 'Leadership for school restructuring', *Educational Administration Quarterly*, 30 (4), 498–518.

Leithwood, K., Day, C., Sammons, P., Harris, A. and Hopkins, D. (2006) *Seven Strong Claims about Successful School Leadership*, London, DfES.

McTavish, D. (2003) 'Aspects of public sector management: a case study of further education ten years from the passage of the Further and Higher Education Act', *Educational Management and Administration*, 31 (2), 175–187.

Newland, C. (1995) 'Spanish American elementary education 1950–1992: bureaucracy, growth and decentralisation', *International Journal of Educational Development*, 15 (2), 103–114.

Woods, P., Bennett, N., Harvey, J. and Wise, C. (2004) 'Variabilities and dualities in distributed leadership: findings from a systematic literature review', *Educational Management, Administration and Leadership*, 32 (4), 439–457.

Yukl, G.A. (2002) *Leadership in Organizations, Fifth Edition*, Upper Saddle River, NJ, Prentice-Hall.

2

Models of educational leadership

Introduction

In Chapter 1, we examined the context for educational leadership and management. We also noted the widespread belief that effective leadership is fundamental to successful schools and education systems. While there is an emerging consensus about the main constituents of leadership, there is much less clarity about which behaviours are most likely to produce the most favourable outcomes. Awareness of alternative approaches to leadership is essential in order to inform the design and development of programmes for aspiring and practising leaders. This chapter provides an overview of the main models of educational leadership (Bush and Glover 2002; Bush 2011).

The implementation of the Education Reform Act (1988) and subsequent legislation in England and Wales, and similar moves towards self-management in many other countries, have led to an enhanced emphasis on the *practice* of educational leadership and management (Huber 2004). Heads and principals are inundated with advice and exhortations from politicians, officials, academics and consultants about how to lead and manage their schools and colleges. Many of these prescriptions are atheoretical in the sense that they are not underpinned by explicit values or concepts (Bush 2011).

There is no single all-embracing theory of educational leadership. In part this reflects the astonishing diversity of educational institutions, ranging from small rural primary schools to very large universities and colleges, and across widely different international contexts. It relates also to the varied nature of the problems encountered in schools and colleges, which require different approaches and solutions. Above all, it reflects the multifaceted nature of theory in educational leadership and management. As a result, several perspectives may be valid simultaneously (Bush 2011).

The models discussed in this chapter should be regarded as alternative ways of portraying events. The existence of several different perspectives creates what Bolman and Deal (1997, p. 11) describe as 'conceptual pluralism: a jangling discord of multiple voices'. Each theory has something to offer in explaining behaviour and events in educational institutions. The perspectives favoured by managers, explicitly or implicitly, inevitably influence or determine decision-making. Government bodies also influence, or may determine, which models can be used in leading and managing schools and colleges. Hoyle and Wallace (2005, p. 9) argue that 'policies embodied in the educational reform movement of the past two decades have brooked little compromise, relying on the excessive resort to leadership and management, that we will term "managerialism", to ensure implementation'.

The various theories of educational leadership reflect very different ways of understanding and interpreting events and behaviour in schools and colleges. They also represent what are often ideologically based, and certainly divergent, views about how educational institutions ought to be managed. Waite (2002, p. 66) refers to 'paradigm wars' in describing disagreements between academics holding different positions on theory and research in educational administration. The models discussed in this chapter are broad compilations of the main theories of educational leadership and are based on a systematic review of the literature and research (Bush and Glover 2002; Bush 2011).

Classifying models of educational leadership

Bush (2011) has presented and classified theories of educational leadership and management for over 25 years (see also Bush and Glover 2002). The vast literature on leadership has generated a number of alternative, and competing, models. Some writers have sought to cluster these various conceptions into a number of broad themes or 'types'. The best known of these typologies is that by Leithwood et al. (1999), who identified six 'models' from their scrutiny of 121 articles in four international journals. Bush and Glover (2002) extended this typology to eight models. These are among the ten leadership models shown in Table 2.1.

Table 2.1 Typology of leadership models (adapted from Bush 2011)

Leadership model	Main features
Instructional	Focuses on the leadership of teaching and learning
Managerial	Focuses on task completion within a hierarchical framework
Transactional	Focuses on exchange transactions between leaders and teachers
Transformational	Focuses on securing the commitment of teachers to the goals of the organisation's leaders
Participative	Focuses on leadership being shared with teachers and stakeholders
Distributed	Focuses on leadership being independent of formal roles
Moral	Focuses on the values and beliefs of leaders
Emotional	Focuses on individual motivation, and interpretation of events
Postmodern	Focuses on subjective interpretation of events
Contingent	Assumes that leadership approaches are contingent on the context and the nature of events

The rest of this chapter will examine these models and assess their significance for leadership practice in a wide range of educational contexts. It should be noted that these are not the only types of leadership discussed in the literature (see, for example, Davies 2004) but the authors believe that the ten leadership models featured in Table 2.1 are the most significant.

Instructional leadership

Instructional leadership differs from the other models reviewed in this chapter because it focuses on the direction of influence, rather than its nature and source. The increasing emphasis on managing teaching and learning as the core activities of educational institutions has led to this approach being emphasised and endorsed, notably by the English NCSL (2001) which included it as one of its ten leadership propositions.

Leithwood et al. (1999) point to the lack of explicit descriptions of instructional leadership in the literature and suggest that there may be different meanings of this concept. Hallinger and Lee (2014) claim that the principal's instructional leadership 'is essential for the improvement of teaching and learning in schools' but adds that 'the practice of instructional leadership remains both poorly understood and outside the main job description of the principal'.

Southworth (2002, p. 79) says that 'instructional leadership . . . is strongly concerned with teaching and learning, including the professional learning of teachers as well as student growth'. Bush and Glover's definition stresses the direction of the influence process:

> Instructional leadership focuses on teaching and learning and on the behaviour of teachers in working with students. Leaders' influence is targeted at student learning via teachers. The emphasis is on the direction and impact of influence rather than the influence process itself. (2002, p. 10)

Southworth's (2002) qualitative research with primary heads of small schools in England and Wales shows that three strategies were particularly effective in improving teaching and learning:

- modelling
- monitoring
- professional dialogue and discussion.

Southworth (2002) also concurs with Hill (2001) that 'school leaders may lack sufficient knowledge of teaching and learning to provide adequate, let alone successful, instructional leadership' (p. 87). Similarly, Hallinger and Lee (2014) comment that 'the expectation for principals to act as instructional leaders represents a major change from traditional practice' in many countries. In Thailand, for example, 'principals have been viewed as line managers within the hierarchy of a highly centralized national system of education' rather than as innovators or instructional leaders (ibid.).

Despite these comments, instructional leadership is a very important dimension because it targets the school's central activities, teaching and learning. Indeed, Hallinger (2009, p. 1) claims that 'instructional leadership has recently been reincarnated as a global phenomenon in the form of "leadership for learning"', a more distributed approach, which suggests that many leaders may be involved in leading learning.

Instructional leadership is significant because it targets the main purpose of educational organisations. It may also be undergoing a renaissance in England (NCSL 2001) and globally (Hallinger 2009). However, it may be perceived as narrow because it underestimates other aspects of school life, such as socialisation, student health and welfare, and self-esteem (Bush 2011, p. 18).

Managerial leadership

Leithwood et al.'s definition below shows that managerial leadership is essentially 'top down', with authority closely aligned to the formal roles of leaders:

> Managerial leadership assumes that the focus of leaders ought to be on functions, tasks and behaviours and that if these functions are carried out competently the work of others in the organisation will be facilitated . . . Authority and influence are allocated to formal positions in proportion to the status of those positions in the organisational hierarchy. (1999, p. 14)

School and college principals have power and authority as a direct result of their senior positions, regardless of their personal qualities. This 'positional power' is reinforced by the hierarchy within and beyond schools.

Dressler's (2001, p. 175) review of leadership in Charter schools in the USA shows the significance of managerial leadership: 'Traditionally, the principal's role has been clearly focused on management responsibilities'.

It is significant to note that this type of leadership does not include the concept of vision, which is central to most leadership models. Managerial leadership is focused on managing existing activities successfully rather than visioning a better future for the school. This approach is very suitable for school leaders working in centralised systems as it prioritises the efficient implementation of external imperatives, notably those prescribed by higher levels in the hierarchy.

Bureaucracy, and by implication managerial leadership, is the preferred model for many education systems, including the Czech Republic (Svecova 2000), China (Bush et al. 1998), Greece (Kaparou 2013), Israel (Gaziel 2003), Poland (Klus-Stanska and Olek 1998), the Seychelles (Purvis 2007), South Africa (Bush 2007), Slovenia (Becaj 1994) and much of South America (Newland 1995).

Managerial leadership has certain advantages, notably for bureaucratic systems, but there are difficulties in applying it too enthusiastically to schools and colleges because of the professional role of teachers. If teachers do not 'own' innovations but are simply required to implement externally imposed changes, they are likely to do so without enthusiasm, leading to possible failure (Bush 2011, p. 50).

Managerialism

The shift in the language of school organisation to favour 'leadership' at the expense of 'management' is partly semantic (Bush 2008) but also reflects anxiety about the dangers of value-free management, focusing on efficiency for its own sake, what Hoyle and Wallace (2005, p. 68) describe as 'management to excess':

> Effective leadership and management 'take the strain' by creating structures and processes which allow teachers to engage as fully as possible in their key task. Managerialism, on the other hand, is leadership and management to excess. It transcends the support role of leadership and, in its extreme manifestation, becomes an end in itself.

Managerial leadership is the model which provides the greatest risk of a managerialist approach to school organisation. By focusing on functions, tasks and behaviours, there is the possibility that the aims of education will be subordinated to the managerial aim of greater efficiency. Simkins (2005, pp. 13–14) claims that managerialist values are being set against traditional professional values. He refers to 'an impoverished concept of purpose' within education that values measurable outcomes over those that are more elusive but more valuable. He also criticises the imposition of models of leadership and management that emphasise individual accountability, rigid planning and target-setting as the prime means of organisational control. He expresses concern about the authority and autonomy of professionals being replaced by the power of managers to establish agendas and determine modes of work.

Evidence of a managerialist approach to education may be found in English and Scottish further education (Lumby 2003; McTavish 2003), in universities (Allen 2003; Brehony and Deem 2005) and in schools (Hoyle and Wallace 2007; Rutherford 2006). Goldspink (2007, p. 29) aligns managerialism with 'New Public Management' and adds that 'tight linkage between teachers, schools and the centre is seen as both desirable and achievable'. Managerial leadership is an essential component of successful schools and colleges but it should complement, not supplant, values-based approaches. Effective management is essential but value-free managerialism is inappropriate and damaging.

Transactional leadership

Miller and Miller (2001, p. 182) define transactional leadership as 'leadership in which relationships with teachers are based upon an exchange for some valued resource. To the teacher, interaction between administrators and teachers is usually episodic, short-lived and limited to the exchange transaction'. Exchange is an established political strategy for members of organisations. Heads and principals possess authority arising from their positions as the formal leaders of their institutions. They also hold power in the form of key rewards such as promotion and references. However, the head requires the co-operation of staff to secure the effective management of the school. An exchange may secure benefits for both parties to the arrangement.

Judge and Piccolo (2004, p. 755) say that there are three dimensions of transactional leadership:

- *contingent reward*: the degree to which the leader sets up constructive engagement with followers

- *management by exception – active*: active leaders monitor follower behaviour, anticipate problems, and take corrective actions

- *management by exception – passive*: passive leaders wait until the behaviour has caused problems before taking action.

The major limitation of transactional leadership is that it does not engage staff beyond the immediate gains arising from the exchange. It does not produce long-term commitment to the values and vision being promoted by school leaders.

Transformational leadership

Leithwood et al. argue that transformational leadership is based around the commitment and capacity of organisational members. Higher levels of personal commitment to organisational goals, and greater capacities for accomplishing those goals, are assumed to result in extra effort and greater productivity' (Leithwood et al. 1999, p. 9).

Leithwood (1994) conceptualises transformational leadership along eight dimensions:

- building school vision

- establishing school goals

- providing intellectual stimulation

- offering individualised support

- modelling best practices and important organisational values

- demonstrating high performance expectations
- creating a productive school culture
- developing structures to foster participation in school decisions.

Leithwood's (1994) research suggests that there is some empirical support for the essentially normative transformational leadership model. He reports on seven quantitative studies and concludes that 'transformational leadership practices, considered as a composite construct, had significant direct and indirect effects on progress with school-restructuring initiatives and teacher-perceived student outcomes' (p. 506). Subsequently, Leithwood and Jantzi (2006) drew on data from a four-year study of England's National Literacy and Numeracy Strategies to show that transformational leadership produced significant effects on teachers' classroom practices, but not on student achievement.

The transformational model is comprehensive in that it provides a normative approach to school leadership, which focuses primarily on the process by which leaders seek to influence school outcomes rather than on the nature or direction of those outcomes. However, it may also be criticised as being a vehicle for control over teachers and more likely to be accepted by the leader than the led (Chirichello 1999). Allix (2000) goes further and alleges that transformational leadership has the potential to become 'despotic' because of its strong, heroic and charismatic features. He believes that the leader's power ought to raise 'moral qualms' and serious doubts about its appropriateness for democratic organisations.

The contemporary policy climate within which schools have to operate also raises questions about the validity of the transformational model, despite its popularity in the literature. The English system increasingly requires school leaders to adhere to government prescriptions, which affect aims, curriculum content and pedagogy, as well as values. There is 'a more centralised, more directed, and more controlled educational system [that] has dramatically reduced the possibility of realising a genuinely transformational education and leadership' (Bottery 2001, p. 215).

Hoyle and Wallace (2005, p. 151) refer to the inconsistencies of the 'transformational rhetoric-transmissional reality' gap underlying English government prescriptions for practice, 'promoted through government-sponsored training and scrutinized in practice through OFSTED surveillance'. Bottery (2004, p. 17) adds that 'there is much to question' in assessing transformational leadership, arguing that it transforms and corrupts reality.

When transformational leadership works well, it has the potential to engage all stakeholders in the achievement of educational objectives. The aims of leaders and followers coalesce to such an extent that it may be realistic to assume a harmonious relationship and a genuine convergence leading to agreed decisions. When 'transformation' is a cloak for imposing the leader's values, or for implementing the prescriptions of the government, then it lacks legitimacy:

> The strongest advocacy of a transformational approach to reform has come from those whose policies ensure that the opportunity for transformation is in fact denied to people working in schools. (Hoyle and Wallace 2005, p. 128)

Participative leadership

Hoyle and Wallace (2005, p. 124) say that participation refers to the opportunities that staff members have for engaging in the process of organisational decision-making. This model is underpinned by three assumptions:

- Participation will increase school effectiveness.

- Participation is justified by democratic principles.

- In the context of site-based management, leadership is potentially available to any legitimate stakeholder (Leithwood et al. 1999, p. 12).

Sergiovanni (1984, p. 13) points to the importance of a participative approach. This will succeed in 'bonding' staff together and in easing the pressures on school principals. 'The burdens of leadership will be less if leadership functions and roles are shared and if the concept of *leadership density* were to emerge as a viable replacement for principal leadership'.

Savery et al. (1992) demonstrate that deputy principals in Western Australia wish to participate in school decision-making although their desire to do so varied across different types of decision. They conclude that 'people are more likely to accept and implement decisions in which they have participated, particularly where these decisions relate directly to the individual's own job' (p. 24).

Distributed leadership

Distributed leadership has become the normatively preferred leadership model in the twenty-first century. Gronn (2010, p. 70) states that 'there has been an accelerating amount of scholarly and practitioner attention accorded [to] the phenomenon of distributed leadership'. An important starting point for understanding this phenomenon is to uncouple it from positional authority. As Harris (2004, p. 13) indicates, 'distributed leadership concentrates on engaging expertise wherever it exists within the organization rather than seeking this only through formal position or role'.

Gronn (2010) refers to a normative preference for distributed leadership but cautions that this does not necessarily mean any reduction in the scope of the principal's role. Indeed, Hartley (2010, p. 271) argues that 'its popularity may be pragmatic: to ease the burden of overworked headteachers'.

A key issue in assessing the practice of distributed leadership is to consider how it is distributed. Bennett et al. (2003, p. 3) claim that distributed leadership is an emergent property of a group or network of individuals in which group members pool their expertise. Harris (2004, p. 19), referring to an English study of ten English schools facing challenging circumstances (Harris and Chapman 2002), says that there should be 'redistribution of power', not simply a process of 'delegated headship'. However, Hopkins and Jackson (2002) argue that formal leaders need to orchestrate and nurture the space for distributed leadership to occur, suggesting that it would be difficult to achieve without the active support of school principals.

Ghamrawi (2011), drawing on her research in Lebanese secondary schools, refers to the important role of subject leaders in distributing leadership to teachers. However, heads and principals retain much of the formal authority in schools, leading Hartley (2010, p. 282) to conclude that 'distributed leadership resides uneasily within the formal bureaucracy of schools'.

The interest in, and support for, distributed leadership is predicated on the assumption that it will bring about beneficial effects that would not occur with singular leadership. Leithwood et al.'s (2006) important study of the impact of school leadership led to the articulation of 'seven strong claims' about successful school leadership. One claim is that school leadership has a greater influence on schools and students when it is widely distributed. Leithwood et al. (2006, p. 12) show that multiple leadership is more effective than solo leadership. 'Total leadership accounted for a quite significant 27 per cent variation in student achievement across schools' (Leithwood et al. 2006, p. 12). Hallinger and Heck (2010) also found that distributed leadership was significantly related to growth in student learning. These are important findings but more such research is required before a causal relationship can be established with confidence.

The existing authority structure in schools and colleges provides a potential barrier to the successful introduction and implementation of distributed leadership. Hartley (2010) suggests that the origins of distributed leadership were essentially pragmatic and a response to the extra responsibilities imposed on schools as site-based management took root in many countries from the 1990s. However, he also notes that the requirements of the standards agenda, in England and elsewhere, mean that bureaucracy remains powerful and limits the scope for distributed leadership. Fitzgerald and Gunter (2008) also refer to the residual significance of authority and hierarchy and note the 'dark side' of distributed leadership – managerialism in a new guise. These reservations suggest that an appropriate climate is an essential precondition for meaningful distributed leadership.

Moral leadership

This model assumes that the critical focus of leadership ought to be on the values, beliefs and ethics of leaders themselves. Authority and influence are to be derived from defensible conceptions of what is right or good (Leithwood et al. 1999, p. 10). Sergiovanni claims 'administering' is a 'moral craft' (1991, p. 322).

West-Burnham (1997) discusses two approaches to 'moral' leadership. The first he describes as 'spiritual' and relates to 'the recognition that many leaders possess what might be called "higher order" perspectives. These may well be . . . represented by a particular religious affiliation' (p. 239). West-Burnham's (1997) second category is 'moral confidence', the capacity to act in a way that is consistent with an ethical system and is consistent over time.

Gold et al.'s (2003) research in English primary, secondary and special schools provides some evidence about the nature of the values held and articulated by heads regarded as 'outstanding' by Ofsted inspectors. They point to the inconsistency between 'the technicist and managerial view of school leadership operationalised by the Government's inspection regime' and the heads' focus on 'values, learning communities and shared leadership' (p. 127). Gold et al. (2003, p. 136) conclude that their case study heads 'mediate the many externally-generated directives to ensure, as far as possible, that their take-up was consistent with what the school was trying to achieve'.

Sergiovanni (1991) argues that both moral and managerial leadership are required to develop a learning community:

> In the principalship the challenge of leadership is to make
> peace with two competing imperatives, the managerial and the
> moral. The two imperatives are unavoidable and the neglect of
> either creates problems. Schools must be run effectively if they

are to survive . . . But for the school to transform itself into an institution, a learning community must emerge . . . [This] is the moral imperative that principals face. (p. 329)

Emotional leadership

Crawford (2009) discusses the emerging model of emotional leadership. She stresses that emotion is concerned with individual motivation and interpretation of events, rather than emphasising the fixed and the predictable, and criticises much of the current literature on leadership for underestimating this dimension. 'The educational leadership literature rarely considers headship from the perspective of the headteacher – in other words, "what does it feel like to be in that role?". This is probably because such subjectivity is viewed, in an accountability culture, as suspect' (ibid., p. 15). Crawford (2009) adds that emotion is socially constructed and stresses the importance of individual interpretation of events and situations: 'perception is reality'.

Beatty (2005, p. 124) also notes the importance of emotional leadership and contrasts it with bureaucratic approaches. 'Emotional silence may be the most powerful self-replicating mechanism of bureaucratic hierarchy – in schools and elsewhere.' She adds that hierarchical stratifications and silos of specialisation are anathema to the creation of dynamic learning communities. 'To overcome the anachronistic view of leadership as located exclusively at the top is itself an emotional challenge' (ibid., p. 125). Crawford (2009, p. 164) concludes that 'educational leadership cannot, and does not, function without emotion'.

Postmodern leadership

Keough and Tobin (2001, p. 2) say that 'current postmodern culture celebrates the multiplicity of subjective truths as defined by experience and revels in the loss of absolute authority'. They identify several key features of postmodernism:

- Language does not reflect reality.

- Reality does not exist; there are multiple realities.

- Any situation is open to multiple interpretations.

- Situations must be understood at local level with particular attention to diversity (ibid., pp. 11–13).

Grogan and Simmons (2007, p. 39) stress that postmodern leadership developed as a reaction to 'universal' formal or scientific theories: 'A post-modern stance on educational leadership questions the very notion of seeking truth and objectivity in research'.

The postmodern model offers few clues to how leaders are expected to operate. The most useful point to emerge from such analyses is that leaders should respect, and give attention to, the diverse and individual perspectives of stakeholders. They should also avoid reliance on the hierarchy because this concept has little meaning in such a fluid organisation.

Sackney and Mitchell (2001, pp. 13–14) stress the centrality of individual interpretation of events while also criticising transformational leadership as potentially manipulative: 'Leaders must pay attention to the cultural and symbolic structure of meaning construed by individuals and groups . . . postmodern theories of leadership take the focus off vision and place it squarely on voice'. Instead of a compelling vision articulated by leaders, there are multiple visions and diverse cultural meanings.

Contingent leadership

The models of leadership examined earlier in this chapter are all partial. They provide valid and helpful insights into one particular aspect of leadership. However, none of these models provide a complete picture of school leadership. As Lambert (1995, p. 2) notes, there is 'no single best type'.

The contingent model provides an alternative approach, recognising the diverse nature of school contexts and the advantages of adapting leadership styles to the particular situation, rather than adopting a 'one size fits all' stance:

> This approach assumes that what is important is how leaders
> respond to the unique organizational circumstances or problems
> . . . there are wide variations in the contexts for leadership and
> that, to be effective, these contexts require different leadership
> responses. (Leithwood et al. 1999, p. 15)

Yukl (2002, p. 234) adds that 'the managerial job is too complex and unpredictable to rely on a set of standardised responses to events. Effective leaders are continuously reading the situation and evaluating how to adapt their behaviour to it'. Leadership requires effective diagnosis of problems, followed by adopting the most appropriate response to the issue or situation (Morgan 1997). This reflexive approach is particularly important in periods of turbulence when leaders need to be able to assess the situation carefully and react as appropriate, rather than relying on a standard leadership model.

Implications for leading and managing people

Leadership can be understood as a process of influence, based on clear values and beliefs, and leading to a 'vision' for the school. The vision is articulated by leaders who seek to gain the commitment of staff and stakeholders to the ideal of a better future for the school, its students and stakeholders.

Each of the leadership models discussed in this book is partial. They provide distinctive but unidimensional perspectives on school leadership. The ten models, adapted from Leithwood et al. (1999) and Bush and Glover (2002), collectively suggest that concepts of school leadership are complex and diverse. They provide clear normative frameworks by which leadership can be understood but relatively weak empirical support for these constructs. They are also artificial distinctions, or 'ideal types', in that most successful leaders are likely to embody most or all of these approaches in their work (Bush 2011).

This analysis provides a starting point for linking the models to the leadership and management of people. Much depends on the nature of the educational system where leadership is exercised. If the principal's role is mainly about the implementation of policy determined outside the school, for example by national, provincial or local government, then the principal may have to focus primarily on developing 'managerial leadership'. This is the expectation in many developing countries and those in Eastern Europe. In such systems, school leaders often have little influence on key aspects of 'people' management, such as recruitment and selection, pay, promotion and working conditions, and performance appraisal. However, they can and should influence other important dimensions, such as internal deployment, motivation and job satisfaction, and school-based induction and development.

A weakness of such an approach, however, is that it is rarely focused on the key task of managing teaching and learning and it does not require sustained engagement with school-level stakeholders. As a result, school and student outcomes may be disappointing and governments may become concerned about their inability to compete effectively in a global economy. Improving the quality of learning requires a focus on 'instructional leadership'. This means working with teachers to improve the quality of teaching and learning through such processes as evaluation of test scores, monitoring teaching and observation of classroom practice. This requires consideration of school and college culture, so that such processes are regarded as constructive, not punitive, and are welcomed, not resented, by teachers.

An instructional leadership approach involves changing the mindset of leaders to regard the processes of teaching and learning as central to their role, rather than simply leaving such matters to classroom teachers. As we noted earlier, however, this model relates to the direction rather than the process of leadership. While encouraging leaders to focus on teaching and learning, it offers little guidance on how they should do so (Bush 2011).

To address the limitations of the instructional model, it makes sense to link it to an approach that addresses the process as well as the direction of leadership. Transformational leadership is currently in vogue as it accords closely with the present emphasis on vision as the central dimension of leadership. Successful leaders are expected to engage with staff and other stakeholders to produce higher levels of commitment to achieving the goals of the organisation which, in turn, are linked to the vision. As Miller and Miller (2001, p. 182) suggest, 'through the transforming process, the motives of the leader and follower merge'. Good leaders seek to ensure that vision is genuinely the product of a shared process, not the imposition of the leaders' values on other staff.

Moral leadership has similar characteristics to transformational leadership in its emphasis on developing the commitment of followers, but its distinctive element is the focus on values and moral purpose. Leaders are expected to behave with integrity and to develop and support goals underpinned by explicit values. The main difficulty arises when staff or stakeholders do not support the values of leaders. Faith schools seek to overcome such problems by trying to recruit only those staff who share the beliefs of the school's leaders and sponsors.

Participative leadership is likely to be effective in increasing the commitment of participants and in the development of teamwork, but the price may be an increase in the time taken to reach agreement, and there may be difficulties for the formal leader, who remains accountable for decisions reached through the collective process. This model suggests that leaders need to invest time in building consensus within the teaching team.

Distributed leadership is currently fashionable, and appears to provide a way of sharing tasks while also empowering and developing people. The challenge for principals is how to allow colleagues to lead, while also ensuring that tasks are completed and accountability to external stakeholders is maintained. This is likely to require a careful and contextualised balance between 'top-down' and 'bottom-up' approaches, described as 'hybrid' by Gronn (2010).

The transactional leadership model assumes that relationships with teachers and other stakeholders are based on a process of exchange. Leaders offer rewards or inducements to followers rather than seeking to improve their commitment or motivation, as in the transformational model. The main limitation of the transactional model is that the exchange is often short-term and limited to the specific issue under discussion. It does not produce long-term commitment to the values and vision being promoted by school leaders. While a measure of exchange is inevitable for school leaders, principals should focus on enhancing intrinsic motivation as well as extrinsic rewards.

Postmodern leadership focuses on multiple individual perceptions. There is no absolute truth, only a set of individual insights. There are multiple visions and diverse cultural meanings instead of a single vision enunciated by leaders. This model serves to stress the need for an approach to 'people' management which recognises and celebrates the individuality of teachers and other staff. Emotional leadership suggests a similar approach, but also encourages recognition that feelings are as important as 'facts' in leading and managing people.

Contingent leadership acknowledges the diverse nature of school contexts and the advantages of adapting leadership styles to the particular situation, rather than adopting a 'one size fits all' stance. Contingent leadership is not a single model but represents a mode of responsiveness, which requires effective diagnosis followed by careful selection of the most appropriate leadership style. It is pragmatic rather than principled and can be criticised for having no overt sense of the 'big picture'. However, the message for leaders is that they should adopt a flexible approach in their work with teachers and other staff, adapting their approaches to the situation, the event, and the specific needs and background of the people they are responsible for managing.

References

Allen, D. (2003) 'Organisational climate and strategic change in higher education: organisational insecurity', *Higher Education*, 46 (1), 61–79.

Allix, N.M. (2000) 'Transformational Leadership: Democratic or Despotic?', *Educational Management and Administration*, 28 (1), 7–20.

Beatty, B. (2005) 'Emotional leadership', in Davies, B. (ed.), *The Essentials of School Leadership*, London, Paul Chapman Publishing.

Becaj, J. (1994) 'Changing bureaucracy to democracy', *Educational Change and Development*, 15 (1), 7–14.

Bennett, N., Harvey, J., Wise, C. and Woods, P. (2003) *Distributed leadership: a desk study*, Nottingham, NCSL.

Bolman, L.G. and Deal, T.E. (1997) *Reframing organisations: artistry, choice and leadership*, San Francisco, Jossey Bass.

Bottery, M. (2001) 'Globalisation and the UK competition state: no room for transformational leadership in education?', *School Leadership and Management*, 21 (2), 199–218.

Bottery, M. (2004) *The Challenges of Educational Leadership*, London, Paul Chapman.

Brehony, K. and Deem, R. (2005) 'Challenging the post-Fordist/flexible organisation thesis: the case of reformed organisations', *British Journal of Sociology of Education*, 26 (3), 395–417.

Bush, T. (2007) 'Educational leadership and management: theory, policy and practice', *South African Journal of Education*, 27 (3), 391–406.

Bush, T. (2008) 'From management to leadership: Semantic or meaningful change?', *Educational Management, Administration and Leadership*, 36 (2), 271–288.

Bush, T. (2011) *Theories of Educational Leadership and Management, Fourth Edition*, London, Sage.

Bush, T. and Glover, D. (2002) School Leadership: Concepts and Evidence, Nottingham, NCSL.

Bush, T., Coleman, M. and Si, X. (1998) 'Managing secondary schools in China', *Compare*, 28 (2), 183–196.

Chirichello, M. (1999) 'Building Capacity for Change: Transformational Leadership for School Principals', Paper presented at ICSEI Conference, 3–6 January, San Antonio.

Crawford, M. (2009) *Getting to the Heart of Leadership: Emotion and Educational Leadership*, London, Sage.

Davies, B. (2004) *The Essentials of School Leadership*, London, Paul Chapman Publishing.

Dressler, B. (2001) 'Charter School Leadership', *Education and Urban Society*, 33 (2), 170–185.

Fitzgerald, T. and Gunter, H. (2008) 'Contesting the orthodoxy of teacher leadership', *International Journal of Leadership in Education*, 11 (4), 331–341.

Gaziel, H. (2003) 'Images of leadership and their effects upon school principals' performance', *International Review of Education*, 49 (5), 475–486.

Ghamrawi, N. (2011) 'Trust me: Your school can be better – A message from teachers to principals', *Educational Management, Administration and Leadership*, 39 (3), 333–348.

Gold, A., Evans, J., Earley, P., Halpin, D. and Collarbone, P. (2003) 'Principled principals? Values-driven leadership: evidence from ten case studies of "outstanding" school leaders,' *Educational Management and Administration*, 31 (2), 127–138.

Goldspink, C. (2007) 'Rethinking educational reform: a loosely coupled and complex systems perspective', *Educational Management, Administration and Leadership*, 35 (1), 27–50.

Grogan, M. and Simmons, J. (2007) 'Taking a critical stance in research', in Briggs, A. and Coleman, M. (eds), *Research Methods in Educational Leadership and Management, Second Edition*, London, Sage.

Gronn, P. (2010) 'Where to next for educational leadership?' in Bush, T., Bell,

L. and Middlewood, D. (eds), *The Principles of Educational Leadership and Management,* London, Sage.

Hallinger, P. (2009) *Leadership for 21ˢᵗ Century Schools: From Instructional Leadership to Leadership for Learning,* Hong Kong, Hong Kong Institute of Education.

Hallinger, P. and Heck, R. (2010) 'Leadership for learning: Does distributed leadership make a difference in student learning?', *Educational Management, Administration and Leadership,* 38 (6), 654–678.

Hallinger, P. and Lee, M. (2014) 'Mapping instructional leadership in Thailand: Has education reform impacted on principal practice?', *Educational Management, Administration and Leadership,* 42 (1).

Harris, A. (2004) 'Distributed leadership and school improvement: leading or misleading?', *Educational Management, Administration and Leadership,* 32 (1), 11–24.

Harris, A. and Chapman, C. (2002) *Effective Leadership in Schools Facing Challenging Circumstances: Final Report,* Nottingham, NCSL.

Hartley, D. (2010) 'Paradigms: How far does research in distributed leadership "stretch"?', *Educational Management, Administration and Leadership,* 38 (3), 271–285.

Hill, P. (2001) 'What Principals Need to Know About Teaching and Learning', University of Melbourne, paper presented to the National College for School Leadership Think Tank, London.

Hopkins, D. and Jackson, D. (2002) 'Building the capacity for leading and learning', in Harris, A., Day, C., Hadfield, M., Hopkins, D., Hargreaves, A. and Chapman, C. (eds), *Effective Leadership for School Improvement,* London, Routledge.

Hoyle, E. and Wallace, M. (2005) *Educational Leadership: Ambiguity, Professionals and Managerialism,* London, Sage.

Hoyle, E. and Wallace, M. (2007) 'Educational reform: an ironic perspective', *Educational Management, Administration and Leadership,* 35 (1), 9–25.

Huber, S. (2004) 'Context of research', in Huber, S. (ed.), *Preparing School Leaders for the 21ˢᵗ Century: An International Comparison of Development Programs in 15 Countries,* London, RoutledgeFalmer.

Judge, T. and Piccolo, R. (2004) 'Transformational and transactional leadership: A meta-analytical test of their relative validity', *Journal of Applied Psychology,* 89 (5), 755–768.

Kaparou, M. (2013) *Instructional leadership in England and Greece: a cross-country comparative approach,* unpublished Ph.D thesis, Coventry, University of Warwick.

Keough, T. and Tobin, B. (2001) 'Postmodern Leadership and the Policy Lexicon: From Theory, Proxy to Practice', paper for the Pan-Canadian Education Research Agenda Symposium, 22–23 May, Quebec.

Klus-Stanska, D. and Olek, H. (1998) 'Private education in Poland: breaking the mould', *International Review of Education,* 44 (2–3), 235–249.

Lambert, L. (1995) 'New directions in the preparation of educational leaders', *Thrust for Educational Leadership,* 24 (5), 6–10.

Leithwood, K. (1994) 'Leadership for school restructuring', *Educational Administration Quarterly,* 30(4), 498–518.

Leithwood, K. and Jantzi, D. (2006) 'Transformational leadership for large-scale reform: Effects on students, teachers and their classroom practices', *School Effectiveness and School Improvement,* 17 (1), 201–227.

Leithwood, K., Jantzi, D. and Steinbach, R. (1999) *Changing Leadership for Changing Times*, Buckingham, Open University Press.

Leithwood, K., Day, C., Sammons, P., Harris, A. and Hopkins, D. (2006) *Seven Strong Claims about Successful School Leadership*, London, DfES.

Lumby, J. (2003) 'Distributed leadership in colleges: leading or misleading?', *Educational Management and Administration*, 31 (3), 283–293.

McTavish, D. (2003) 'Aspects of public sector management: a case study of further education: ten years from the passage of the Further and Higher Education Act,' *Educational Management and Administration*, 31 (2), 175–188.

Miller, T.W. and Miller, J.M. (2001) 'Educational leadership in the new millennium: a vision for 2020', *International Journal of Leadership in Education*, 4 (2), 181–189.

Morgan, G. (1997) *Images of Organization*, Newbury Park, California, Sage.

National College for School Leadership (2001) *Leadership Development Framework*, Nottingham, NCSL.

Newland, C. (1995) 'Spanish American elementary education 1950–1992: bureaucracy, growth and decentralisation', *International Journal of Educational Development*, 15 (2), 103–114.

Purvis, M.T. (2007) *School Improvement in a Small-Island Developing State: The Seychelles*, unpublished Ph.D. thesis, University of Warwick.

Rutherford, C. (2006) 'Teacher leadership and organisational structure', *Journal of Educational Change*, 7 (1–2), 59–78.

Sackney, L. and Mitchell, C. (2001) 'Postmodern expressions of educational leadership', in Leithwood, K. and Hallinger, P. (eds), *The Second International Handbook of Educational Leadership and Administration*, Dordrecht, Kluwer.

Savery, L., Soutar, G. and Dyson, J. (1992) 'Ideal decision-making styles indicated by deputy principals', *Journal of Educational Administration*, 30 (2), 18–25.

Sergiovanni, T. (1984) 'Leadership and excellence in schooling', *Educational Leadership*, 41 (5), 4–13.

Sergiovanni, T.J. (1991) *The Principalship: a reflective practice perspective*, Needham Heights, MA, Allyn and Bacon.

Simkins, T. (2005) 'Leadership in education: "What works and what makes sense?"', *Educational Management, Administration and Leadership*, 33 (1), 9–26.

Southworth, G. (2002) 'Instructional leadership in schools: reflections and empirical evidence', *School Leadership and Management*, 22 (1), 73–91.

Svecova, J. (2000) 'Privatisation of education in the Czech Republic', *International Journal of Educational Development*, 20, 127–133.

Waite, D. (2002) 'The "paradigm wars" in educational administration: an attempt at transcendence', *International Studies in Educational Administration*, 30 (1), 66–81.

West-Burnham, J. (1997) 'Leadership for learning: reengineering "mind sets"', *School Leadership and Management*, 17 (2), 231–243.

Yukl, G.A. (2002) *Leadership in Organizations, Fifth Edition*, Upper Saddle River, NJ: Prentice-Hall.

3

Leading and managing the whole workforce

Introduction

Leading and managing people in educational institutions no longer means being responsible for simply the teachers and lecturers employed in them, but for all those who work there, in whatever capacity. This is particularly true in developed countries, especially in those that operate under national educational systems which have devolved responsibility for management to schools and colleges, i.e. autonomous or semi-autonomous institutions. In countries such as England and Wales, the USA, Canada, Scotland and to some extent Australia and New Zealand, those staff in a support role form an important part of a school's or college's organisation and development. Consequently, the research and literature related to these staff is largely confined to such countries. Although the importance of, for example, school bursars and secretaries, librarians and caretakers/janitors has always been acknowledged, little literature exists before 1990. In the countries mentioned above, since the 1990s there has been a particular interest in those who work in direct support of teachers. Kerry and Kerry (2003, p. 71) point to a Kansas State list of duties for staff known then as 'paraprofessionals' that dates back to 1977, but in many developing countries, the issue of unqualified teachers is far more pressing than the roles of other staff (see, for example, Middlewood 2003 on South Africa, and Dalin and Rust 1994 on Columbia, Ethiopia and

Bangladesh). Literature concerning those in a support role for teachers in many countries is very limited, and in some countries such staff simply do not exist, except for those offering clerical support. Other support is usually given through the use of volunteers such as parent helpers and others (for the example of South Africa, see Lumby et al. 2003).

The use of volunteers is beyond the scope of this chapter, which focuses on the leadership and management of paid employees in schools and colleges. It examines who such staff are, what they do, and the issues that are most relevant to their effectiveness. It should be noted of course that most of the areas concerning the leading and managing of people examined in other chapters of this book apply equally to these staff.

The recent and current context

In the developed countries referred to earlier where school- or college-based management has evolved since the 1980s and 1990s, there has been a considerable growth in the numbers of employees other than teachers. In England, for example, the number of support staff more than doubled between 1996 and 2006, and had trebled by 2011, while the number of teachers increased by ten per cent over the same period. Clearly, much of this increase related to schools organising their own budgets, resources and general operational arrangements. A seminal research report in the early period of devolved budget management (Mortimore et al. 1994) examined this and found that:

- schools were appointing people specifically to manage the resources and finance (mainly in secondary schools)

- they were investing more in various kinds of curriculum support staff (mainly in primary schools).

That report found that concern for value for money was the overriding factor in these developments.

In addition, in the late 1990s and early 2000s, the greater emphasis on community involvement for schools, including community schools in the USA and in Scotland and extended schools in England and Wales, meant that there were new areas of service provision by schools which needed additional staff. These included closer links with the local community, other local public services, businesses and industry, as well as parents. As schools were encouraged to be 'at the heart of the community', they needed employees who had different skills from those needed in the classroom, and who had different experiences and backgrounds, as well as availability to service, for example, provision in the evenings, at weekends and during school holidays. Some Full Service Extended Schools (FSES) in England and Wales became 'one stop' services for their local communities, employing a number of staff of different kinds.

The other development in this period has been the changing of titles of those undertaking specific roles. 'Classroom assistants' became 'teaching assistants' (TAs) with relevant qualifications being introduced. For example, schools in England and Wales can have a higher level teaching assistant (HLTA), and in some schools the role of bursar has evolved into that of business manager. However, the generic term for those employed in schools other than teachers remains more diverse. In North America, the term 'paraeducators' is now widely used, whereas in the UK 'support staff' appears more common. The 1994 report used the term 'associate staff' but it has not been universally adopted, although it is used quite widely in post-statutory institutions such as further education colleges. What does appear to be agreed is that any use of a descriptor such as 'non-teaching' staff is to be rejected, since describing role holders in terms of what they do *not* do seems wholly inappropriate. The term 'support staff' will be used in this chapter for consistency, while we recognise the validity of various other terms.

Common National Occupational Standards were drawn up by 2001 'for all staff in England, Scotland, Wales and Northern Ireland who work with teachers in classrooms supporting the learning process in primary, special and secondary schools' (LGNTO 2001). The final official recognition was the UK government's proposal (DfES 2003) that from September 2003 teachers would not be required to do a number of administrative tasks (for example, photocopying, examination entries, displays, cataloguing resources, etc.). There was the further proposal that assistants, with training, should take over supervision of classes on occasions, which, perhaps inevitably, brought divided reactions from teachers' unions.

Because of the complex situation described above, much current literature focuses more on the operational aspects of the management of support staff and less upon a strategic view of what is in the best interests of pupil learning and therefore the best way to lead and manage these staff. Most research has focused on what assistants actually do (for example, Moyles and Suschitzky 1997; Wilson et al. 2003). It is appropriate now to try to describe the various kinds of support staff in schools, identify some of the issues in leading and managing them, and propose principles for effective practice in their leadership and management.

Who are support staff?

Classification is most helpfully done by task and purpose, especially because several of these tasks officially coming under different roles are actually done by the same people. It is quite common for someone to have two separate employment contracts in one school, for example one as a cleaner and one as a midday supervisor. Various classifications have been made, such as by Bush and Middlewood (2005), Bubb and Earley (2004), and Middlewood and Parker (2009), but the situation is constantly evolving. The following is seen as helpful for our discussion here (with no priorities intended between the groups):

- Group A: Those relating directly to teaching and learning and child development
    - teaching assistants (TAs) and higher level teaching assistants (HLTAs)
    - special needs assistants (SNAs) and learning support assistants (LSAs)
    - language assistants – including those supporting pupils whose first language is not the national language, and those supporting pupils from minority groups such as travellers' children
    - nursery nurses
    - specialist coaches in sport, music, various arts
    - learning mentors
    - counsellors, welfare officers and medical staff
    - youth workers and various community staff, such as youth justice workers
    - cover supervisors

- Group B: Those working in technical areas
    - design and technology technicians, art technicians
    - science technicians
    - librarians and resource centre managers

- Group C: Those working in administration
    - bursars and business managers
    - secretarial staff
    - clerical and office staff
    - receptionists
    - examination invigilators

- Group D: Those concerned with the environment
  - premises managers
  - caretakers and maintenance staff
  - cleaners
  - catering and kitchen staff
  - lunchtime supervisors

Inevitably, some categories overlap. The last named role, lunchtime supervisors, began historically for the purposes of simply maintaining order at meal times, but in many schools it has evolved into a useful role in the area of child behaviour. This of course underpins what can be seen as the key to effective leadership and management of all people in the school or college, including *all* those in the above groups, that is, remembering that the purpose of the institution is to enhance effective learning, and therefore every single post should be viewed in that light. The cleanliness of the buildings, the manner in which meals are taken, the efficient use of the budget and everything else ultimately serve this purpose.

Although most literature focuses on schools, the roles of employees other than lecturers in further education colleges have also developed since greater funding flexibility was introduced. Kedney and Brownlow (1994, p. 12) note that such roles were becoming:

- more flexible

- more involved directly in support of students

- more likely to offer guidance and support

- more likely to be directly concerned with instruction, supervision and design.

Later Simkins and Lumby (2002, p. 19), also referring to English further education colleges, note that 'Role distinctions between academic and other staff may also be becoming more blurred'.

Since the leaders' responsibility is for the whole workforce, staff relationships are crucial and issues such as motivation, job satisfaction and team working are explored in other chapters of this book. One of the clearest examples is that of teacher and teaching assistant, where an effective relationship is essential to the development of the pupils' learning because its effects have an immediate impact. Middlewood and Parker (2001, p. 198) suggest that the relationship could operate at three levels:

- the compensatory level where the assistant relieves pressure on the teacher by doing certain tasks

- the interpretative level where the learners are helped to understand the task set by the teacher

- the extension level where the learner needs to understand what comes next.

Kamen (2008, pp. 3–4) suggests the levels are:

- at pupil level, for example respond to pupil needs, reward and praise pupils

- at teacher level, for example give feedback about pupils, help monitor progress

- at school level, for example work with parents, attend staff meetings

- at curriculum level, for example understand learning theories, interpret literacy strategies.

Such models can not only help both teachers and assistants to clarify their working relationships but also allow leaders and managers to decide what skills and qualities are needed at each specific level and thereby help to determine what training and development might be most effective.

In thinking about leading and managing the whole workforce, there are firstly some basic organisational matters to be considered, before looking at some more complex issues.

Organisational issues in the leadership and management of support staff

Who should lead and manage support staff?

It could be argued that, given the diversity of roles in the above classification, there is a risk of having too many managers, but it is important that the responsibility is clear in any organisation. Middlewood (1997, p. 188), writing about staff development, asks whether the needs of a science technician, for example, could be best met by considering that person as a member of the science departmental team or as a member of the school's support staff. A reasonable answer is that both are essential but there is potential tension in the situation for the technicians and their managers.

Each of the above categories of support staff may be viewed as a team but designated leaders and managers vary. In many organisations, there is an office manager who leads the clerical/administration team, and premises staff have a Head of Premises or equivalent to lead that team. However, this is not usually the case with midday supervisors, and technicians are usually managed by a teacher in charge of the relevant curriculum area. Most LSAs who support pupils with special educational needs (SEN) are led by the school or college's head of learning support (a senior teacher or lecturer) or, in the case of smaller schools, by the teacher who is SEN co-ordinator (SENCO). This learning support will normally be a separate department to which both teachers and support staff belong. In many schools and colleges a member of the leadership team has overall responsibility for support staff. However, Curtis (2002, p. 5) describes how, in one school, a specific department was created for support staff:

> With the business manager as its head, the support staff department at Churchdown School was born. Technicians, site management staff, lunchtime supervisors, secretarial staff, the librarian, the receptionist, catering staff and cleaners all stood on an equal footing with teachers. They now have department meetings and have a head of department to whom they can turn.

This department is different from other teaching departments because it is about the same size (80 people) as the entire teaching staff; therefore, a number of its processes are necessarily different, for example, identifying training needs, performance management interviews. Two of the key advantages of this department appear to be the status and value that its existence gives to support staff and the vehicle it offers for allowing support staff views to be represented and acted upon. However, research by Argyri (2011) across a very large secondary school showed that opinion was divided between support staff from all the different areas of the school as to whether such a department would be able to meet their specific needs as successfully as specialist departments would. Nevertheless the idea of the status being raised was widely endorsed.

Training and development

All staff in a school or college may be perceived as having an entitlement to training, but whereas the training and development of teachers has generated a whole literature in its own right, including relevant journals, the training of certain groups of support staff is much less widespread.

Naylor (1999) notes that the training he described for lunchtime supervisors was rare, probably no more than one school in 20 being estimated as providing them with training of any kind, regardless of its quality.

The concern therefore for leaders and managers is to ensure that effective and relevant training is available to support staff of all kinds in a way that is 'enriching', as Stoll et al. (2003, p. 126) describe it: 'Involve them, training them to perform roles that will enhance the school, build their personal efficacy, use their skills . . .' Moreover, it is one thing to offer support staff training, but, as Bedford et al. (2008. p. 9) note, there were 'no specific training programmes to support teachers working with [support staff] in this new partnership,' thus implicitly conveying the message that support staff needed training but teachers did not.

As other chapters in this book show, the importance of training and development is also that it contributes to the 'collective learning' (Stoll et al. 2003, p. 140) of the organisation. Those in support roles may have access to aspects of the organisation's culture which need to be explored and developed. Using this access can have practical value for leaders who wish to move the organisation forward as a whole. Middlewood (1999) describes how John, an LSA in a special school, joined an in-house course for staff and undertook a piece of in-house research on pupil behaviour between lessons, as a result of which the school re-examined its whole practice in this area. John had access to the pupils in a way which teachers could not have and was able therefore to gain additional insights. More structured, relevant and consistent training for support staff clearly brings additional benefits to the organisation. Ryall and Goddard's (2003) case studies of the training of midday assistants and specialist teaching assistants led in both cases to the conclusion that:

> investment in the training of support staff is worthwhile both for the individuals and the organisation . . . The school has to reflect on the implications emerging from the training and modify their structures and procedures to maximise benefits. It is an investment that is well worth the cost. (p. 78)

Career structure and development

Various studies (Wilson et al. 2003; Gunter 2008; Lowe 2009) show that, for classroom support staff, levels of pay are low, many contracts are temporary and there is no career structure. This, ironically, means that those receiving training can become among the most frustrated if no development opportunities are given for them to use the received benefits.

However, as attention was paid to the issue of reducing teachers' workloads in England and Wales (DfES 2003), significantly increased opportunities seemed likely to emerge for various support staff to have access to training to enable them to gain precise and coherent qualifications and to plan career progression. New foundation degrees began in a few higher education (HE) institutions in 2001 offering TAs the chance to study, in a work-based link between schools and HE, for a qualification as a higher level assistant, an associate teacher and, for those who wished, to proceed to gain full qualified teacher status (QTS). The high demand for places on these courses has underlined the need for them but also the frustration at the lack of other opportunities offered. Official evaluations of these degrees (for example, Foreman-Peck and Middlewood 2002) indicate that they are likely to expand as well as be refined. However, apart from those staff wishing to proceed to QTS, there is still generally a lack of a properly structured career progression. Most support staff are on fixed-term contracts (Lowe 2009) and many feel undervalued considering the responsibilities they have (Hammersley-Fletcher and Lowe 2011). As Groom (2006) notes, the roles have undergone a transformation, but there has not been an accompanying change in development opportunities.

Lack of access to professional practices

The undervaluing mentioned above is felt outside of schools. In further education, Simkins and Lumby (2002) show that little attention is paid to support staff and Lumby (2001) found an intensely felt 'them and us' culture between lecturers and support staff.

This undervaluing of support staff has often included lack of formal processes, such as induction (Middlewood 1999, p. 129), appraisal (Balshaw and Farrell 2002), mentoring, access to training and development, promotion opportunities, and in some cases job descriptions (Bland and Follett 2007); effectiveness can be limited by a lack of formal or even informal appraisal of performance. However, undervaluing can reveal itself in other less overt ways that are reflected in the culture of the organisation. Effectiveness in deployment of support staff can be hampered by 'entrenched attitudes and traditional working practices,' (Attwood and Bland 2012, pp. 87).

Leaders and managers may reflect upon the actual practice of what is commonly stated in organisations about 'equally valuing all staff' by asking the following questions:

- Do all staff have equal access to the staffroom and facilities?

- Do 'staff lists' reflect hierarchical values?

- Do 'staff' photographs include all members of staff?

- Are staff events, including social occasions, open to all staff?

- Are achievements of support staff recognised in the same way as those of others?

One important consideration sometimes overlooked is that many support staff tend to live within the school's or college's immediate community, compared with teachers and lecturers who are able to travel a considerable distance to work. This means that support staff are potentially powerful voices within the local community and should be valued as such – not least because of their importance in informal 'word of mouth' marketing!

Where members of support staff feel undervalued, the effect on their self-esteem can be significant, but there are ways in which the contribution made by them can be acknowledged. Williams et al. (2001, p. 56) describe a case study in which a head teacher deliberately adopted strategies to enhance the self-esteem of midday supervisors:

> Midday supervisors are difficult to recruit, but having got together a team I set out to build up the self-esteem of the group and raise the profile of the job. I appointed an intelligent and caring MDSA and sent her for training in first aid and managing challenging behaviour. We had daily briefings before lunch to update her on children causing concern. I gave her a budget to choose new uniforms in agreement with the others. The other members of the team were offered options on a rota basis and began to ask, 'When is it my turn for training?' *I allow them odd days off (without pay) to take up cheaper holidays within school time.* Staff meetings are held after lunch once per term and problems are raised with me. I now have a committed team and a list of people wanting to join!

This example contains strategies both of formal processes (giving access to training) and informal recognition (giving days off for cheaper holidays).

While there is comparatively little research into support staff in Europe, research that has been done has important implications for its perceived value. While Kerry's (2001) study of paraprofessionals in Portugal found them to be well integrated, the focus in the Czech Republic on using assistants to support an ethnic minority (Romany children) had significant effects. On the one hand, the assistants enhanced the Romany children's education significantly; on the other, the fact that they had assistants rather than teachers raised the same ethical issue as was raised about support staff being used to meet the needs of students of racial, ethnic and language minority groups in the USA, i.e. 'Is one of the constructs of the support staff role that they are to be seen as second class instructors for second class students?' (Kerry and Kerry 2003, p. 70).

However, what is very interesting to note is that as schools and colleges became more autonomous, there was one category of support staff which grew significantly in status and benefited from the formalising of career development, secure contracts and an appropriate salary structure. This category was those staff administering the finance and business side of a school or college's operations, such as bursars or business managers. The school or college bursar in fact has become a member of the senior leadership team in many schools (especially secondary) and colleges. Courses and programmes leading to diplomas and even degrees have flourished and school bursars have their own dedicated journal in the UK. The huge importance of effective and efficient management of finance and resources made this inevitable, and it is not likely to decrease in the context of new types of increasingly autonomous educational institutions emerging in, for example, England and the USA.

Issues for leaders and managers to consider

Working on the premise that all employees are entitled to be led and managed in a sensitive, professional and efficient way, it is clear that support staff in educational organisations require many of the same principles to be applied to them as any other members of staff, in order for pupil or student performance to improve. However, the following principles, which are proposed for leaders and managers to examine when managing the workforce as a whole, may need special consideration in relation to support staff.

Considering the role of the employee in relation to the institution's key purpose

As with all staff, the purpose of the role of *any* employee in relation to the institution's key purpose of effective learning needs to be considered first of all during any restructuring, job description, role adjustment, new appointment, performance assessment or reward. The first question is always whether the job is needed. Evidence, for example, relating to the use of TAs during a period of considerable growth in numbers mentioned earlier, is mixed. Not only did teachers report that they worked just as many hours as without an assistant but the five-year study by Blatchford et al. (2007, p. 21) showed that the growth in the use of assistants in primary school classrooms had had 'no measurable impact on pupil attainment'. However, Harris et al. (2008) found that the changes in arrangements concerning TAs had made a positive difference to pupils' achievement. While there may be other factors to be considered, leaders need to be clear about how the appointment of a person in any post will bring something extra to the school or college that benefits learning.

Seeing the way support staff are utilised as an indicator of the organisation

The way in which support staff are utilised in the school or college may be seen as a significant indicator of the organisation in two ways:

- It can shed light on the organisational culture and the values espoused. As noted above, a school which claims each person is of equal value but fails in any of the above ways to treat support staff with equal dignity is contradicting itself. Balshaw and Farrell (2002, p. 101) argue that a school which wishes to develop inclusive practice with its pupils should ensure that staff with apparently lower status feel as included as any pupils; 'where they feel as included as others, the likelihood is that the pupils will feel that they are fully included in the classroom and learning environment'. If a more democratic workplace is to be developed, these staff need to feel their contributions are valued, and structures, systems and relationships need to exist to ensure this happens.

- It can also be argued that the deployment of support staff in an educational institution can send a message about the nature of the kind of education provided there. Gunter (2007) argues that while the use of assistants in classes was allowing teachers to design new schemes of work, it had potential consequences for the philosophies underpinning education and had the effect of distancing teachers from the classroom. Also, Hammersley-Fletcher and Lowe (2011, p. 79) speculate whether the growing use of people other than teachers to deliver the curriculum could 'lead to the delivery of a more technocratic curriculum.' Hoyle and Wallace (2007) comment on the irony of TAs having actually added to the workload of teachers, thereby leading to more functional and less reflective teaching. Similarly, Bubb and Earley (2004, p. 98) use the example of cover supervisors in schools as a double-edged weapon in the fight for efficient use of time in classrooms. Thus, pupils do not miss out when a teacher is absent because they receive a downloaded pre-prepared lesson, but, if it is that easy, is it 'an erosion of the profession and the making of cheaper education'? Likewise, Graves's (2013, p. 19) study of the impact of HLTAs in schools suggested that their work with learners meant that the teacher's redefined role 'even lacked variety and in some senses autonomy'.

Being aware of ethical implications

Most leaders will be aware of the various sensitivities involved when someone is asked to do the job of someone who is paid much more than they are, such as an assistant taking a class (see Hammersley-Fletcher and Lowe 2011; Emira 2011). They will also be conscious of the need to show that qualifications are important and should not be undermined through inappropriate deployment of less qualified staff. Moreover, external perceptions can affect not only the morale of those involved but also the reputation of a place where, for example, a less privileged group are 'only' served by a support staff member, not by a teacher. In addition, the provision of the formal professional processes mentioned earlier can be seen as a moral entitlement, as well as effective practice. It should be stressed that this applies to dealing with poor as readily as effective performance. As Fidler and Atton (1999) show, the poor performance of a receptionist at a school and college cannot be tolerated any more than that of a teacher or lecturer. If it is, it gives out the signal that that particular job or task does not matter and, by implication, the people affected do not matter either.

Recognising the special abilities of support staff

While giving equal value to all employees, it is important to recognise the special abilities of support staff. What is required of support staff demands particular skills specific to the job as well as a number of attributes common to all or most effective employees. If these are to be acknowledged and used effectively, it is important that they are not seen as a 'watered down' version of the skills of teachers or lecturers. In healthcare, for example, surgeons have high-level skills but paramedics such as ambulance staff have particular skills which surgeons do not possess because each is specific to the job they do. Yet, ultimately, the patient is likely to need both. Similarly, in the case of support staff and the teachers, they will work best as a team when their complementary roles and skills are recognised and used accordingly. Indeed, any idea that assistants are all inherently frustrated teachers is dispelled by research undertaken with assistants (for example, Foreman-Peck and Middlewood 2002; Emira 2011). Many support staff are clear they want to be in their roles because they are important and fulfilling. They believe their roles are just as important as the teachers', but bring a different dimension to the learning process. Some of the people working in community or extended schools as learning mentors, counsellors and youth justice workers are well qualified – some are graduates – but choose to work in specific roles. Those interviewed by Middlewood and Parker (2009) 'nearly all conveyed the passion and realisation that their contributions, however small, were making a difference and that made the job worthwhile' (ibid., p. 67).

Similarly, Hammersley-Fletcher and Lowe (2011, p. 80) quote a teaching assistant:

> Teaching assistants have a better understanding of children on a personal level and build closer relationships while simultaneously providing equal access to education for all.

Similarly, effective midday supervisors employ a whole range of specific skills relevant to the situations that they manage. A case study by Ryall and Goddard (2003, p. 74) identified 'use of effective communications with pupils and teaching staff and strategies for behaviour management including the non-confrontational handling of misbehaviour' as key elements in the improvement of this category of support staff. From this case study emerged also the significant issue that to enable these skills to be effectively deployed, there were several things that school leaders needed to address. For example, supervisors had in many contexts authority to punish but none to reward, and received no feedback from teachers to whom they referred disciplinary problems (p. 75). It was hardly surprising that these staff were perceived by children as negative and by teachers as ineffective. The involvement of the supervisors in the revision of procedures, sanctions and rewards proved invaluable.

Some schools and colleges have increasingly found that support staff have all the personal skills required to be a personal tutor for secondary or post-16 students. There is no reason why such a person cannot provide as effective pastoral support for an adolescent as any teacher since it is likely to be life experience that is drawn on in that role. In a large secondary school, Middlewood et al. (2005) found examples of support staff who were seen as effective tutors, and their 'qualifications' included being a grandparent, an auntie, an elder brother, as well as having worked in, for example, local industry, voluntary services, and having travelled extensively! For specialist advice, the students can be referred elsewhere, as indeed they are when subject teachers are tutors.

To be able to use them effectively, leaders need to be aware of the support staff's own perceptions of their roles, which are broadly in three categories:

- those who see the role as essentially one carrying out the teachers' instructions
- those who see the role as important in its own right
- those who see the role as a stepping stone to gaining full teacher status.

While the last group can be supported towards gaining the relevant qualifications, the second group needs careful encouragement and structured support to ensure their special contributions are recognised and used.

Offering leadership and management opportunities to support staff

Many support staff will potentially be members of three kinds of teams within their schools or colleges:

- teams of teachers where support staff contribute on specific issues, for example a specific child, a computer problem or a resource recommendation
- teams which are joint meetings of teachers and support staff
- teams of support staff only.

There is every reason why staff should gain experience, and many do, of leading the third type of team. Emira's (2011) study shows that the majority of TAs carried out duties which they firmly believed involved management and/or leadership responsibilities and suggested that: 'Building their leadership capacities to a certain degree is likely to maximise the use of their skills, allow them to express their views and make them feel they are valued team members' (ibid., p. 171).

Conclusion

The effective leader will wish to develop a staffing model for the future of the particular school or college, based upon the most effective way of enhancing pupil/student learning and continuing to improve achievement. This model will inevitably include a range of employees with a variety of skills, some of which cannot necessarily be foreseen at present because of the evolving nature of learning in the twenty-first century and consequent evolving ways of supporting this. Just as the role of the teacher will develop, so will that of all those in supporting roles.

However, particularly in developed countries, as workforces change according to government legislation, leaders need to be aware of the risk of being so busy implementing government initiatives that they do not see the implications of their impact on the kind of education being offered. The reflective and strategic leader is therefore mindful of focusing on the kind of education being offered first, and then developing the workforce most appropriate to help achieve it. It is certain that support staff will play a vitally important role in that.

References

Argyri, J. (2011) *The Effective Management of Associate Staff*, unpublished MA dissertation, Warwick, University of Warwick.

Attwood, T. and Bland, K. (2012) 'Deployment and impact of higher level teaching assistants – how do small scale studies fit into the bigger picture?' *Management in Education*, 26 (2), 82–88.

Balshaw, M. and Farrell, P. (2002) *Teaching Assistants*, London, David Fulton.

Bedford, J., Jackson, C. and Wilson, E. (2008) 'New partnerships for learning: teachers' perspectives on their developing professional relationships with TAs in England', *Journal of In-Service Education*, 34 (1), 7–25.

Bland, K. and Follett, J. (2007) 'An investigation into the use and deployment of HLTAs in a Northamptonshire Technology College', available at www.northampton.ac.uk/438/ (accessed November 2012).

Blatchford, P., Bassett, R., Brown, P. and Martin, C. (2007) 'The Role and Effects of Teaching Assistants in English Primary Schools (Years 4 to 6)', *British Educational Research Journal*, 33 (1), 5–26.

Bush, T. and Middlewood, D. (2005) *Leading and Managing People in Education*, London, Sage.

Bubb, S. and Earley, P. (2004) *Leading and Managing Continuing Professional Development*, London, Paul Chapman Publishing.

Curtis, R. (2002) 'The management of support staff', *Headship Matters*, (20), 5–6, London, Optimus Publishing.

Dalin, P. and Rust, V. (1994) *How Schools Improve*, London, Cassell.

DfES (2003) *Time for Standards – Raising Standards and Tackling Workload: A National Agreement*, London, DfES.

Emira, M. (2011) 'I am more than just a TA!' *Management in Education*, 25 (4), 163–174.

Fidler, B. and Atton, T. (1999) *Poorly Performing Staff in Schools and How to Manage Them*, London, Routledge.

Foreman-Peck, L. and Middlewood, D. (2002) *A Formative Evaluation of the*

Foundation Degree Arts – Learning and Teaching (Schools), Northampton, University College Northampton.

Graves, S. (2013) 'Chameleon or Chimera? The role of the HLTA in a remodeled workforce in English schools', *Educational Management Administration and Leadership*, 41 (1), 68–89.

Groom, B. (2006) 'Building relationships for learning: the developing role of the teaching assistant', *Support for Learning*, 21 (4), 199–203.

Gunter, H. (2007) 'Remodelling the school workforce in England: a study in tyranny', *Journal for Critical Education Policy Studies*, 5 (1), 1–11.

Gunter, H. (2008) 'Policy and Workforce Reform in England', *Educational Management Administration and Leadership*, 36 (2), 253–270.

Hammersley-Fletcher, L. and Lowe, M. (2011) 'From general dogsbody to whole -class delivery – the role of the primary school teaching assistant within a moral maze', *Management in Education*, 25 (2), 78–81.

Harris, A., Ghent, K. and Goodall, J. (2008) *Beyond Workforce Reform: Raising Achievement*, London, Specialist Schools and Academies Trust.

Hoyle, E. and Wallace, M. (2007) 'Educational Reform: an ironic perspective', *Educational Management, Administration and Leadership*, 35 (1), 9–25.

Kamen, T. (2008) *Teaching Assistant's Handbook, Second Edition*, London, Hodder Education.

Kedney, B. and Brownlow, S. (1994) *Funding Flexibility*, Mendip Paper 62, Blagdon, Staff College.

Kerry, T. (2001) *Working with support staff*, London, Pearson Education.

Kerry, C. and Kerry, T. (2003) 'Government policy and the effective employment and deployment of support staff in UK schools', *International Studies in Educational Administration*, 31 (1), 65–81.

Local Government National Training Organisation (LGNTO) (2001) *National Occupational Standards for Teaching/Classroom Assistants*, London, Local Government National Training Organisation.

Lowe, M. (2009) 'Learning Support Assistant and Teaching Assistant – the Same or Different? A study of the support role in Schools and Further Education', paper presented at the BERA Conference, Manchester University.

Lumby, J. (2001) *Managing Further Education: A Learning Enterprise*, London, Paul Chapman Publishing.

Lumby, J., Middlewood, D. and Kaabwe, S. (eds) (2003) *Managing Human Resources in South African Schools*, London, Commonwealth Secretariat.

Middlewood, D. (1997) 'Managing staff development', in Bush, T. and Middlewood, D. (eds), *Managing People in Education*, London, Paul Chapman Publishing.

Middlewood, D. (1999) 'Engendering change', in Middlewood, D., Coleman, M. and Lumby, J., *Practitioner Research in Education*, London, Paul Chapman Publishing, pp. 119–136.

Middlewood, D. (2003) 'Teacher professionalism and development', in Lumby, J., Middlewood, D. and Kaabwe, S. (eds), *Managing Human Resources in South African Schools*, London, Commonwealth Secretariat.

Middlewood, D. and Parker, R. (2001) 'Managing curriculum support staff for effective learning', in Middlewood, D. and Burton, N. (eds), *Managing the Curriculum*, London, Paul Chapman Publishing, pp. 190–203.

Middlewood, D. and Parker, R. (2009) *Leading and Managing Extended Schools*, London, Sage.

Middlewood, D., Parker, R. and Beere, J. (2005) *Creating a Learning School*, London, Paul Chapman Publishing.

Mortimore, P., Mortimore, J. and Thomas, H. (1994) *Managing Associate Staff*, London, Paul Chapman Publishing.

Moyles, J. and Suschitzky, W. (1997) *Jill of All Trades*, London, ATL Publications.

Naylor, D. (1999) 'The professional development needs of mid-day assistants', *Professional Development Today*, 3 (1), 51–60.

Ryall, A. and Goddard, G. (2003) 'Support staff in primary schools: reflections upon the benefits of training and implications for schools', *Education 3–13*, 31 (1), 72–78.

Simkins, T. and Lumby, J. (2002) 'Cultural transformation in further education? Mapping the debate', *Research in Post-Compulsory Education*, 7 (1), 9–25.

Stoll, L., Fink, D. and Earl, L. (2003) *It's About Learning (and It's About Time!)*, London, RoutledgeFalmer.

Williams, S., Macalpine, A. and McCall, C. (2001) *Leading and Managing Staff through Challenging Times*, London, Stationery Office.

Wilson, V., Schlapp, U. and Davidson, J. (2003) 'An extra pair of hands? Managing classroom assistants in Scottish primary schools', *Educational Management and Administration*, 31 (2), 189–205.

Part II

Key Concepts

Organisational cultures

Introduction: defining culture

The concept of culture has become increasingly significant in education since the 1970s and into the twenty-first century. Lumby (2012, p. 576) comments that it has 'retained a tenacious hold on the literature'. This enhanced interest may be understood as an example of dissatisfaction with the limitations of those leadership and management models which stress the structural and technical aspects of schools and colleges. The focus on the intangible world of values and attitudes is a useful counter to these bureaucratic assumptions and helps to produce a more balanced portrait of educational institutions.

Culture relates to the informal aspects of organisations rather than their official elements. It focuses on the values, beliefs and norms of individuals in the organisation and how these individual perceptions coalesce into shared meanings. Culture is manifested by symbols and rituals rather than through the formal structure of the organisation:

> Beliefs, values and ideology are at the heart of organisations. Individuals hold certain ideas and value-preferences which influence how they behave and how they view the behaviour of other members. These norms become shared traditions which are communicated within the group and are reinforced by symbols and ritual. (Bush 2011, p. 170)

However, Lumby (2012) cautions that defining culture is 'notoriously difficult'. She also notes that culture, climate and ethos may be used interchangeably by some authors.

The developing importance of culture arises partly from a wish to understand, and operate more effectively within, this informal domain of the values and beliefs of teachers, support staff and other stakeholders. Morgan (1997) and O'Neill (1994) both stress the increasing significance of cultural factors in leadership and management. The latter charts the appearance of cultural 'labels' and suggests why they have become more prevalent:

> The increased use of such cultural descriptors in the literature of educational management is significant because it reflects a need for educational organizations to be able to articulate deeply held and shared values in more tangible ways and therefore respond more effectively to new, uncertain and potentially threatening demands on their capabilities . . . In this sense the analysis and influence of organizational culture become essential management tools in the pursuit of increased organizational growth and effectiveness. (O'Neill 1994, p. 116)

The shift towards self-management in many countries reinforces the notion of schools and colleges as unique entities with their own distinctive features or 'culture'. It is inevitable that self-management will lead to greater diversity and, in England, the widespread introduction of academies and 'free schools', independent of local government, weakens the notion of an education 'system', while strengthening the individuality of educational institutions. Lumby (2001) also notes the impact of new funding models on culture in English further education colleges. Caldwell and Spinks (1992) argue that there is 'a culture of self-management'. The essential components of this culture are the *empowerment* of leaders and their acceptance of *responsibility*.

Societal culture

Most of the literature on culture in education relates to organisational culture and that is also the main focus of this chapter. However, there is also an emerging literature on the broader theme of national or societal culture. Given the globalisation of education, issues of societal culture are increasingly significant, but Bottery (2004, p. 36) warns of 'cultural globalisation', where standardisation arises from uncritical adoption of international, usually Western, norms and values. Walker (2010,

p. 178) notes that 'culture can be applied in big picture terms to nations, societies, religious or ethnic groups'. Walker and Dimmock refer to issues of context and stress the need to avoid 'decontextualized paradigms' in researching and analysing educational systems and institutions:

> It is clear that a key factor missing from many debates on educational administration and leadership is context . . . context is represented by societal culture and its mediating influence on theory, policy and practice. (2002, p. 2)

Walker and Dimmock are by no means alone in advocating attention to issues of context. Bush et al. (1998, p. 137) referring to their study of school management in China, stress that 'all theories and interpretations of practice must be "grounded" in the specific context . . . before they can be regarded as useful'.

Dimmock and Walker (2002, p. 71) have given sustained attention to these issues and provide a helpful distinction between societal and organisational culture:

> Societal cultures differ mostly at the level of basic values, while organizational cultures differ mostly at the level of more superficial practices, as reflected in the recognition of particular symbols, heroes and rituals. *This allows organizational cultures to be deliberately managed and changed,* whereas societal or national cultures are more enduring and change only gradually over longer time periods. School leaders influence, and in turn are influenced by, the organizational culture. Societal culture, on the other hand, is a given, being outside the sphere of influence of an individual school leader. (Our emphasis)

Dimmock and Walker (2002) identify seven 'dimensions' of societal culture, each of which is expressed as a continuum. Bush and Qiang (2000) apply four of these to Chinese education:

1   *Power distributed/power concentrated*: power is either distributed more equally among the various levels of a culture or is more concentrated. In China, *power is concentrated* in the hands of a limited number of leaders. 'The principal has positional authority within an essentially bureaucratic system . . . China might be regarded as the archetypal high power-distance (power-concentrated) society' (p. 60).

2   *Group-oriented/self-oriented*: people in self-oriented cultures perceive themselves to be more independent and self-reliant. In group-

oriented cultures, ties between people are tight, relationships are firmly structured and individual needs are subservient to the collective needs. Chinese culture is *group oriented*. 'Collective benefits [are] seen as more important than individual needs' (p. 61).

3   *Consideration/aggression*: in aggression cultures, achievement is stressed, competition dominates and conflicts are resolved through the exercise of power and assertiveness. In contrast, consideration societies emphasise relationships, solidarity and resolution of conflicts by compromise and negotiation. Chinese culture stresses *consideration* rather than aggression. 'The Confucian scholars advocate modesty and encourage friendly co-operation, giving priority to people's relationships. The purpose of education is to mould every individual into a harmonious member of society' (p. 62).

4   *Male influence/female influence*: in some societies, the male domination of decision-making in political, economic and professional life is perpetuated. In others, women have come to play a significant role. *Patriarchal leadership* dominates in education, business, government and the Communist Party itself. There were no women principals in the 89 secondary schools in three counties of the Shaanxi province studied by Coleman et al. (1998), who attribute such inequalities to the continuing dominance of patriarchy. In contrast, in the Seychelles, the Minister of Education, most senior civil servants and almost all heads are women (Bush, Purvis and Barallon 2008).

Societal culture is one important aspect of the context within which school leaders must operate. Leaders and managers must also be aware of organisational culture, which provides a more immediate framework for leadership action. Principals and others can help to shape culture but they are also influenced by it.

Central features of organisational culture

Organisational culture has the following major features (Bush 2011):

1   It focuses on the *values and beliefs* of members of organisations. These values underpin the behaviour and attitudes of individuals within schools and colleges but they may not always be explicit. These individual beliefs coalesce into shared values: 'Shared values, shared beliefs, shared meaning, shared understanding, and shared

sensemaking are all different ways of describing culture' (Morgan 1997, p. 138).

This does not necessarily mean that individual values are always in harmony with one another. Morgan (1997, p. 137) suggests that 'there may be different and competing value systems that create a mosaic of organizational realities rather than a uniform corporate culture'. Dissonance is more likely in large, multipurpose organisations such as colleges and universities but Nias et al. (1989) note that it may also exist in primary education. Fullan and Hargreaves (1992, pp. 71–72) argue that some schools develop a 'balkanized' culture made up of separate and sometimes competing groups: teachers in balkanized cultures attach their loyalties and identities to particular groups of their colleagues. The existence of such groups in a school or college often reflects and reinforces very different group outlooks on learning, teaching styles, discipline and curriculum. Bates (2006, p. 160) stresses that culture is not unified but 'a complex mosaic of negotiation (and sometimes rebellion), constantly shaped by the exercise of power'.

Staff working in sub-units, such as departments, may develop their own distinctive 'subculture' and middle leaders may wish to cultivate this as a way of developing and enhancing team effectiveness. However, as Fullan and Hargreaves (1992) imply, such subcultures may not be consistent with the whole-school or -college culture.

2   Organisational culture emphasises the development of *shared norms and meanings*. The assumption is that interaction between members of the organisation, or its subgroups, eventually leads to behavioural norms that gradually become cultural features of the school or college. Nias et al.'s (1989, pp. 39–40) research shows how group norms were established in their case-study schools:

> As staff talked, worked and relaxed together, they began to negotiate shared meanings which enabled them to predict each other's behaviour. Consequently each staff developed its own taken-for-granted norms.

These group norms sometimes allow the development of a monoculture in a school with meanings shared throughout the staff – 'the way we do things around here'. We have already noted, however, that there may be several subcultures based on the professional and personal interests of different groups. These typically have internal coherence but experience difficulty in relationships with other groups whose behavioural norms are different.

Wallace and Hall (1994, pp. 28 and 127) identify senior management teams (SMTs) as one example of group culture with clear internal norms but often weak connections to other groups and individuals:

> SMTs in our research developed a 'culture of teamwork' . . . A norm common to the SMTs was that decisions must be reached by achieving a working consensus, entailing the acknowledgement of any dissenting views . . . there was a clear distinction between interaction inside the team and contact with those outside . . . [who] were excluded from the inner world of the team.

Wallace (2002, p. 174) argues the need for strong links between the senior leadership team (SLT) and other staff, 'which win their respect' and 'reduce the headteacher's isolation from staff colleagues'. This issue was a central theme of research on high performing leadership teams in England (Bush and Glover 2012). Most of their case study schools gave considerable attention to developing and maintaining good links with other staff. At one secondary school, for example, SLT offices are spread around the school to facilitate interaction. Hall and Wallace (1996) show the dangers of SLTs being seen as remote from the rest of the school and almost all of Bush and Glover's (2012) case study schools appear to have worked hard to ensure cohesion. However, this raises questions about whether such strategies are used to underpin senior leaders' power, and to undermine sub-groups.

3   Culture is typically expressed through *rituals and ceremonies* which are used to support and celebrate beliefs and norms. Schools, in particular, are rich in symbols such as assemblies, prize-givings and corporate worship. 'Symbols are a key component of the culture of all schools . . . [they] have expressive tasks and symbols which are the only means whereby abstract values can be conveyed . . . Symbols are central to the process of constructing meaning' (Hoyle 1986, pp. 150–152).

Schein (1997, p. 248) argues that 'rites and rituals [are] central to the deciphering as well as to the communicating of cultural assumptions'.

4   Organisational culture assumes the existence of *heroes and heroines* who embody the values and beliefs of the organisation. These

honoured members typify the behaviours associated with the culture of the institution. Campbell-Evans (1993, p. 106) stresses that heroes or heroines are those whose achievements match the culture: 'Choice and recognition of heroes . . . occurs within the cultural boundaries identified through the value filter . . . The accomplishments of those individuals who come to be regarded as heroes are compatible with the cultural emphases.' This feature is evident in South Africa, for example, where the huge interest in school sport means that sporting heroes are identified and celebrated. This was noted in a Durban school visited by one of the authors, where numerous photographs of former student Shaun Pollock, the South African fast bowler were on display and a room was named after him. In celebrating the achievements of this cricketing 'hero', school managers are seeking to emphasise the centrality of sporting achievement to the ethos and culture of the school.

These four 'central features' are not of equal significance. Hofstede (1984) distinguishes between 'deep culture', the shared values of organisational members, and 'shallow culture', the visible signals of culture. Values and norms are the core components of culture while symbols, rituals and heroes are manifestations of it.

Developing a culture of learning in South Africa

As we noted earlier (see page 54), societal or national culture underpins the organisational culture of individual schools and colleges. Nowhere is this more apparent than in South African schools where the predominant culture reflects the wider social structure of the post-apartheid era. Decades of institutionalised racism and injustice have been replaced by an overt commitment to democracy in all aspects of life, including education. Ngcobo (2003) addresses issues of cultural diversity and discusses nine dimensions of African culture: spirituality, harmony, movement, verve, affect, communalism, expressive individualism, oral tradition and social time perspective – time as social rather than material space.

Ngcobo (2003) notes that these cultural features are very different from European cultures. Such cultural differences became particularly significant as some schools began to change their racial composition in response to the South African Schools Act (1996), which made it illegal to deny admission to students on the basis of race, and as a consequence of internal and international migration. Former white schools, with a predominantly 'European' culture, began to assimilate learners, and to a lesser extent educators, from different cultural backgrounds. Ngcobo (2003) gives two contrasting examples of how school leaders responded to these cultural changes. One high school avoided cultural diversity by dividing the premises into two sections, white and black, while another adopted a different approach, aiming at cultural diversity and encouraging learners and staff to express and celebrate their own cultures.

During the apartheid era, many of the 'black' schools became centres of resistance to the unpopular regime. Both learners and educators were frequently absent to take part in protest activity or simply because they were demoralised by government policies. They were also deeply concerned about the inequitable funding regimes for different racial groups. As a result, it became difficult for school principals to establish and sustain a 'culture of learning' in township and many deep rural schools. Both educators and learners became more involved with the struggle than with their own learning and teaching. They did not want to co-operate with a racist system even if they were disadvantaged by such a stance.

Bush and Anderson's (2003) survey of school principals in the KwaZulu-Natal province shows that they wanted 'to develop a culture of learning'. Its ongoing absence in many South African schools illustrates the long-term and uncertain nature of cultural change. The long years of resistance to apartheid education have to be replaced by a commitment to teaching and learning if South Africa is to thrive in an increasingly competitive world economy. However, educational values have to compete with the still prevalent discourse of struggle and also have to reconcile the diverse value systems of the different subcultures in South Africa's integrated schools. Recent research (Bush and Glover 2012b; Bush et al. 2011) shows that factionalism and intra-staff disputes continue to undermine teaching and learning in some township schools, and create serious challenges for school leaders.

Leadership and culture

We noted earlier (see page 56) that societal culture is beyond the control of educational leaders but heads and principals are able to influence organisational culture. Lumby (2001, p. 143) notes that 'understanding culture in any college is therefore a question of decoding the signals to arrive at the central beliefs of the organisation'. Arguably, senior leaders have the main responsibility for generating and sustaining culture and communicating core values and beliefs both within the organisation and to external stakeholders (Bush 1998; 2011). Heads and principals have their own values and beliefs arising from many years of successful professional practice. They are also expected to embody the culture of the school or college. As Schein (2011, p. xi) asserts, 'I doubt that there is a manager or scholar alive that does not take the concepts of climate and culture seriously'. Spillane (2006) also notes the widespread adherence to the notion of a charismatic leader, who can transform culture and produce significant school improvement. However, Walker (2010, p. 194) warns that 'there is no recipe or guidebook for building learning cultures; it is not that simple'.

Schein (1997, p. 211) argues that cultures spring primarily from the beliefs, values and assumptions of founders of organisations. Nias et al. (1989, p. 103) suggest that heads are 'founders' of their school's culture. They refer to two of their English case study schools where new heads dismantled the existing culture in order to create a new one based on their own values. The culture was rebuilt through example: 'All the heads of the project schools were aware of the power of example. Each head expected to influence staff through his/her example. Yet their actions may also have been symbolic of the values they tried to represent.' Nias et al. (1989) also mention the significance of co-leaders, such as deputy heads and curriculum co-ordinators, in disseminating school culture.

One of the ways in which leaders can shape or change culture is through the appointment of other staff who have the same values and beliefs, leading to cultural consonance. In this view, the staff selection process provides an opportunity to set out the values of the school, or its leaders, in the hope that those who hold similar values will be attracted to the post while others will be deterred from making or pursuing an application. Over time, the culture of the school will shift in the direction sought by the principal. The literature on collegiality (for example, Bush 2011) shows that leaders are more likely to cede power to others when they are confident that their own educational values will not be compromised by doing so.

Foskett and Lumby (2003) point out that staff selection processes are themselves subject to cultural variables. They distinguish between 'universalistic' and 'particularistic' approaches to selection. The universalistic approach, as discussed in Chapter 9 of this volume, for example, attempts to match applicants to objective criteria and is thought to be 'more successful in identifying the best match to the vacant post' (Foskett and Lumby 2003, p. 71). This contrasts with the particularistic approach adopted, for example, in Africa and in China. Here, 'selection is shaped by the personal affiliation of the players, for example kinship, religion, ethnic or political similarities' (ibid., p. 70). This approach is likely to be successful in ensuring that the appointees have similar values to the leaders.

Using cultural criteria to appoint new staff may help to modify culture but the established staff, and inertia, may still ensure that change is highly problematic. Reynolds (1996, pp. 153–154) refers to one school where the prevailing culture was 'posing severe difficulties for any purported change attempts'. He points to 'multiple barriers to change' including:

- staff wanting 'top down' change and not 'ownership'
- 'we've always done it this way'
- individual reluctance to challenge the prevailing culture
- staff blaming children's home background for examination failure
- numerous personality clashes, personal agendas and fractured interpersonal relationships.

This example illustrates the difficulty of attempting to impose cultural change. Hargreaves (1999, p. 59) comments that 'most people's beliefs, attitudes and values are far more resistant to change than leaders typically allow'. He identifies three circumstances when culture may be subject to rapid change:

- The school faces an obvious crisis, for example a highly critical inspection report or falling pupil numbers, leading to the prospect of staff redundancies or school closure.

- The leader is very charismatic, commanding instant trust, loyalty and fellowship. This may enable cultural change to be more radical and be achieved more quickly.

- There is a new leader, particularly if the new leader succeeds a very poor principal. Staff will be looking for change to instil a new sense of direction.

These points may also apply to sub-units and subcultures. Hargreaves (1999, p. 60) concludes that, 'if none of these special conditions applies, assume that cultural change will be rather slow'. Leaders also have responsibility for sustaining culture, and cultural maintenance is often regarded as a central feature of effective leadership.

Limitations of organisational culture

The concept of organisational culture contributes several useful elements to the leadership and management of people in schools and colleges.

The focus on the informal dimension is a valuable counter to the rigid and official components of the formal models. By stressing the values and beliefs of participants, culture reinforces the human aspects of management rather than the structural elements. However, this approach has three significant weaknesses (Bush 2011):

1   The notion of 'organisational culture' may simply be the imposition of the leaders' values on other members of the organisation. The search for a monoculture may mean subordinating the values and beliefs of some participants to those of leaders, or the dominant group. 'Shared' cultures may be simply the values of leaders imposed on less powerful people. Morgan (1997, pp. 150–151) refers to 'a process of ideological control' and warns of the risk of 'manipulation':

> Ideological manipulation and control is being advocated as an essential managerial strategy . . . such manipulation may well be accompanied by resistance, resentment and mistrust.

Prosser (1999, p. 4) refers to the 'dark underworld' of school culture and links it to the concept of micropolitics: 'The micropolitical perspective recognized that formal powers, rules, regulations, traditions and rituals were capable of being subverted by individuals, groups or affiliations in schools'. Hargreaves (1999, p. 60) uses the term 'resistance group' to refer to sub-units seeking to subvert leaders and their intended cultural change. However, this may simply be a legitimate attempt to enunciate the specific values of, for example, departmental culture.

2   The portrayal of culture may be unduly mechanistic, assuming that leaders can determine the culture of the organisation (Morgan 1997). While they have influence over the evolution of culture by espousing desired values, they cannot ensure the emergence of a monoculture. As we have seen, secondary schools and colleges may have several subcultures operating in departments and other sections. This is not necessarily dysfunctional because successful sub-units are vital components of thriving institutions, and successful middle-level leadership and management are increasingly regarded as essential to school and college effectiveness (Harris 2002; Briggs 2003).

   In an era of self-managing schools and colleges in many countries, lay influences on policy are increasingly significant. Governing bodies often have the formal responsibility for major decisions and they share in the creation of institutional culture. This does not mean simple acquiescence to the values of the head or principal. Rather, there may be negotiation leading to the possibility of conflict and the adoption of policies inconsistent with the leader's own values.

3   Symbols may misrepresent the reality of the school or college. Hoyle (1986) suggests that schools may go through the appearance of change but the reality continues as before:

> A symbol can represent something which is 'real' in the sense that it . . . acts as a surrogate for reality . . . in reality the system carries on as formerly. (p. 166)

Schein (1997, p. 249) also warns against placing too much reliance on ritual.

> When the only salient data we have are the rites and rituals that have survived over a period of time, we must, of course, use them as best we can . . . however . . . it is difficult to decipher just what assumptions leaders have held that have led to the creation of particular rites and rituals.

Conclusion: people and culture

The belief that schools and colleges are unique entities is gaining ground as people increasingly recognise the importance of the specific contexts, internal and external, which provide the frameworks within which leaders and managers must operate. Despite the pressures of globalisation, understanding and managing the school context is a vital dimension of leadership in the twenty-first century. Values and beliefs are not universal and a 'one size fits all' model does not work for nations any more than it does for schools.

The recognition that school and college development needs to be preceded by attitudinal change is also salutary, and is consistent with the view that teachers must feel 'ownership' of change if it is to be implemented effectively. Externally imposed innovation often fails because it is out of tune with the values of the teachers who have to implement it.

The emphasis on values and symbols may also help to balance the focus on structure and process in many of the other models. The informal world of norms and ritual behaviour may be just as significant as the formal elements of schools and colleges. 'Even the most concrete and rational aspects of organization – whether structures, hierarchies, rules, or organizational routines – embody social constructions and meanings that are crucial for understanding how organization functions day to day' (Morgan 1997, p. 146).

Culture also provides a focus for organisational action. Effective leaders often seek to influence values so that they become closer to, if not identical with, their own beliefs. In this way, they hope to achieve widespread support for, or 'ownership' of, new policies. By working through this informal domain, rather than imposing change through positional authority or political processes, heads, principals and other leaders, including middle managers, are more likely to gain support for innovation.

An understanding of both societal and organisational culture also provides a sound basis for leading and managing people in education. In many countries, schools and colleges are becoming multicultural, and recognition of the rich diversity of the cultural backgrounds of students, parents and staff is an essential element in school management. Similarly, all educational organisations have certain distinctive features and understanding and managing this cultural apparatus is vital if leadership is to be 'in tune' with the prevailing norms and values. An appreciation of the relevance of both societal and organisational culture, and of the values, beliefs and rituals that underpin them, is just as important as consideration of organisational structure, the focus of the next chapter.

References

Bates, R. (2006) 'Culture and leadership in educational administration: A historical study of what was said and what might have been', *Journal of Educational Administration and History*, 38 (2), 155–168.

Bottery, M. (2004) *The Challenges of Educational Leadership*, London, Paul Chapman Publishing.

Briggs, A. (2003) 'Finding the balance: exploring the organic and mechanical dimensions of middle managers' roles in English further education colleges', *Educational Management and Administration*, 31 (4), 421–436.

Bush, T. (1998) 'Organisational culture and strategic management', in Middlewood, D. and Lumby, J. (eds), *Strategic Management in Schools and Colleges*, London, Paul Chapman Publishing.

Bush, T. (2011) *Theories of Educational Leadership and Management, Fourth Edition*, London, Sage.

Bush, T. and Anderson, L. (2003) 'Organisational culture', in Thurlow, M., Bush, T. and Coleman, M. (eds), *Leadership and Strategic Management in South African Schools*, London, Commonwealth Secretariat.

Bush, T. and Glover, D. (2012a) 'Distributed leadership in action: Leading High Performing Leadership Teams in English Schools', *School Leadership and Management*, 32 (1), 21–36.

Bush, T. and Glover, D. (2012b) 'Leadership development and learning outcomes: Evidence from South Africa', *Journal of Educational Leadership, Policy and Practice*, 27 (2), 3-15.

Bush, T. and Qiang, H. (2000) 'Leadership and culture in Chinese education', *Asia Pacific Journal of Education*, 20 (2), 58–67.

Bush, T., Qiang, H. and Fang, J. (1998) 'Educational management in China: an overview', *Compare*, 28 (2), 133–140.

Bush, T., Purvis, M.T. and Barallon, L. (2008) 'Leadership development in small-island states', in Lumby, J., Pashiardis, P. and Crow, G. (eds.), *International Handbook on the Preparation and Development of School Leaders*, New York, Routledge.

Bush, T., Duku, N., Glover, D., Kiggundu, E., Msila, V. and Moorosi, P. (2011) *The Impact of the National ACE Programme on School and Learner Outcomes*, Pretoria, Department of Basic Education.

Caldwell, B. and Spinks, J. (1992) *Leading the Self-Managing School*, London, Falmer Press.

Campbell-Evans, G. (1993) 'A values perspective on school-based management', in Dimmock, C. (ed.), *School-Based Management and School Effectiveness*, London, Routledge.

Coleman, M., Qiang, H. and Li, Y. (1998) 'Women in educational management in China: experience in Shaanxi province', *Compare*, 28 (2), 141–154.

Dimmock, C. and Walker, A. (2002) 'School leadership in context – societal and organizational cultures', in Bush, T. and Bell, L. (eds), *The Principles and Practice of Educational Management*, London, Paul Chapman Publishing.

Foskett, N. and Lumby, J. (2003) *Leading and Managing Education: International Dimensions*, London, Paul Chapman Publishing.

Fullan, M. and Hargreaves, A. (1992) *What's Worth Fighting for in Your School?*, Buckingham, Open University Press.

Hall, V. and Wallace, M. (1996) 'Let the team take the strain: lessons from research into senior management teams in secondary schools', *School Organisation*, 16 (3), 297–308.

Hargreaves, D. (1999) 'Helping practitioners explore their school's culture', in Prosser, J. (ed.), *School Culture*, London, Paul Chapman Publishing.

Harris, A. (2002) 'Effective leadership in schools facing challenging circumstances', *School Leadership and Management*, 22 (1), 15–26.

Hofstede, G. (1984) *Culture's Consequences: International Differences in Work-Related Values*, Newbury Park, CA, Sage.

Hoyle, E. (1986) *The Politics of School Management*, Sevenoaks, Hodder and Stoughton.

Lumby, J. (2001) *Managing Further Education: Learning Enterprise*, London, Paul Chapman.

Lumby, J. (2012) 'Leading organizational culture: Issues of power and equity', *Educational Management, Administration and Leadership*, 40 (5), 576–591.

Morgan, G. (1997) *Images of Organization*, Newbury Park, CA, Sage.

Ngcobo, T. (2003) 'Managing multicultural contexts', in Lumby, J., Middlewood, D. and Kaabwe, E. (eds), *Managing Human Resources in South African Schools*, London, Commonwealth Secretariat.

Nias, J., Southworth, G. and Yeomans, R. (1989) *Staff Relationships in the Primary School*, London, Cassell.

O'Neill, J. (1994) 'Organizational structure and culture', in Bush, T. and West-Burnham, J. (eds), *The Principles of Educational Management*, Harlow, Longman.

Prosser, J. (1999) *School Culture*, London, Paul Chapman Publishing.

Reynolds, D. (1996) 'Turning round ineffective schools: some evidence and some speculations', in Gray, J., Reynolds, D., Fitz-Gibbon, C. and Jesson, D. (eds), *Merging Traditions: The Future of Research on School Effectiveness and School Improvement*, London, Cassell.

Schein, E. (1997) *Organizational Culture and Leadership*, San Francisco, CA, Jossey-Bass.

Schein, E. (2011) 'Preface', in Ashkanasy, N., Wilderson, C. and Petersen, M. (eds.), *Handbook of Organizational Culture and Climate*, Thousand Oaks, CA, Sage.

Spillane, J. (2006) *Distributed Leadership*, San Francisco, CA: Jossey Bass.

Walker, A. (2010) 'Building and leading learning cultures', in Bush, T., Bell, L. and Middlewood, D., *The Principles of Educational Leadership and Management, Second Edition*, London, Sage.

Walker, A. and Dimmock, C. (2002) 'Introduction', in Walker, A. and Dimmock, C. (eds), *School Leadership and Administration: Adopting a Cultural Perspective*, London, Routledge-Falmer.

Wallace, M. (2002) 'Modelling distributed leadership and management effectiveness: Primary school senior management teams in England and Wales', *School Effectiveness and School Improvement*, 13 (2), 163–186.

Wallace, M. and Hall, V. (1994) *Inside the SMT: Teamwork in Secondary School Management*, London, Paul Chapman Publishing.

5

Organisational structures and roles

Introduction: the nature and purpose of organisational structure

Structure refers to the formal pattern of relationships between people in organisations. It expresses the ways in which people relate to each other in order to achieve organisational objectives. Structure is often represented by diagrams or charts which show the authorised pattern of relationships between members of the organisation. However, there is a tension between the focus on structure and the individual characteristics which people bring to their workplaces. If structure is regarded as a framework for individual role holders, it must also reflect the perspectives of these individuals. As Lumby (2001, p. 82) suggests:

> 'the very concept of an organisational structure is problematic, as the organisation is a theoretical concept which exists in reality only as a set of buildings and people . . . Whatever the "structure" on paper, the reality will be a maelstrom of loosely connected beliefs and activities'.

Despite this recognition of the importance, and variability, of individuals, all organisations have some form of structure which is recognisable and provides the framework for organisational activity. Lumby (2001, p. 83) extends the notion of structure to embrace the external environment which interacts with the organisation and may enable or constrain its activities.

Fidler (1997) argues that structures have two overarching purposes: control and co-ordination. Structures are often tightened in an attempt to achieve greater control. Changing school management structures is one of the ways in which new principals can exert their influence over the school or college. However, creativity is more likely to be encouraged with a looser framework designed to co-ordinate rather then to control. Fullan (1999, p. 5) notes that too little structure creates chaos while too much leads to 'gridlock'. Lumby (2001, p. 85) concludes that 'any structure will be a compromise which cannot achieve all that is required. It may be necessary to identify the primary objectives the structure is to achieve from the myriad that are possible'.

Structures and hierarchy

An abiding feature of structure is its emphasis on hierarchy. Organisations are almost always portrayed in terms of a vertical, or pyramidal, structure. Briggs's (2002, p. 66) 'generalised hierarchy of management in further education colleges' includes middle managers as being at the third or fourth tier of the college hierarchy. They are subordinate to the principal and the senior management team but superordinate to staff working in their teams. Harper (2000) also emphasises the dominance of hierarchy in English further education. Her study of 107 such colleges leads her to conclude that 'one broad type of structure has become dominant which . . . has become labelled as "the new college hierarchy"':

> In the new college hierarchy no two colleges are identical.
> However, the common features are that the senior management team most typically consists of a chief executive and two, three or four senior managers, each accountable for one or more broad areas of operational management. Academic and support functions are centralised and middle managers coordinate varying aspects of support for teaching and learning within flatter organisational structures. (p. 434)

Lumby's (2001) work in this sector suggests that the hierarchy is being modified as college principals respond to funding constraints. 'Management posts have been deleted, leading to flatter organisations' (p. 86). Despite this trend, Lumby (2001, p. 92) notes that 'some degree of bureaucratic hierarchy will always assert itself' and that structural change is often presented as a way of 'softening the rather negative connotations of hierarchy' (p. 91).

The pervasiveness of hierarchy is demonstrated by its prevalence in other sectors of education. Smith (2002) joins with Deem (2000) to note that higher education structures are highly managerial and bureaucratic, notably in the new, or statutory, universities. Wallace and Hall's (1994) study of secondary school management teams also shows the significance of hierarchy. Within such teams, 'distinctions between levels of individual management responsibility variably reflected the formal status hierarchy within each team' (p. 50). Heads are superordinate because of their overall responsibility for the school, leading to a 'major hierarchical distinction' (p. 52) at one school, while the most "senior" deputy acted in the head's absence, contributing to 'a perception of hierarchy' (p. 52). This research demonstrates that, even in ostensibly collaborative frameworks, such as teams, hierarchy remains a powerful determinant of structure and process (see Chapter 8).

More recent research on senior leadership teams, by Bush and Glover (2012a), shows that structures are influenced by two considerations: how leadership responsibilities are distributed and the size of the team. They note a trend towards larger and more diverse teams, and towards integrated structures where academic and pastoral dimensions are linked.

Hierarchy is a dominant feature of structure in many other countries. In South Africa, for example, there are at least three levels external to the school (national, provincial and district). There are also powerful bureaucratic constraints on the nature of internal structures, with prescriptions about the number of management posts, and on the size and composition of SMTs (Bush et al. 2010). Bush et al. (1998) note that in China there is 'a complex and elaborate structure with five separate levels external to the school' (p. 133) and bureaucratic requirements for the nature of internal structures.

The growing interest in distributed leadership, and in new models of leadership, has loosened the links between structure and hierarchy in the twenty-first century. In England, new forms of organisation, such as federations and academy chains, have extended structures beyond the school boundary, and widened the scope of leadership (Bush 2011a). Similarly, interest in networks, and other forms of partnership, offer alternative ways of conceptualising structure, with a reduced focus on hierarchy (Briggs 2010; Townsend 2010). Harris (2010) and Gronn (2010) use the term 'configuration' to describe the more fluid arrangements associated with distributed and teacher leadership. This notion does not supplant structure but offers a more flexible framework for understanding the nature of educational organisations.

The determinants of structure

A significant determinant of structure, as noted above, is the extent to which organisations are able to design or modify it to meet institutional needs. The central control in China means that there is little scope for local initiative, and structures are very similar in all schools. The administrative structure has four main divisions:

- the principal's office, including one vice-principal in schools with 12–24 classes and two vice-principals in larger schools

- the Teaching Affairs section, responsible for the management of teaching and political (or moral) education

- the General Affairs section, responsible for infrastructure, including finance, buildings and equipment

- the school factory or farm, whose profits contribute to school income (Bush et al. 1998).

There is also a parallel Communist Party structure headed by a branch secretary in each school. Bush et al. (1998) note that the structure is unwieldy, with limited scope for principals to influence its design, or to modify it as circumstances change.

In England, structure is usually one of the discretionary elements of organisations. Leaders inherit structure but are free to adapt it to meet local needs:

> The internal management structures of colleges, and the contexts in which they operate, are . . . largely developed in response to local management need, and shaped by the philosophies of those who manage them. (Briggs 2002, p. 64)

The institutional context is a major variable in determining structure. Scale is one key dimension and larger organisations tend to have more complex structures. This is illustrated by one college, studied by Briggs (2002), whose staff refer to 'imperfections and frustrations' (p. 71), which can be attributed to the college being both large and located on several sites.

Lumby (2001) shows how English colleges use the management structure as a tool for cultural change. Of the 164 colleges responding to her survey, only four had not restructured within the previous six years. Most had done so more than once in a 'belief in the efficacy of achieving the right structure to support effective management' (p. 82).

Wildy and Louden (2000), referring to restructuring in the USA, point to three dilemmas for school principals:

1   The *autonomy* dilemma – principals are expected to share power with professional colleagues.
2   The *efficiency* dilemma – principals are expected to minimise the wastage of resources such as time, energy and commitment. This requirement conflicts with the pressures for participation.
3   The *accountability* dilemma – the principal has to be answerable to the district. This requirement also limits the scope for autonomy and participation.

School structures are likely to be a compromise, taking account of each of these dilemmas. In South Africa, accountability to the district is a key constraint on structure (Bush et al. 2011). In England, there may be a strong rhetorical commitment to participation and 'distributed leadership', but a residual reliance on formal structure. Wallace and Hall (1994) show that their six case study secondary schools 'all exhibited a strong commitment among members to a team approach to management' while retaining a significant measure of hierarchy both within, and external to, their senior management teams. The nature and significance of structure may also be influenced by gender. Coleman's (2002) study of English secondary school headteachers suggests that women are more likely than men to favour collaboration and teamwork.

Structures and organisational theory

Structure is an important aspect of the theory of educational leadership and management. The treatment of structure varies according to the conceptual assumptions underpinning each theory (Bush 2011b).

Bureaucracy

As we have noted, most organisational structures in education, particularly those in secondary schools and colleges, tend to be consistent with bureaucratic assumptions and some could be regarded as pictorial representations of bureaucracy. The hierarchical pyramid, referred to earlier, is based on bureaucratic theories (Bush 2011b). This is reflected in the structure of English further education colleges (Lumby 2001). It is also evident in New Zealand where Fitzgerald (2009, p. 53) refers to 'the bureaucracy of leadership' and 'the insistent practice that leadership is connected with hierarchy'. She complains about the 'tyranny of bureaucracy that leaves little time for leadership' (ibid., p. 63) and concludes that 'the organization and hierarchy of schools replicates industrial models of working that differentiates people and activities according to position' (ibid., p. 64). Saiti (2009, p. 396) makes a similar point about Greece, arguing that its education system has become 'a bureaucracy in the negative sense – one of a narrow hierarchy', which cannot be 'instantly responsive to a more fluid and distributed approach to leadership' (ibid., p. 399). Goldspink (2007, p. 30), drawing on research in South Australian schools, concludes that 'the assumption that educational systems are or should be approached as formal command and control hierarchies . . . has been shown to be unrealistic'.

Collegiality

An alternative to hierarchy is a collegial structure. In this model, structures are flattened and communication tends to be lateral rather than vertical, reflecting the view that all teachers should be involved in decision-making and 'own' the outcome of discussions. Authority in collegial structures is based on professional expertise rather than formal position. Ad hoc working parties, rather than committees whose membership is determined by position, may be more effective in promoting collegiality, as Brown et al. (1999, p. 323) suggest in relation to English secondary schools. 'We have working parties who report back to faculties after consultation with the senior management team and collaborative policies are produced and implemented.'

There is some evidence of collegiality even within the largely bureaucratic structures prevalent in China and South Africa. Chinese schools have teaching and research groups (*jiaoyanzu*) which operate on the 'assumption that teachers would work together in almost every aspect of their work' (Paine and Ma 1993, p. 676). In many South African schools, there is at least a rhetorical commitment to shared decision-making. Some SMTs in the Limpopo and Mpumalanga provinces held regular meetings to discuss school priorities and practice but, significantly, some met rarely, if at all, suggesting weak collegiality at best (Bush et al. 2010). Cameron's (2005, p. 328) study of a secondary school in the USA showed that collaborative working led to tensions, notably for the principal, who felt the need to 'negotiate the policies in which she believes strongly, rather than leave them to the unpredictable nature of the shared governance'.

Referring to English further education, Harper (2000, p. 442) suggests that 'team-based, non-hierarchical structures are far more appropriate for today's changing environment' but warns that 'flat organisations, by their very nature, present few opportunities for promotion, whereas in a Weberian bureaucracy there is a clearly defined career structure'.

English primary schools usually have flat and unstratified structures. Teachers are accountable directly to the head, rather than via an intermediate authority, limiting the extent and importance of the hierarchy, and providing the potential for distributed leadership (Bush and Glover 2012a).

Distributed leadership

Distributed leadership de-emphasises formal structure, preferring to stress relationships and informal arrangements. Harris (2010, p. 59) notes that 'a common misinterpretation is to position distributed leadership as the antithesis of top-down, hierarchical leadership'. Rather, it involves both vertical and lateral dimensions of leadership practice, and leadership moves between formal and informal leadership positions (ibid., p. 60). As we noted earlier, Harris (2010) and Gronn (2010) both use the term 'configuration' to describe leadership arrangements within a distributed model, while the latter also stresses the 'hybrid' nature of structure, linking individual and shared leadership. Townsend (2010) shows that networks, which might be regarded as a specific form of distributed leadership, involve voluntary collaboration rather than a more formal arrangement. Briggs (2010, p. 252) distinguishes between hierarchy and partnerships. 'Collaborative leadership offers a fundamental conceptual shift to a focus upon equity, mutuality and shared educational purpose'. Grant (2006, p. 514) notes the links between distributed and teacher leadership and claims that the latter 'is critical in the transformation of South African schools'.

Hartley (2010, p. 271) offers a cautious review of distributed leadership, noting that 'the reason for its popularity may be pragmatic, to ease the burden of over-worked headteachers'. This implies that this mode of leadership may be little more than disguised delegation, a means of allocating work to colleagues. He also notes that distributed leadership has 'fewer demarcations' but still has to co-exist with the formal structure. 'The "heterarchy" of distributed leadership resides uneasily within the formal bureaucracy of schools' (ibid., p. 282).

Bolden et al. (2009) note that leadership in UK higher education is widely distributed, but add that it has a wide variety of interpretations. They distinguish between 'devolved' distributed leadership, formal mechanisms for the distribution of roles and responsibilities, and 'emergent' processes of collaborative and informal leadership. They conclude that it may be 'most influential through its rhetorical value' and assert that it is 'not a successor to individual leadership' (ibid., p. 275).

Bush and Glover (2012a, p. 21), drawing on their study of high performing leadership teams, say that 'the work of effective senior leadership teams is an important manifestation of distributed leadership'. They distribute leadership in ways which give them a strong collective overview of teaching and learning. However, they caution that leaders may use the term 'distributed leadership' as it is more 'acceptable' than delegation. Genuine distributed leadership is more likely where 'there are high levels of trust and shared values' (ibid., p. 34).

Micropolitics

The departmental structure of many secondary schools and colleges may allow micropolitics to thrive with sub-units competing for resources and influence (Bush 2011b). The formal structure becomes the setting for conflict between interest groups and the structure may be subject to change through a process of bargaining and negotiation. 'Organisational structure[s] . . . are often best understood as products and reflections of a struggle for political control . . . organisational structure is frequently used as a political instrument' (Morgan 1997, pp. 175–176). Deal (2005, p. 114) advises leaders to use structure as a political asset. 'Politically, it is a way for leaders to consolidate power, reward allies or punish opponents.'

Goldspink (2007, p. 40) stresses the 'rich multi-dimensional coupling' of schools and colleges. This is often linked to the sectional interests of the different sub-units. This is evident, for example, in the Netherlands where there are two parallel structures representing subject departments and student guidance units. Imants et al. (2001, p. 290) argue that these are 'conflicting sub-structures', leading to tension, fragmentation and barriers between teachers of different subjects. Micropolitics are also evident in Wildy and Louden's (2000) study of high schools in the USA, where the case study principals worked with a 'balkanised senior staff group'.

There is also significant evidence of micropolitics influencing structure in England. This is often related to scale, as Bolton (2000, p. 57) suggests in relation to higher education. 'Larger units – those with more than, say, 30 staff – tend in any case to form themselves into interest groups or cliques.'

In further education, micropolitical 'territories' (Briggs 2005) exist while Lumby (2001, p. 89) points out that restructuring can be seen as 'an internal political process of reshaping power'. Harper (2000, p. 443) claims that 'there are serious conflicts between managers and lecturers in the sector'. Referring to Scottish further education colleges, McTavish (2006, p. 421) mentions 'micro-political factors' influencing roles and working patterns.

Salo's (2008) study of Finnish nursery schools is interpreted through a micropolitical lens, a continuing struggle for control, power and influence. He asks if meetings are 'arenas in which heads realize their formal power?' (ibid., p. 505), and concludes that any single model is partial and incomplete. This example illustrates the ease with which apparently collegial frameworks, such as meetings, can become the settings for micropolitical activity. In this model, the structure may be unstable and be subject to change as different interest groups seek to shape it to their advantage.

Subjective models

Subjective models regard organisational structure as an outcome of the interaction of participants rather than a fixed entity. Structure is a product of the behaviour of individuals and serves to explain the relationships between members of organisations. Subjective theories stress the different meanings placed on structure by individuals. Structural change may be ineffective if it does not address the underlying concerns of individuals. 'We are forced to see problems of organisational structure as inherent not in "structure" itself but in the human meanings and purposes which support that structure' (Greenfield 1973, p. 565).

Lumby's (2001, pp. 82–83) study of English further education colleges addresses this issue. 'As the goals and experience of each individual are unique, from the subjective standpoint, an organisation cannot exist as a coherent whole, but merely as the sum of the range of different perspectives and experiences.'

Ambiguity

Ambiguity models regard organisational structure as problematic. Institutions are portrayed as aggregations of loosely coupled sub-units with structures that may be both ambiguous and subject to change (Bush 2011b). One aspect of this process is the extent of participation in committees and working parties. People who are members of such committees may not participate regularly, may arrive late or leave early. 'One consequence of such structural ambiguities is that decisions may be possible only where there are enough participants. Attempts to make decisions without sufficient participation may founder at subsequent stages of the process' (Bush 2011b, p. 160).

Large organisations are particularly prone to structural ambiguity. Briggs (2002, p. 70) refers to a 'mismatch of role expectations' in English further education and subsequently adds that 'ambiguity and role overload are common features of the managers' situation' (Briggs 2005, p. 46). Lumby (2001, p. 100) states that, 'whether the official place within the structure of any role had changed or not, the way the role was seen by the role holder and by others continued to change, and was likely to be subject to ambiguity, conflict and overload'.

Culture

Structure may be regarded as the physical manifestation of the culture of the organisation. 'There is a close link between culture and structure: indeed they are interdependent' (Stoll 1999, p. 40). The values and beliefs of the institution are expressed in the pattern of roles and role relationships established by the school or college.

The larger and more complex the organisation, the greater the prospect of divergent meanings, leading to the development of sub-cultures, and the possibility of conflict between them (see Chapter 4). Lumby (2012), comments that assumptions that there is a single integrated culture within schools is not a credible position, and that subcultures are inevitable. If there is a dominant culture, this is likely to be as a result of the exercise of overt or covert power. Subcultures are evident in English further education where managers are perceived to have a different value system from that of academic staff (Randle and Brady 1997; Harper 2000). Elliott (1996) contrasts the student-centred pedagogic culture of lecturers with the managerialist culture of managers.

Leadership and management roles

Structure is usually expressed in two distinctive features of the organisation. First, there is a pattern of committees and working parties which have regular or ad hoc meetings. Secondly, individual roles are established and there is a prescribed or recommended pattern of relationships between role holders. The relationship between structure and management roles is deceptively simple. As Hall (1997, p. 61) explains, 'functionalist views of role theory suggested that, as long as a school's or college's purposes and structures could be identified, roles could be ascribed and subsequent behaviour predicted'. However, Lumby (2001,

p. 95) notes the limitations of this view. 'Each individual will have a job description which delineates duties and responsibilities, but this is at best only a sketchy approximation of their role. The concept of role is more dynamic and exists at the interface of formal duties and responsibilities, the expectations of the role set and the status accorded to the role by the players.'

James et al. (2007, p. 577) make three important points about organisational roles:

1   Roles as practices cannot be assigned in the way that roles as social positions can, as they require individual agency.
2   The assigning of a role requires a boundary to delineate the responsibilities associated with the role.
3   Individuals take up both formal roles (for example, subject leader) and informal roles (for example, 'hero' or 'scapegoat').

A distinction can be made between 'role-taking', accepting the role as it is presented, and 'role-making', actively reconstructing it (Hall 1997). In the former model, roles are used to match people with tasks and responsibilities through job descriptions and other formal processes. In the latter approach, individuals behave differently from their job descriptions by responding to both the expectations of their role set and their own interpretation of the requirements of the post. 'Teachers, lecturers and principals, within the framework of their understanding of others' expectations of their roles, attempt to interpret them in ways which are comfortable, rewarding and manageable' (Hall 1997, p. 64).

Briggs (2002, p. 69) notes that role expectations varied according to management level in her study of middle managers in colleges:

• Senior managers expected middle managers to translate strategy into action.

• Middle managers saw themselves as 'bridging the gap', by interpreting college objectives.

• Team members saw the middle managers as 'bridges and brokers' and 'information managers'.

One team member expressed the dilemma more starkly, referring to middle managers 'mediating between those who actually do the work and those who institute unworkable policies' (p. 70). Middle managers are affected by all three sets of perceptions as all contribute to their received role.

Smith's (2002) study of English universities shows that middle managers have to balance academic leadership with line management. While most of his respondents regarded these dimensions as of equal significance, a significant minority disagreed, with those from chartered universities stressing academic leadership while those in the newer statutory universities gave primacy to line management. Subsequently, Smith (2005, p. 455) differentiated between head of department (HoD) roles in the two universities. He noted that the HoD in the chartered university focused on research, including 'having the highest research rating we can get'. In contrast, the statutory university HoD focused on staff management and administration.

Robinson (2011) stresses that the advent of federations, and executive headships, has had a fundamental impact on the role of school leaders in England. While many of the heads in her study claimed to be distributed leaders, within and across schools, some commented on the uncertainty over who leads the school when the executive head is off-site. She adds that 'the level and type of distribution was contingent on circumstances and headteachers watched its effects on the school with care' (ibid., p. 74).

These changes all point to the need for a flexible approach in interpreting the role of teachers, leaders and managers in educational organisations. Leaders and managers need to recognise that skills and talent can be found throughout the school or college and are not located only in the upper echelons of the hierarchy. Creativity is most likely to be facilitated by reducing the emphasis on formal structures and through empowering all staff.

Leadership and management roles are also contingent on the cultural context. In China, for example, the concept of *chung* (faithfulness) means that middle leaders and teachers are highly respectful towards their principals, leading to 'a hierarchical structure in which the views of the headteacher are paramount' (Mercer and Ri 2006, p. 117). In the relatively new context of Slovenia, the principal's leadership is influenced by 'prevailing (post-independence) values and beliefs', linked to the wider European heritage (Pang 2006, p. 323).

Role conflict and ambiguity

The need to respond to differing expectations often leads to role strain, conflict or ambiguity. Role strain occurs when individual expectations are either contradicted or not shared with others. Hall (1997, p. 69) regards role strain as 'inevitable' given the nature and scale of change in education. This also links to the problem of role overload where expectations increase to the point where strain, and sometimes stress, is evident. This can be seen in primary schools where headship may be not just a job but a way of life (Southworth 1995). It is also evident in further education where 'role overload was reported as universal and serious, leading to severe stress for staff' (Lumby 2001, p. 101).

Role conflict occurs when there are contradictory expectations held for a person occupying a particular position. The conflict can occur between roles, within a role or within a role set (Hall 1997). Briggs (2002) says that strain or conflict can occur when there is a lack of role clarity. Smith (2002) makes a similar point in relation to the problem of managing 'difficult' members of staff in higher education. He refers to Bolton's (2000, p. 62) explanation of this issue:

> The main culprit is the vagueness of the academic contract which implicitly acknowledges that research creativity cannot be predicated on a nine to five basis and that excellence in teaching cannot be imparted. If the HoD [head of department] decides, therefore, to question formally the performance of a particular member of staff, he or she will be faced with a major stumbling block – where is the written statement of what, in detail, is expected or required?

Role ambiguity occurs when an individual is uncertain about the precise nature of the role at any given time. This can be a particular problem for teachers undertaking management roles for the first time, usually without any specific preparation for their new responsibilities. Briggs (2005, p. 46) claims that role overload and ambiguity are 'common features of the [middle] managers' situation' in further education, a view endorsed by Lumby (2001).

The ubiquitous presence of role strain, conflict, ambiguity and overload suggests that leading and managing educational organisations is a thankless task, and it is little surprise that there are many early retirements and that there is a succession planning problem in England and some other countries (Bush 2011c) (see Chapter 14). However, the situation is less bleak than might be imagined. The many uncertainties create the space and 'structural looseness' to enable managers to shape their roles according to their own sense of what is important, taking account of, but not slavishly following, the expectations of others. Given the changing educational landscape, individual interpretation of roles is essential if they are to be creative and innovative. Hall (1997) and Lumby (2001) both point to the value of utilising 'space' flexibly to enhance the role:

There is a positive side to role ambiguity. It is located in the space it allows for an individual to shape his or her own role. (Hall 1997, p. 72)

The gains from the creativity and energy of people liberated to build their own part of the organisation outweighed the disadvantages of the disagreements that arise as a consequence. (Lumby 2001, p. 97)

However, Bush and Glover's (2012, p. 30) research in English schools shows that 'unity is a signature feature of high performing teams'. They add that 'role clarity is central' and that individual responsibilities should be linked to the school's strategic aims (ibid., p. 28).

Conclusion: linking structure and role

Structures are familiar elements of educational organisations. Because they are usually on 'display' as figures or charts, they provide an apparently clear description of school or college management. Structure also expresses the formal set of roles and role relationships within an organisation, setting out management responsibilities and accountabilities for all to see. These pictorial representations of structure, based essentially on the bureaucratic model, are also remarkably similar across educational contexts, leading to the misleading assumption that educational management operates in the same way regardless of national or school culture. The reality is much more complex and raises important questions about the validity of both structure and management roles.

1   The formal structure, expressed in a 'solid' form, may be misleading because it takes little account of the differing interpretations of participants. When a manager leaves and is replaced, the new person rarely operates in the same way as the predecessor. Rather, new managers bring their own unique mix of values, qualifications and experience to interpret the role in their own way. This serves to modify the role and also produces subtle but important changes to the structure itself. The structure influences role behaviour but does not determine it.

2   The essentially Weberian structure (Bush 2011b) also raises wider questions about the nature of school and college management. The various points in the hierarchy are inevitably represented by role rather than person, 'principal' not 'Ann Smith' or 'Joseph Wong'. This means that the apparent structure remains unchanged as

people move in or out of the organisation but it also implies a lack of respect for individual talents and personalities. The assumption is that people are 'role-takers' rather than 'role-makers', but the evidence is that successful leaders and managers in the twenty-first century require space to create and recreate their roles in response to changing demands from the external environment.

3   The bureaucratic structure also underestimates the significance of alternative portrayals of school and college organisation. By emphasising hierarchy and vertical accountability, it neglects lateral and participative models, such as teamwork and distributed leadership. It also downplays the potential for ambiguity and micropolitics to undermine the formal structure and, by adopting a 'one size fits all' model, underestimates the importance of societal and organisational culture.

These reservations demonstrate the limitations of bureaucratic structures and formal roles as the 'building blocks' of schools and colleges. However, they do not mean that structure is redundant. It provides an essential framework for organisational leadership and management, and a valuable starting point for new teachers, leaders and managers. As long as structure can be *interpreted* flexibly, and is capable of being adapted to accommodate new people and a rapidly changing context, it remains helpful and relevant in understanding organisations and in helping them to operate effectively. Formal structures have their limitations but they are remarkably resilient.

References

Bolden, R., Petrov, G. and Gosling, J. (2009) 'Distributed leadership in higher education: rhetoric and reality', *Educational Management, Administration and Leadership*, 37 (2), 257–277.

Bolton, A. (2000) *Managing the Academic Unit*, Milton Keynes, Open University Press.

Briggs, A. (2002) 'Facilitating the role of middle managers in further education', *Research in Post-Compulsory Education*, 7 (1), 63–78.

Briggs, A. (2005) 'Middle managers in English further education colleges: understanding and modelling the role', *Educational Management, Administration and Leadership*, 33 (1), 27–50.

Briggs, A. (2010) 'Leading educational partnerships: new models for leadership?', in Bush, T., Bell, L. and Middlewood, D. (eds), *The Principles of Educational Leadership and Management, Second Edition*, London, Sage.

Brown, M., Boyle, B. and Boyle, T. (1999) 'Commonalities between perception and practice in models of school decision-making in secondary schools', *School Leadership and Management*, 21 (2), 199–218.

Bush, T. (2011a) 'Succession planning in England: New leaders and new forms of leadership', *School Leadership and Management*, 31 (3), 181–198.

Bush, T. (2011b) *Theories of Educational Leadership and Management, Fourth Edition*, London, Sage.

Bush, T. (2011c) 'Succession planning and leadership development: Comparing English and South African approaches', *Compare*, 41 (6), 785–800.

Bush, T. and Glover, D. (2012b) 'Distributed leadership in action: Leading high performing leadership teams in English schools', *School Leadership and Management*, 32 (1), 21–36.

Bush, T., Kiggundu, E. and Moorosi, P. (2011) 'Preparing new principals in South Africa: the ACE: School Leadership Programme', *South African Journal of Education*, 31 (1), 31–43.

Bush, T., Qiang, H. and Fang, J. (1998) 'Educational management in China: an overview', *Compare*, 28 (2), 133–141.

Bush, T., Joubert, R., Kiggundu, E. and Van Rooyen, J. (2010) 'Managing teaching and learning in South African schools', *International Journal of Educational Development*, 30 (2), 162–168.

Cameron, D.H. (2005) 'Teachers working in collaborative structures: A case study of a secondary school in the USA', *Educational Management, Administration and Leadership*, 33 (3), 311–330.

Coleman, M. (2002) *Women as Headteachers: Striking the Balance*, Stoke-on-Trent, Trentham Books.

Deal, T.E. (2005) 'Poetical and political leadership', in Davies, B. (ed.), *The Essentials of School Leadership*, London, Paul Chapman.

Deem, R. (2000) *'New Managerialism' and the Management of UK Universities*, End of Award Report, Economic and Social Research Council.

Elliott, G. (1996) *Crisis and Change in Vocational Education and Training*, London, Jessica Kingsley.

Fidler, B. (1997) 'Organisational structure and organisational effectiveness', in Harris, A., Bennett, N. and Preedy, M. (eds), *Organisational Effectiveness and Improvement in Education*, Buckingham, Open University Press.

Fitzgerald, T. (2009) 'The tyranny of bureaucracy: Continuing challenges of leading and managing from the middle', *Educational Management, Administration and Leadership*, 37 (1), 51–65.

Fullan, M. (1999) *Change Forces: The Sequel*, London, Falmer.

Goldspink, C. (2007) 'Rethinking educational reform: A loosely coupled and complex systems perspective', *Educational Management, Administration and Leadership*, 35 (1), 27–50.

Grant, C. (2006) 'Emerging voices on teacher leadership: Some South African views', *Educational Management, Administration and Leadership*, 34 (4), 511–532.

Greenfield, T. (1973) 'Organisations as social inventions: rethinking assumptions about change', *Journal of Applied Behavioural Science*, 9 (5), 551–574.

Gronn, P. (2010) 'Where to next for educational leadership?', in Bush, T., Bell, L. and Middlewood, D. (eds), *The Principles of Educational Leadership and Management, Second Edition*, London, Sage.

Hall, V. (1997) 'Management roles in education', in Bush, T. and Middlewood, D. (eds), *Managing People in Education*, London, Paul Chapman Publishing.

Harper, H. (2000) 'New college hierarchies? Towards an examination of organisational structures in further education in England and Wales', *Educational Management and Administration*, 28 (4), 433–446.

Harris, A. (2010) 'Distributed leadership: Evidence and implications', in Bush, T., Bell, L. and Middlewood, D. (eds), *The Principles of Educational Leadership and Management, Second Edition*, London, Sage.

Hartley, D. (2010) 'Paradigms: How far does research in distributed leadership "stretch"', *Educational Management, Administration and Leadership*, 38 (3), 271–285.

Imants, J., Sleegers, P. and Witziers, B. (2001) 'The tension between organisational sub-structures in secondary schools and educational reform', *School Leadership and Management*, 19 (2), 213–222.

James, C., Connolly, M., Dunning, G. and Elliot, T. (2007) 'Systematic leadership for schools and the significance of systemic authorisation', *Educational Management, Administration and Leadership*, 35 (4), 573–588.

Lumby, J. (2001) *Managing Further Education: Learning Enterprise*, London, Paul Chapman Publishing.

Lumby, J. (2012) 'Leading educational culture: Issues of power and equity', *Educational Management, Administration and Leadership*, 40 (5), 576–591.

McTavish, D. (2006) 'Further education management, strategy and policy: Institutional and public management dimensions', *Educational Management, Administration and Leadership*, 34 (3), 411–428.

Mercer, D. and Ri, L. (2006) 'Closing the gap: The role of head of department in Chinese secondary schools', *Educational Management, Administration and Leadership*, 34 (1), 105–120.

Morgan, G. (1997) *Images of Organisation*, Newbury Park, CA, Sage.

Paine, L. and Ma, L. (1993) 'Teachers working together: a dialogue on organisational and cultural perspectives of Chinese teachers', *International Journal of Educational Research*, 19, 675–697.

Pang, N. (2006) 'The organizational values of Gimnazija in Slovenia', *Educational Management, Administration and Leadership*, 34 (3), 319–343.

Randle, K. and Brady, N. (1997) 'Further education and the new managerialism', *Journal of Further and Higher Education*, 21 (2), 229–239.

Robinson, S. (2011) 'Primary headteachers: New leadership roles inside and outside the school', *Educational Management, Administration and Leadership*, 39 (1), 63–83.

Saiti, A. (2009) 'The development and reform of school administration in Greece: A primary school perspective', *Educational Management, Administration and Leadership*, 37 (3), 378–403.

Salo, P. (2008) 'Decision-making as a struggle and a play: On alternative rationalities in schools as organisations', *Educational Management, Administration and Leadership*, 36 (4), 495–510.

Smith, R. (2002) 'The role of the university head of department: a survey of two British universities', *Educational Management and Administration*, 30 (3), 293–312.

Smith, R. (2005) 'Departmental leadership and management in chartered and statutory universities', *Educational Management, Administration and Leadership*, 33 (4), 449–464.

Southworth, G. (1995) *Looking into Primary Headship: A Research Based Interpretation*, Lewes, Falmer Press.

Stoll, L. (1999) 'School culture: black hole or fertile garden for school improvement?', in Prosser, J. (ed.), *School Culture*, London, Paul Chapman Publishing.

Townsend, A. (2010) 'Leadership and educational networks', in Bush, T., Bell,

L. and Middlewood, D. (eds), *The Principles of Educational Leadership and Management, Second Edition*, London, Sage.

Wallace, M. and Hall, V. (1994) *Inside the SMT: Teamwork in Secondary School Management*, London, Paul Chapman Publishing.

Wildy, H. and Louden, W. (2000) 'School restructuring and the dilemmas of principals' work', *Educational Management and Administration*, 28 (2) 173–184.

Leading and Managing for Diversity

Introduction

In the previous editions of this book on managing people in education, there has been a chapter on equal opportunities. In societies generally, as well as in educational discourse, the concept forming 'equal opportunity for all' has been overtaken, or indeed absorbed, within the broader concepts of 'diversity' and 'inclusion'. This chapter briefly examines this particular development, and then attempts to define what are meant by 'diversity' and 'inclusion'. It then addresses some of the fields within which these concepts are significant in education. It examines some of the reasons why they are important to leaders and managers and describes some of the strategies employed to influence them. Finally, it reflects on some of the issues and problems that need to be considered.

From equal opportunities to diversity

Limitations of equal opportunities

Awareness of equal opportunities in the developed world today relates very much to the legislation which is bound up with it, which was enacted during the second half of the twentieth century, and is regularly adapted and developed. The Human Rights Act (1998), for example, has brought the legislation of many European countries into force in the UK and affected the rights of individuals there. The key rights likely to affect those working in education may include:

- the right to respect for private and family life
- the right of freedom of expression
- the right of freedom of thought, conscience and religion
- the right not to be subjected to degrading treatment
- the right to a fair and public hearing within a reasonable time by an independent and impartial tribunal established by law (adapted from Gold 2001).

A focus on legislation inevitably leads to an emphasis on the indicators of success of implementing equal opportunities policies being largely numerical. Thus schools and colleges, like other organisations in the UK, Europe and North America, are required to monitor staff appointments and keep records for submission to show to what extent their employees reflect the application of equal opportunities, i.e. the number of those from ethnic minorities, balance of gender, able and disabled, and where applicable, age range. This monitoring can have at least two distinct disadvantages, according to Middlewood and Lumby (1998, p. 35).

- It defines 'success' in terms of the *current* system, which may have some highly unsatisfactory features in practice.

- It may encourage leaders and managers to focus on certain forms of discrimination while ignoring others. Furthermore, Gagnon and Cornelius (2000, p. 4) suggest that if weight of numbers becomes a primary indicator of a need to get equality of opportunity, then certain groups will simply never gain a voice that is listened to. Such legislation, often including the contentious issues of legislating for quotas of particular minority groups, did have some successes of course. For example, a law passed in Norway, which insisted that 40 per cent of members of all business executive boards should be female, has been seen to have completely changed the attitudes towards leadership in business (Fugerland 2011). Legislation, in such cases, can be seen as simply a tool for accelerating a desirable process so that it eventually becomes a fact of life and the law is irrelevant.

Using the issue of women's equality in Australia as her example, Summers (2003) argues that it is tempting for developed countries, having reached a certain level of equality through debate, rhetoric and legislation, to relax the emphasis. Having raised the issue in public consciousness, and the number of women in senior positions in government, business or public service organisations having increased, public focus can move elsewhere. The problem with this, she argues, is that it is only the situation of *some* women that has improved and many others remain disempowered.

However, the main limitation of a focus on equal opportunity and its concern with legislation is that it perceives the issues it attempts to deal with as problems, such as discrimination against specific minority groups. Inevitably, legislation is updated as different issues arise for specific groups. In education, since the 1980s in particular, concern for equality of access and opportunity for all learners, especially those with SEN, led to a huge emphasis on 'inclusive' education. In the concern to indicate that many such learners were not treated as 'separate', there was a considerable move to close many special schools throughout the UK and focus on integrating apparently disadvantaged learners into mainstream schools or colleges. Gains (2001, p. 177) describes this legislation over twelve years (from 1988 to 2000) as turning 'a stroll into a stampede', and with others (O'Brien 2001; Hornby 2001), believes it illustrates the folly of offering a single, apparently simple solution to a situation which involves the rich complexity of the needs of individual people. He argues for replacing the 'current (2001) obsession with "inclusion" to a focus on "diversity"'.

In the twenty-first century, the focus on diversity has indeed become of major interest for leaders, managers and all employers, not just in education but *also* in business and politics and most fields of human social and professional activity.

Diversity

Diversity may be seen as accepting that the uniqueness of each individual contributes to the richness of the experience of all of us as human beings in a community or society. It follows, therefore, that no single simple structure or organisational mechanism can be established, which meets the needs of the huge range of individuals involved. Therefore, addressing leadership and management for diversity, the topic for this chapter, would seem to also address 'responsible inclusion' (Vaughn and Schumm 1995). A focus on diversity recognises the differences between individuals and sees this as a richness or an asset, whereas a focus on equal opportunities sprang from dealing with problematic issues. Another big difference, highlighted by Wilson and Iles (1999), was that diversity is 'individual focused', whereas equal opportunities is 'group focused'. However, the underpinning issue in all areas of diversity, inclusion and equal opportunities is a concern for equity, and the emphasis and meaning of leading and managing for diversity is perhaps trying to achieve 'equity through difference' (Jones 2000, p. 155). The ultimate task of leaders may be to 'institutionalise the valuing of difference' (Lumby with Coleman 2007, p. 107).

Benefits of a focus on diversity

The 'business case'

The example of Norway mentioned earlier, where the number of women in the country's boardrooms increased significantly, illustrates the argument for diversity being an asset in terms of simple numbers. Prior to this change, companies were 'fishing in half of the talent pool; now they have access to the whole pool. It makes no business sense to exclude half the population from leadership'. (Fugerland 2011, p. 15).

This key principle of having access to a much wider range of talent and ability can clearly apply to the empowerment of all groups of people often seen as minority or disadvantaged. The Diversity Champions Programme in the UK currently involves over six hundred and fifty major employers, including all the armed services, the public sector, and MI5. Employers realise that they operate in global markets where almost every colleague or client will be different and that workforces that reflect the wider public are more likely to improve the public or consumer services that they deliver. Although this programme began as a reaction to discrimination against gay and lesbian employees, it now embraces the diversity of all people potentially disadvantaged by: gender, ethnicity, disability, age or religion.

Cohesion

Since the key element in diversity is that of equity, a major advantage compared with a focus on equal opportunities is that it seeks to promote cohesion through a celebration of difference, instead of being concerned with the problems of groups 'other than' the majority. The focus on separate groups can lead at worst to tokenism and people being treated as 'invisible', majority/minority splits and 'us versus them' attitudes. Detached subgroups can function almost independently from the majority (Shelton 2003). All these can be recognised in wider society and, potentially at least, in any institution, including educational ones. A focus on diversity, with its recognition of the special abilities of each individual, not only offers a larger pool of new ideas and opinions (see above) but also a lower likelihood of groupthink and a greater sense of institutional cohesion.

Problems with a focus on diversity

Discrepancy between policy and practice

While the principle of valuing everyone equally is widely accepted, it is 'not the lived experience of many individuals' (Lumby with Coleman 2007, p. 29). In a study of education for pupils with disabilities in Malawi, for example, the principal finding was 'the mismatch between policy and practice', with many well-written policies in place, but the experience of many learners and teachers bearing little resemblance to these (Kamchedzera 2008, p. 143). Booth's (2000) review of international developments since a 1990 World Conference on Disability in Education showed considerable inequality existing and that learners with disabilities continued to be the most excluded from education. The more recent World Conference on Disability in 2012 in Stockholm emphasised the huge scale of the problem, with an estimate of one billion people (or fifteen per cent of the population) having a disability. Such a scale can only emphasise the need for individual institutions to try to close the 'gap' between their stated policies and their practice.

Diversity as an issue for management

Research by Lumby et al. (2005) in the post-compulsory sector in England, found that several institutions perceived diversity as something to be 'managed' and gave it higher or lower importance accordingly. In some cases a diversity manager or co-ordinator existed. This practice of course indicates that diversity is something that can be managed separately, just like any other 'subject', and therefore fails to convey the message that diversity is an issue which should permeate the whole of any institution and any curriculum.

Such an approach leads Morrison et al. (2006, p. 243) to suspect that diversity management may be no more than 'the emperor donning a new set of invisible clothes to reduce the impact of inequality concerns and absorb new patterns of legislation-induced accountability'.

Significance of diversity in educational organisations

Important as the focus on diversity may be in any kind of organisation, it can be argued that it has a particular significance in educational institutions, such as schools, colleges and universities.

There are four main arguments for this, each of them linked to what many see as the key moral purpose of education, i.e. to improve the human condition, both by developing people's understanding and knowledge in the institution's immediate society and thereby contributing to progress on a wider scale.

First, future citizens need to be able to see, in the adults who guide their learning, *role models* who embody the future and improved state. If all that they see in the world presented by their learning environment is that which reinforces what has been, they will learn or deduce that this is the preferred state.

This may include such extremes as:

- only women teach very young children

- only men can be school caretakers or janitors

- only able-bodied people can teach

- only adults of certain races can hold senior positions

- only heterosexual people can excel at certain sports.

In a school or college, therefore, pupils and students need ideally to have the opportunity to see the embodiment of diversity in the way adults on the staff hold particular roles and perform in those roles according to what they do, not who they are. Without this opportunity, the tendency to stereotype certain roles and tasks according to certain types of people is difficult to avoid. The issue of positive discrimination whereby appointments are made on the basis to bolster the balance on a staff between different groups, has been a factor in addressing this issue for schools and colleges in particular contexts. In an evaluation of a Masters course for black and minority ethnic (BME) students (Coleman and Campbell-Stephens 2009), the vast majority were adamant they did not want positive discrimination, but valued the opportunity to meet as a group because of their shared interests.

Secondly, as an educational institution responsible for children and young people, a school or college can provide the best learning environment for them by having a staff which has the *richness of diversity*, bringing together the various strengths of different types and groups of people. For example, a staff which has good representation of both genders should theoretically bring the respective strengths of women and of men to education and its leadership and management.

An equally relevant example relates to the range of strengths that could exist in a staff that is ethnically diverse. While much debate centres on the value of one ethnic cultural approach compared to another, particularly Western models being transposed to Asian or Eastern cultures (Foskett and Lumby 2003), a more important argument concerns the possibility of utilising the strengths of both – or more – cultures. There are possibilities, at least ideally, in a staff with elements of, for example,

- Japanese group ethic

- Chinese work ethic

- African collaborative approaches

- Western problem-solving abilities

all being represented through various personnel, thus exposing pupils and students to all the possibilities inherent in these. Again, the above list is stereotypical, representing what have been seen as the dominant features of particular cultures, not exclusive to them.

Thirdly, educational organisations have by their very nature a *moral* imperative to lead change since their task is helping with the formation of the next generation(s). Therefore, they should offer signs of that improved future via the environment and ethos within which their learners and employers operate. The ways in which they are led and managed is the clearest signal to their adult employees about what the future is seen to be.

Fourthly, and by far the most important, a focus on diversity which permeates the whole ethos, as well as the strategic and operational processes of a school or college, encourages and fosters those values which are central to positive human development, such as respect for others, equity, social justice, critical thinking and tolerance.

Some issues for educational leadership

Understanding context: national level

While gender, for example, may be treated as an issue for equal opportunities legislation in Western societies, it is a more complex phenomenon in segregated societies and in patriarchal or collective societies where motherhood and age are equated with status and authority. Thus, Debroux (2003) argues that work practices in Japan are based on a mutual agreement, which can be silent and implicit, between leaders and employees which are reflective of widespread social norms. Accordingly, women have to accept to play forever a subordinate role in the labour market.

In segregated societies, such as Iran (Afshar 1992) and Saudi Arabia (Al-Khalifa 1992), face-to-face meetings between men and women at work may be avoided with a reliance on telephone or writing. In Pakistan, separate institutions exist for females, including a women's university with only women in leadership positions (Shah 1998). In such contexts, equal opportunities idealism, as discussed earlier, is not relevant; it becomes more of an issue of valuing those employees equally, once the initial separations have been made.

Despite the United Nations Bill of Rights, homosexuality still remains a criminal offence in a few countries and a morally and culturally despised state in several more. As noted earlier, inequalities in the treatment of disabled children are widespread, and attitudes to youth and old age differ markedly between, for example, Western and Eastern societies.

Understanding context: international level

Leaders will be aware of their school or college's own community context and if they themselves are of a minority group, the challenge to develop a focus on diversity is even greater, being both personal as well as role driven. The female head of a special school in Birmingham described her struggle: 'it's three times the battle being a woman, an Asian woman in a male-dominated society and then a head in a racialist community' (Abrol 1999, p. 65).

However, it is worth considering the situation for leaders where a school or college is structured, either by design (for example, a faith school) or by geographical context, so that a diverse composition is not a possibility.

In a local community where the population is wholly white, for example some rural areas in certain north European countries, the challenge to present to the students an awareness of a society which is diverse and pluralist may be made more difficult when there are no staff role models to demonstrate this. One headteacher of a school in rural Somerset, in an all-white small town, describes how she agonised over the appointment of the school's first black member of staff, not because she was not able, but because it was a relatively low status job and it might send out the wrong signals to the students, who, according to the headteacher, only had the first chance to actually meet a non-white person if they went to university.

> She (the applicant) was the best person, but how I wished the post was that of Head of Department! I felt that this was the first black member of staff that the students had ever seen and their risk of forming stereotypes – of reinforcing them – was huge. (Gardiner 2004, p. 3)

This headteacher stressed that the school made every effort to heighten students' awareness through the curriculum, both in school and out of school, but that eventually the presence of that one black person in school made a huge impact on their consciousness.

However, two other examples, both from faith schools, emphasise that some leaders approach the move to focus on diversity in quite different ways, either by actually underlining the exclusivity of their religion, or by suggesting it is the business of the state and not the educational institution.

In a study of an Ultra-Orthodox Jewish College, Starr-Glass and Schwartzbaum (2002, p. 198) suggest that 'diversity can best be appreciated through the examination of self and of our own socially constructed world rather than through the differences of others'. In the curriculum, the college does not offer studies of other religions or philosophies. The approach is to offer and develop through all core courses critical examination of social reality and 'academic values that transcend sectarian division' (ibid.). This, it is claimed, leads to perspectives that 'recognise difference and acknowledge plurality . . . which represent our efforts to promote the conditions for diversity' (ibid.). The students are therefore seen as empowered to make wider choices because of their appreciation of the social nature of inclusion. The personal choices made by students will be guided by their specific faith but within the context of maximum creative expression in adjusting effectively to the society they live in.

In contrast, research carried out by McNamara and Norman (2010) in post-primary schools in the Republic of Ireland found that there 'was little indication at leadership level that concerns about social justice and equity were leading to a willingness to take potentially controversial initiatives and this timidity seems to percolate down through the staff structure' (ibid., p. 545).

The bulk of schools in Ireland are faith-based, overwhelmingly Catholic. As in the Jewish example above, the schools inevitably reflect the ethos of the Church. However, while the increasingly diverse state has enacted legislation to protect the rights of minorities, the schools, in reflecting the Church's teachings, were not able to be free from the constraints of these teachings. For example, while the legislation provides for adequate sex education for all, the Church's attitude to homosexuality as a 'moral evil' (Ratzinger 1986) was a complication. The research found that 'significant levels of homophobic bullying in schools' occurred with only a limited response from leaders and staff.

These three examples illustrate the dilemmas faced by some leaders of institutions with specific contextual issues which potentially militate against a desire to inculcate social justice, and inclusiveness and diversity in their learners and teachers.

Building a focus on diversity

While legislation may require leaders to pay attention to such issues as ethnicity, religion, disability, gender, age and sexual orientation, an institution committed to diversity and inclusion will also ensure that its valuing of people extends to all areas of people management. For example:

- part-time employees (see Young and Brooks 2004)
- employees on a fixed-term contract
- voluntary workers
- those in low paid or low status jobs
- those called to stand in for staff in an emergency, such as 'supply' or 'cover' staff.

All these categories have the right to have their work valued as making a contribution to the institution's maintenance or development. While this valuing cannot normally be done in terms of finance or contracts, it is the task of leaders to try to ensure that these people feel their work is recognised and appreciated.

Some of the above categories may themselves directly relate to the issues of equity and diversity, since many voluntary workers may be retired and elderly, and members of ethnic minorities may often be in low status jobs. The challenge for leaders, therefore, is to focus in all management processes on the people as individuals in their own right. Indeed, some opponents of positive discrimination agree that it is not the individual that matters, but the job itself. Thus, McElroy (1992) argues that quota systems for employment of women stigmatise women as inferior by rendering it uncertain as to whether they owe any positions of prestige to personal merit or merely to their gender. She also points out the resentment in a workforce of those who have been passed over in favour of the appointee. Both she and Papps (1992) argue that the key element in employment is the value that is placed on the work itself, irrespective of who does it.

As the preface to this book noted, diversity is not only the topic for this chapter but permeates all the areas dealt with in separate chapters throughout the book, including all the leadership and management processes. In recruitment and selection, for example, common sense may suggest that informal networks could be an effective way of appointing low status employees.

However, a careful judgement has to be made to avoid discriminating against anyone's access of opportunity. For example, jobs with low pay are invariably filled by people living near the school or college since travelling long distances is likely to be uneconomic; thus advertising for cleaning or catering staff may reasonably be confined to local outlets. However, a part-time teaching post may be different. Parker-Jenkins (1994) describes how the following were among the procedures followed when recruiting and selecting for a part-time post:

- To ensure as wide a field for recruitment as possible, advertisements were placed in locations outside those which only people in the 'normal' educational circles would reach.

- References were not required since those who have been absent from the labour market – or never in it – might feel reluctant to apply because of the lack of 'appropriate' referees.

- Candidates who did not necessarily follow the conventional format of application were still considered if their suitability matched the job criteria.

As Middlewood (1997) points out, such part-time posts are the very ones which offer opportunities to recruit from unconventional backgrounds, thus widening students' access to a range of staff.

Similarly, in induction and mentoring, the assumption should be avoided that someone of a minority group should have someone of the same minority as a mentor. 'The female headteachers . . . were generally advocates for mentoring, although half of them reported having been mentored by a man' (Coleman 2002, p. 143). In fact, the evidence concerning cross-gender mentoring is mixed. Davidson and Cooper (1992, p. 87) advocate same gender mentoring because it can encourage development of female leaders. Similarly, with BME staff, the evidence of effectiveness is also used. For example, Abrol (1999) describes how both English and Asian managers had been greatly supportive of her as an Asian female head in Birmingham, England, but her informal mentor and friend had been the woman who had been the first Asian secondary headteacher there.

The support of those staff with a physical disability needs similar attention. One teacher in a wheelchair, appointed to work in a primary school in Wales, was allocated a mentor and reported that she felt that her mentor, while being friendly, undoubtedly patronised her by 'taking care' of her and 'looking after' her, something which she felt her mentor would not have done for an able-bodied teacher and which distorted the mentor/mentee relationship (Jenkins 2004). In such cases, the issue is not one of same or different minority group as mentor, but is likely to be one of either selecting a suitable person or of appropriate training.

In terms of situations which may affect the performance of staff, Jenkins (2004) refers to some other interesting examples, all of which came from the actual experiences of her colleagues and pose potential dilemmas for leaders and managers.

- The woman returning from maternity leave is anxious to leave school promptly for the next few weeks. Should special allowance be made for her concerning after-hours meetings for that period?

- The Muslim lecturer, during the period of Ramadan, is weak and 'lightheaded' by the evening because of fasting. Can she be expected to perform her normal duties then?

- The devout Muslim staff need to offer prayers at certain times of the day. Should special arrangements be made, possibly at the expense of others' time?

- Should homosexual men or lesbian women be allowed to 'avoid' certain duties which might place them in a situation where false accusations might be made against them? (adapted from Jenkins 2004).

Such questions are posed, not because there are simple answers, but because in an institution which values diversity there will be a recognition that we are all different and issues of equity, such as those arising in the four contexts described above, can be discussed in a context which respects and values these differences.

Reflections for educational leadership and management

Start with yourself

As Lumby with Coleman (2007, p. 122) suggest, 'changing oneself is the starting point'. However committed as a leader you feel you are, a careful consideration of what you genuinely feel, how this is enacted in your behaviour both in personal and professional terms, and whether this is being accurately communicated to others is a helpful beginning. Perhaps a 360-degree appraisal could help in this respect. In an area such as developing diversity and social justice, there is a need for leaders to critically examine their own beliefs and prejudices and, as all effective leaders do, 'take responsibility rather than blame others for problems' (Baker and Blair 2005, p. 45).

The voice and actions of the leader are of prime importance in promoting diversity and inclusion. While ensuring that those from minority groups are heard, the most powerful voices for celebrating the value of difference are in fact those from the mainstream. Parker-Jenkins et al. (2007, p. 7), in advocating the use of resources about Gypsies, Roma and Travellers, make the point that such resources should be for *all* children, not just those who represent these groups. Montgomery, the Second Sea Lord in the UK Navy (2011) makes the point about acceptance of homosexual people in the armed forces that 'Acceptance is only possible if it's articulated by those who are not gay. It's absolutely fundamental that the mainstream community are those who articulate the message. Otherwise, it's a minority group griping again!' The voice of the leader extolling the value of the individual, each different from the other, is therefore immensely powerful.

Know your local community

Establishing and developing links with the local community 'can offer good opportunities to better equip learners to understand aspects of social cohesion and unity' (Mistry and Sood 2011, p. 128). As research into extended schools shows, knowledge of, and developing links with, the local community can have a profound impact on students' attitudes to whoever is involved in affecting their learning (see Middlewood and Parker 2009). Shah (2006, p. 231) describes the importance of leaders getting to know their communities, and soliciting involvement and collaboration so that the learners 'can develop from where they are to where they can be'.

Avoid being satisfied with increased representation

While increasing the number of role models in staffing through greater representation of different groups is commendable, it should be only the beginning, if indeed one begins there at all. The attraction of this is that it offers 'reasonable progress' (Lumby 2010, p. 222), but is only a step on the road towards a whole-school, or whole-college culture which is imbued with valuing through difference. In this context, avoid stereotyping and be open-minded about what individuals are capable of achieving, regardless of previous experience (Fleming 1998).

Give very careful thought to training on diversity

As noted earlier, 'diversity management' can be a poisoned chalice and training specifically 'for diversity' needs to be extremely carefully thought through and planned. In research in Cyprus, Angelides (2012) found that often informal learning situations were invaluable for promoting inclusiveness and diversity appreciation (see also Dillon and Brandt 2006).

Consider leadership practices throughout

If 'leadership as a social practice is inclusive of all', (Gunter 2006, p. 203), then the more leadership is seen as all pervading, the better this is for diversity and exclusion (see the section on Distributed Leadership in Chapter 2).

Involve pupil/student voice

If diversity and inclusion really are important then the views of the learners are fundamental to illustrating that everyone is worth listening to. The exclusion of those for whom the institution mainly exists makes a travesty of any claim to value the contribution of each individual. Beyond School Councils and such representation is the notion that students 'should be allowed to question and evaluate the equality of service they are receiving and help in a constructive and measured way to improve it' (Piper-Gale and Parker 2011, p. 30).

Consider how democratic the institution is

It can be argued that diversity and inclusion can only really flourish within a democracy. If this is so, the more that democratic values in a school or college can be seen to be embodied and lived through the behaviour of all those working there (learners *and* teachers), the more likelihood there is of difference being valued. In a dictatorship, the views of 'others' are not tolerated; similarly, in a rigidly top-down, authoritarian institution, the difference can be between 'us' and 'them'. With schools and colleges having gained increased autonomy in many countries, there is little likelihood of a true celebration of diversity where leaders are unwilling to recognise that they themselves, while hugely important, are also individuals with differences that they would like respected.

Conclusion

For leaders and managers, developing a focus on diversity is a challenging prospect, but one which is likely to be embraced, because it is so closely related to the inherent values that they bring to their roles. While legislation will always need to be recognised and of course adhered to, more important is the extent to which leaders and mangers are able to facilitate the way diversity can permeate the school's or college's culture and become a guiding principle in each process. The lasting legacy of this will lie in the attitudes and practices of the pupils and students when they become adults making their own impact on society.

References

Abrol, S. with Ribbins, P. (1999) 'Pursuing equal opportunities: a passion for service, sharing and sacrifice', in Rayner, S. and Ribbins, P., *Headteachers and Leadership in Special Education*, London, Cassell.

Afshar, H. (1992) 'Women and work: ideology not adjustment at work in Iran', in Afshar, H. and Dennis, C. (eds), *Women and the Adjustment Policies in the Third World*, Basingstoke, Macmillan. pp. 205–229.

Al-Khalifa, E. (1992) 'Management by halves: women teachers and school management', in Bennett, N., Crawford, M. and Riches, C. (eds), *Managing Change in Education*, London, Paul Chapman Publishing and OUP. pp. 95–106.

Angelides, P. (2012) 'Forms of leadership that promote inclusion in Cypriot schools', *Educational Management Administration and Leadership*, 40 (3), pp. 21–36.

Baker, C. and Blair, M. (2005) 'High Expectations: achieving potential and establishing relationships', in Cole, M. (ed.) *Professional Attributes and Practice*, London, Routledge.

Booth, T. (2000) *Inclusion in Education: Participation of disabled learners*, Canterbury, Christ Church University College.

Coleman, M. (2002) 'Managing for equal opportunities', in Bush, T. and Bell, L. (eds), *Principles and Practice of Educational Management*, London, Paul Chapman Publishing.

Coleman, M. and Campbell-Stephens, R. (2009) 'Factors affecting career progress: perceptions of BME deputy and assistant headteachers from the programme Investing in Diversity,' occasional papers in work-based learning, London, ULE Institute of Education.

Davidson, M. and Cooper, C. (1992) *Shattering the Class Ceiling: The Women Manager*, London, Paul Chapman Publishing.

Debroux, P. (2003) 'The Japanese employment model revisited', in Warner, M. and Joynt, P. (eds), *Managing Across Cultures*, London, Thomson Learning.

Dillon, J. and Brandt, C. (2006) *Outdoor Education: a BAI Roundtable Summary*, London, Centre for Outdoor Education and Schools.

Fleming, P. (1998) 'Asian girls and equal opportunities', *Management in Education*, 12 (4), 7–8.

Foskett, N. and Lumby, J. (2003) *Leading and Managing Education: International Perspectives*, London, Paul Chapman Publishing.

Freeman, A. (1993) 'Women in education', *Educational Change and Development*, 13 (1), 10–14.

Fugerland, B. (2011) 'No sense to exclude half the population from leadership', *Observer Business Equity Review*, June, p. 15.

Gagnon, S. and Cornelius, N. (2000) 'Re-examining workplace equality: the capabilities approach', *Human Resource Management Journal*, 10 (2), 68–87.

Gains, C. (2001) 'Inclusion: decisions, routes and destination', in O'Brien, T. (ed.), *Enabling Inclusion: Blue skies . . . Dark clouds?*, London, The Stationery Office.

Gardiner, G. (2004) 'Staff role models: it's not easy', *Headship Matters*, 26, London, Optimus Publishing.

Gold, R. (2001) 'The Human Rights Act in schools', *Leadership Focus*, 4, 51–52, Cambridge, Hobsons.

Gunter, H. (2006) 'Educational Leadership: the Challenge of Diversity', *Educational Management Administration and Leadership*, 34 (2), 257–268.

Hornby, G. (2001) 'A focus on diversity,' in O'Brien, T. (ed.), *Enabling Inclusion: Blue skies . . . Dark clouds?*, London, The Stationery Office.

Jenkins, K. (2004) 'Can I help you, dear?', *Primary Headship*, (14), London, Optimus Publishing.

Jones, C. (2000) 'Falling between the cracks: what diversity means for black women in Higher Education', *Policy Futures in Education*, 4 (2), 145–159.

Kamchedzera, E. (2008) 'Education of pupils with disabilities in Malawi's secondary schools: policy, practice and experience', in Espinoza, R. and Jones, I. (eds), working papers of the Warwick Seminar Group, Coventry, University of Warwick Institute of Education.

Lumby, J. (2010) 'Leadership for diversity and inclusion', in Bush, T., Bell, L. and Middlewood, D. (eds) 'The Principles of Educational Leadership and Management', London, Sage. pp. 219–235.

Lumby, J. with Coleman, M. (2007) *Leadership and Diversity: challenging theory and practice in education*, London, Sage.

Lumby, J., Muijs, D., Briggs, A., Glover, D., Harris, A., Middlewood, D., Morrison,

M., Sood, K. and Wilson, M. (2005) *Leadership Development and Diversity in the Learning and Skills Sector*, London, LSDA.

McElroy, W. (1992) 'Preferential treatment of women in employment', in Quest, C. (ed.), *Equal Opportunities: A Feminist Fallacy*, London, Institute of Economic Affairs.

McNamara, G. and Norman, J. (2010) 'Conflicts of Ethos: Issues of Equality and Diversity in Faith-based Schools', *Educational Management Administration and Leadership*, 38 (5), 532–546.

Middlewood, D. (1997) 'Managing recruitment and selection', in Bush, T. and Middlewood, D. (eds), *Managing People in Education*, London, Paul Chapman Publishing.

Middlewood, D. and Lumby, J. (1998) *Human Resource Management in Schools and Colleges*, London, Paul Chapman Publishing.

Middlewood, D. and Parker, R. (2009) *Leading and Managing Extended Schools*, London, Sage.

Mistry, M. and Sood, K. (2011) 'Rethinking educational leadership to transform pedagogic practice to improve the attainment of minority ethnic pupils', *Management in Education*, 25 (3), 125–130.

Montgomery, C. (2011) 'Speaking Straight', Speech to Diversity Champions Conference, May.

Morrison, M., Lumby, J. and Sood, K. (2006) 'Diversity and diversity management: messages from recent research', *Educational Management Administration and Leadership*, 34 (3), 277–295.

O'Brien, T. (2001) 'Enabling Inclusion: where to now?' in O'Brien, T. (ed.), *Enabling Inclusion: Blue Skies . . . Dark Clouds?*, London, The Stationery Office.

Papps, I. (1992) 'Women, work and well-being', in Quest, C. (ed.), *Equal Opportunities: A Feminist Fallacy*, London, Institute of Economic Affairs.

Parker-Jenkins, R. (1994) 'Part-time staff recruitment: an equal opportunities dilemma', *Educational Management and Administration*, 8 (2), 3–4.

Parker-Jenkins, R., Hewitt, D., Brownhill, S. and Sanders, T. (2007) *Aiming High: Raising attainment of pupils from culturally diverse backgrounds*, London, Paul Chapman Publishing.

Piper-Gale, J. and Parker, R. (2011) 'Student Research,' in Middlewood, D., Parker, R. and Piper-Gale, J. (eds), *Learning through Research*, Leicester, Beauchamp College.

Ratzinger, J. (1986) 'Letter to the Bishops of the Catholic Church on the Pastoral Care of Homosexual Persons', Rome, Congregation for Doctrine of the Faith.

Shah, S. (2006) 'Leading multi-cultural schools: a new understanding of Muslim Youth Identity,' *Educational Management Administration and Leadership*, 34 (2), 215–237.

Shah, S. (1998) 'Roles and practices of college heads in AJK, Pakistan', unpublished PhD thesis, University of Nottingham.

Shelton, J. (2003) 'Interpersonal concerns in social encounters between majority and minority group members', *Group Processes and Intergroup Relations*, 6 (2), 171–185.

Starr-Glass, D. and Schwartzbaum, A. (2002) 'Seeing diversity in difference: Experiences in an Ultra-Orthodox Jewish college', *Educational Management and Administration*, 3 (3), 189–200.

Summers, A. (2003) *The End of Equality*, Melbourne, Random House.

Vaughn, S. and Schumm, J. (1995) 'Reasonable inclusion for students with learning disabilities', *Journal of Learning Disabilities*, 28 (5), 264–270.

Wilson, E. and Iles, P. (1999) 'Managing diversity: an employment and service delivery challenge', *The International Journal of Public Sector Management*, 12 (1), 27–48.

Young, B. and Brooks, M. (2004) 'Part-time politics: the micropolitical world of part-time teaching', *Educational Management Administration and Leadership*, 32 (2), 129–148.

7

Motivation and job satisfaction

Introduction

Most employees, as well as their leaders and managers, recognise that the way they feel about their work and their job is affected by a number of factors. If they move from one job to another they may feel better or worse about it or, even in the same job, their feelings about the work they do may vary from period to period. It is almost certain that the more positive they feel about the work, the better they will carry it out. This chapter deals with the leader's role in trying to maintain and develop those positive feelings in employees in educational organisations. The ability and strategies to motivate staff, to develop staff morale and to try to ensure job satisfaction are central to the leader's role in raising performance. It is, however, a complex issue. Some of the theories related to motivation and job satisfaction are explored and the barriers to achieving them within organisations are described. While acknowledging the limitations to leaders' influence, the chapter suggests principles for leaders and managers to follow, recognising that perhaps the most significant task is to establish the particular context within which these can flourish. This context is essentially an individualised one, since external factors, often outside the leader's control, may actually work against individual notions of what motivates employees. Nevertheless, effective leaders and managers of staff recognise the crucial importance of motivation and job satisfaction, not least because they acknowledge its significance for their own performance!

Defining the terms

Motivation

Ryan and Deci's (2000, p. 54) relatively straightforward definition of motivation as 'to be motivated means to be moved to do something. A person who feels no impetus or inspiration to act is thus characterized as unmotivated, whereas someone who is energised or activated toward an end is considered motivated.'

Any definition of motivation for application in the workplace is likely to include needs, behaviour, goals and some kind of feedback. These elements closely link with the features associated with performance review or appraisal (dealt with fully in Chapter 12), since effectiveness in that area is ultimately intended to motivate for improved future performance.

There are many theories of motivation, among the best known being Maslow's (1970) hierarchy of needs, McGregor's (1960) 'X' and 'Y' theory and Herzberg's (1966) 'two factor' theory. Middlewood and Lumby (1998) summarise the main theories into three categories:

- *Needs theories*: the Maslow, McGregor and Herzberg theories all fit into this category, each based on the premise that basic needs or impulses within humans are the key to what motivates us. Maslow's hierarchy of needs from 'survival' and 'security' through to 'self-fulfilment' is readily recognisable to many managers. The important aspect of this theory is that satisfaction of needs is sequential and therefore employees cannot be motivated by self-fulfilment unless lower-level needs have been met. There is value for leaders in recognising the range of needs. However, Maslow's insistence on meeting these needs in strict hierarchical order is discredited. McGregor's theory that either people must be pressured by managers because they seek to avoid work or they are self-directed and responsible can be useful in analysing underlying assumptions about the way people behave and may be implicit in staff policies. Sabanci (2008) used McGregor's theory when researching such underlying assumptions of school principals in Turkey and their impact on the principals' attitudes to staff. Among other things, he concludes that leaders could change assumptions according to experience.

- Herzberg suggests that managers need to make staff positively satisfied and remove causes of dissatisfaction but that these two things are independent of each other. His extreme satisfiers are recognition, self-fulfilment and sense of achievement, while the main dissatisfiers were related to conditions at work (pay, relationships with employer), which Herzberg calls the 'hygiene factors'. However, the theory, while offering sensible insights into managing employees, can lead to motivation and satisfaction being confused.

- *Goal theories*: Handy (1993) suggests that all employees make a calculation of costs and benefits of how they act and perform accordingly.

- *Equity theories*: these suggest that employees are primarily motivated by a sense of fair play and that perceptions that they are being treated less fairly than others will demotivate them.

As Middlewood and Lumby (1998) point out, many of these well-known theories originate in the West and probably do not pay enough attention to issues of race and culture. Again, attitudes to, and assumptions about, the adequacy of resources will differ widely, with a consequent effect upon the cultural values held.

Morale

The term morale is normally used to refer to the general state of motivation and well-being among a group of people. Morale will therefore be determined by the overall psychological and physiological state of the staff. Evans (1998, p. 30) describes it as 'a state of mind encompassing all the feelings determined by . . . anticipation of the extent of satisfaction of those needs . . . significantly affecting the work situation'.

Both motivation and morale therefore clearly involve the notion of anticipation and therefore can be related to the individual or group at work looking forward to what is going to happen or to be achieved.

Job satisfaction on the other hand implies an attitude or internal state which is associated with the work an employee *currently* does. Job satisfaction consists of internal reactions developed against the perceptions about the job and job conditions occurring through a system of norms, values and expectations of an individual (see Cerit 2009). For most employees, satisfaction in carrying out the work occurs when what the person doing the work wants and the features of the work coincide, i.e. when the person has expectations of what the work will be and these expectations are met, then that person has job satisfaction.

Job satisfaction and motivation are inextricably linked because staff need to feel they are doing a good job and, when that is established, the leader can build on that to try to motivate them to move forward. If there is basic dissatisfaction, there is little scope for motivation. South Africa's staffing problems in many schools in the second half of the 1990s were largely related to job dissatisfaction. 'A lack of job satisfaction leads to frequent absence from work, behaving aggressively, inclination to quit one's job, and psychological withdrawal from work' (Mwanwenda 1995, p. 85).

The link between job dissatisfaction and absence or withdrawal from work is clear. Blauner (1964) identifies 'meaninglessness' as one of his elements in job dissatisfaction. Essentially where the job is seen as having no point, the eventual extreme logic will be that there is no point in going to work and this can lead to depression and stress. Mwanwenda's (1995) analysis of a specific situation refers to violence in schools and lack of resources but sheer boredom with routine tasks can equally contribute to a job being seen as meaningless. Butt and Lance (2005) found the 'deskilling' of teachers in England, so that some saw teaching as more boring and less creative, and the emphasis on 'performativity' led Ball (2001, p. 212) to argue that this left 'motivations blurred and self-worth slippery'. Fisher (1993) also refers to ancillary workers in education as one of the groups suffering from boredom at work, interestingly noting the advantages of those who worked with children at lunchtime over those who cleaned the empty buildings after working hours.

Blauner's (1964) other key elements in job dissatisfaction are:

- powerlessness – where the employees feel they have no influence on the job done

- isolation – where employees appear not to fit in with any group and behave differently from the norms of the workplace

- self-estrangement – where employees do not see the job as important in their own lives and only the pay earned is relevant.

Factors influencing motivation and job satisfaction

As the abundance of theories suggests, motivation is a very individual matter; since needs and desires are internal states, the task for the leader in trying to analyse those factors influencing staff motivation and morale is complex. Each individual member of staff of a school or college needs to come to work with an understanding that each is valued first and foremost as a person. If not, the implication is that the quality of the staff member's experiences that day will be diminished and performance will suffer.

These factors can be categorised into four groups:

- Individual factors – these include a person's gender, abilities, age and experience, and personal circumstances. These factors are ones over which the leader or manager has no control or influence.

- Social factors – these particularly relate to relationships at work, which teams a person is involved with, mentoring/buddying links, and whether personal relationships are involved or excluded at work. The influence of the leader/manager here is limited to some extent, since employees often choose their own social groups and relationships, although closely structured relationships can be encouraged through work teams, formal mentoring and similar processes.

- Organisational factors – these include the conditions of service, such as facilities and physical resources. They also include workload and work incentives, the fair distribution of these, and structured opportunities for career development. This is the area where the leaders and managers have full responsibility in creating a fair and appropriate working environment.

  It is worth noting that in terms of physical resources, there is no simplistic relationship between plentiful or inadequate resources and motivation or demotivation. As has been variously noted, some teachers in developing countries who work in adverse conditions still thrive. Ladebo (2005, p. 365) notes that despite 'high level noise, broken windows, lack of electricity and pipe-borne water supply, dilapidated buildings, inadequate furniture and teaching materials … some of the teachers still derive pleasure from the job'. As Lumby (2003, p. 155) points out, any simple equations about motivation decreasing in the face of poor conditions 'does not take account of human spirit'.

- Cultural factors – these are what make employees feel they work for an organisation in which they believe. Equal opportunities and inclusion policies in operation will indicate a sense of fairness and consideration for work–life balance will be seen as valuing employees as people. This may be seen as an important long-term aim for leaders, and was discussed in the previous chapter.

Factors affecting the influence of leaders

An analysis of the factors influencing motivation and job satisfaction makes it clear that some of them are controlled by forces external to the school or college and therefore the scope for action by the organisation's leaders is restricted. The most usual external power in this context is national government policy and practice.

Prescribed curriculum

Many countries operate a national curriculum, the content of which (and in some cases the form as well) is prescribed centrally by government departments. This has the effect of removing choice for teachers about what they teach and may well remove creativity and spontaneity from their daily work (Fryer 1996), both of which may be seen for many professionals as essential to motivation and job satisfaction. Along with prescription of content may come an overemphasis on other activities such as testing and recording. In discussing the long hours working culture in Britain, Johnson (2003, p. 65) claims that in educational organisations:

> The core of the problem, however, is that a high proportion of those hours is spent on work that is imposed and considered by the workers unproductive in terms of pupil performance. Much of it is concerned with the recording of activity, required to provide documentary evidence to a distrusting government and its agencies.

Butt and Lance (2005, p. 420) suggest: 'There is no systematic relationship between job satisfaction and hours worked', since a small reduction in hours brought no increase in job satisfaction and 'yet some teachers apparently like working long hours' (ibid.). The nature of the work was clearly critical.

Centralist control

In countries where there is clear and even authoritarian control of the educational system, the roles of those in educational organisations are more inclined towards those of functionaries, following central directives, and the scope for addressing the motivational needs of individuals is inevitably more restricted. In Greece, for example, 'the centralised, bureaucratised and authoritarian system of control over education' (Ifanti 1995, p. 277) has meant a status for teachers as government employees, and with little devolution to regional and local level, the leaders themselves lose motivation. One headteacher in Crete (quoted in Middlewood 2001, p. 184) describes how, if a teacher is absent and no one is prepared to take over, 'the children have no classes – they go home. This encourages a culture in which virtually all teachers send their own children to private extra classes, and many of them take on extra jobs outside their teaching hours. Many actually run private schools for an extra income'.

Similarly, in Greece, Lainas (2010) found that Local Directors of Education were stressed and dissatisfied because of being 'squeezed' between national direction and school principals. In Malta, Bezzina (2001, p. 107) describes how meeting the challenge of moving from a highly centralised system to more local decision-making would be dependent upon the principals' ability to stimulate and motivate their professional colleagues.

Status of educational staff in society

The status of teachers in particular may be quite different in some countries compared with others, simply because of religious and cultural traditions which place a greater or lesser value on learning and education. Reynolds and Farrell (1996, pp. 54–57), in examining a number of studies, list 'the high status of teachers in the Pacific Rim societies' as one of the key factors in the superior educational achievement of students in East Asia, while Lewis (1995) notes the prestige of teaching in Japan as high relative to other professions. Status conferred via a title can be important too. Lumby and Briggs (2002) found that some lecturers employed in sixth form colleges (establishments for 16–19-years-old) much preferred the word 'lecturer' because of its academic associations, although they saw themselves as teaching, not lecturing.

Status is essentially something based on the perceptions of others, and where those that work in schools and colleges perceive themselves as being undervalued in society or by governments, this has clear implications for lower self-esteem and thereby job satisfaction and morale in the workforce. Chapter 3 points to the perceived low status of school support staff in some schools in England and Wales, while Johnson (2003, p. 66) points out that, although government ministers' statements about teachers since 2001 have nearly all been positive, 'teachers believe the contrary' and he suggests that 'the continuation of policies that show a lack of trust in the profession produces the misapprehension'. Müller et al. (2009, p. 593) suggested that 'enhancing the professional image of teachers' was one of the keys to successful change in the system in Switzerland.

In developed countries, since the marketisation of education in the 1980s and 1990s, Ball (2001), Gleeson and Gunter (2001) and Ozga (1995) argue that it is easy for the educational workforce to be marginalised and in some cases scapegoated for the failure to raise standards despite massive restructuring. Ozga's argument is that the workforce can become deskilled and that contributes to 'loss of control over the meaning and purpose of their work' (p. 35). Mather and Seifert (2011) make the same point about the workforce in further education. The phrase 'loss of control' epitomises a potential dilemma for school and college leaders when trying to eliminate Blauner's (1964) 'meaninglessness' from their staff's attitude to work. In a country such as Saudi Arabia, the status of jobs such as teaching may be seen as inferior for men (Bjerke and Al-Meer 1993), hence women are in the majority in the teaching profession. This can clearly have implications for motivation for people considering whether to enter the profession, especially men.

External control over incentives

Whether pay is a significant factor or not in motivating employees in schools and colleges, there is little doubt that lack of pay can be a cause of job dissatisfaction. The issue of performance related pay is covered more fully in the chapter on performance (Chapter 12) but here we may note that the scope for offering incentives, financial or otherwise, may be limited by pay, career progression and promotion structures which are uniform and legislated by government. In countries such as New Zealand, Israel and Singapore, teachers' career structures are formalised so that progression to the next stage depends upon some form of assessment, outside of leaders' control. At one extreme, if the assessment is rigorous and only a minority succeed in progressing, the risk is that those who do not succeed feel demotivated. At the other extreme, if the 'assessment' is ritualistic, with the assumption that all will 'pass', the incentive to work hard for success will be small. The introduction of the threshold assessment in the UK was described by the Secretary of State for Education as an important step in providing a 'well motivated' teaching force (DfEE 1998), and Ingvarson (2001) compares it with a similar move in Australia. He predicted that around 90 per cent would pass and his prediction was correct with 92.5 per cent passing in the first year. 'The assessment gains no respect, there is no recognition and the salary progression quickly becomes automatic, which was what the teacher unions aimed for anyway' (p. 170).

Wong and Wong's (2005) research found that in Hong Kong the dissatisfaction of many teachers with the controlled system of enhancement, sometimes despite sound relationships with leaders at institutional level, meant that the adoption of a more structured reward system was seen as essential to removing or reducing that dissatisfaction.

In countries where progression and pay is automatic, the risk of a 'job for life' culture developing is considerable. In Slovenia, for example, promotion is primarily based on length of service, days of in-service training (unassessed) and additional work (Erculj 2001). While security in a post is important as a basis for satisfaction, it cannot in itself be a motivator for performance.

Importance of leadership at institutional level

Despite the limitations described above, the potential for leaders and managers to make an impact on motivation at institutional level is significant. There are two main reasons for this. The first is simply that motivation *is* an individual issue. National initiatives can never legislate for what employees individually feel or think in their own schools or colleges in the way that the managers in those places can. Figure 7.1 shows a representation of the relative impact of influencers on motivation.

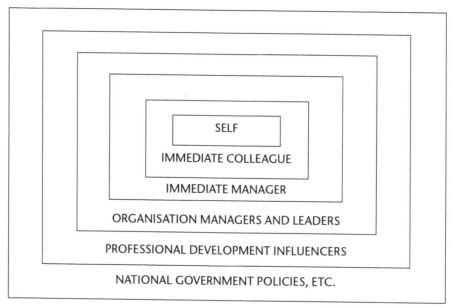

Figure 7.1   Relative impact of influencers on motivation

The significance for leaders of schools and colleges is in realising that the people closest to the individual employee will have the most impact upon motivation. (In some cases, that will be the actual institutional leader of course.) In management terms, the actions of the person with direct responsibility for the employee's work (line manager) are likely to have a more direct impact than those of organisational leaders in getting the best out of that employee.

The second reason is that the evidence is overwhelming that the more immediate the benefit of an action is perceived to be, the greater is likely to be its impact. Not only do people appreciate shorter-term goals (Kakabadse et al. 1988), but adult learners generally need to see practical and relevant outcomes for their learning to be motivated (Brookfield 2005; Reece and Walker 2003).

Furthermore, the actual quality of management at institutional level has been shown to have a direct impact upon staff motivation. Hutchings et al. (2000) found that 40 per cent of demotivated teachers in London schools cited 'poor management' as being central to their demotivation and dissatisfaction. In a survey on *The Quality of Teachers' Working Lives* (2001), the National Foundation for Educational Research (NFER) found that good quality management was very high on the list of factors that were significant for those teachers in the UK who were 'satisfied' or 'very satisfied' with their working lives. Similarly, in Kremer-Hayon and Goldstein's (1990) study of Israeli secondary school teachers, school managers were found to be central to the attitude to work that the teachers had.

Motivational strategies at institutional level

The following may be seen to be relevant to those with responsibility for motivating staff in individual schools and colleges.

Recognising the importance of individuality in motivation

As Whitaker (1997, p. 20) notes: 'In managing, treating all people the same is a recipe for difficulty and disappointment.'

All employees need to be treated appropriately, taking into account as far as possible their personal needs and aspirations. Some of the variations in these needs and aspirations can be appreciated and catered for if attention is paid to the fact that staff can be differently motivated according to the stage of career they are at, their gender, or the culture within which they operate. This is essentially an issue of equal opportunities and inclusion, which is dealt with fully in Chapter 6.

In terms of stages of career

Leithwood (1990) identifies the following career cycle (although it was based on teachers, it is equally relevant to all employees in education):

1   Launching the career.
2   Stabilising: developing mature commitment, feeling at ease, seeking more responsibility.
3   New challenges and concerns, diversifying, seeking added responsibilities.
4   Reaching a professional plateau: reappraisal, sense of mortality, continued striving for promotion *or* stagnating and becoming cynical.
5   Preparing for retirement: focusing, disenchantment or serenity.

Most schools or colleges, even small ones, are very likely to have people on their staff who are at different stages of a cycle such as this. Day et al. (2000) analysed motivating and demotivating factors for UK teachers and if their findings are mapped against Leithwood's career stages, as shown in Table 7.1, it is clear that motivating factors need to be carefully considered by leaders and managers – and demotivating factors avoided – when thinking about each staff member individually.

Table 7.1   Career stages and related motivational issues (based on Leithwood 1990 and Day et al. 2000)

Stage	Phase	Motivational issue
Stage 1	Career launch	Support from senior and middle leaders required
Stage 2	Stabilisation	Avoidance of heavy workloads
Stage 3	New responsibilities	Possibility of progression needed
Stage 4	Reaching plateau	Further advancement, achieving worklife balance
Stage 5	Looking to horizon	Support from institution needed, especially re health, policies and student behaviour

Career stages of course cannot be separated from the stages of human development that individuals move through during their lives. Erikson's (1977) model defines the issue for the ages 30–60 stage of development as being 'generativity versus stagnation'. Since this period covers at present the bulk of a working career in education, it suggests that the ability to enable others to be motivated and renewed is one which is not only valuable to the organisation in fulfilling its goals but also contributes to people leading richer, more fulfilled lives.

In terms of gender

A conventional, perhaps stereotyped view might be that most men work for money and career advancement, whereas women seek job satisfaction, a good working atmosphere and flexibility to fit family life into their careers. Of course, in many education systems, women do not have the same opportunities as men anyway, but the manager still needs to be alert to potential differences in factors affecting motivation for men and for women. Coleman's (2002) research into women as headteachers in England and Wales powerfully brings out the importance of avoiding stereotyping. This has crucial implications for managers of motivation since they need to avoid making assumptions about what motivates someone simply because she is, for example, a single woman who may, according to the stereotype, be a 'career woman [who] are cold, hard and single-minded' (Coleman 2002, p. 86). The most common gender stereotypes relevant to motivation refer to women being seen as wanting to carry the caring role from home into the work situation, and to men as seen wanting to take on more disciplinary and competitive roles. Yet research by Coleman (2002) also suggests that women seeking advancement are often 'pigeonholed' in pastoral or caring roles at a senior level – causing professional frustration.

In terms of different cultures

Harrison's (1995) study, building on the work of Hofstede (1980), suggests that as a country's economy developed so the emphasis on individualism increased with its consequent implications for motivation. However, as Foskett and Lumby (2003, p. 77) point out, this may be undermined by the many conclusions in published studies. They point to Fisher and Yuan's (1998) study which found that satisfaction factors differed considerably, from 'good wages' (China) to 'promotion and growth of skills' (Russia). All these points underline the principle that a universality of imperatives for motivation and satisfaction cannot be assumed.

Providing opportunities for relevant professional development

Professional development and staff learning is fully dealt with in Chapter 13, but it is worth noting here that, since personal growth and development are closely allied to motivational attitudes, leaders and managers will wish to use this as a powerful means of motivating staff. The opportunity to develop skills, gain new ones and demonstrate the ability to learn new ideas and apply them is for adults an important way of gaining the confidence to meet new challenges and adapt to changed situations.

Professional development can be a powerful motivating force even in circumstances where all the usual factors likely to motivate staff appear to be absent. Taylor (2003, p. 9) contrasts the motivational attitudes of the staff of two schools she worked in, both of which were designated to close, and attributes the success of one of them to the leadership shown:

> [An] . . . important thing that the leadership did was to establish
> a very full programme of accredited professional development
> with a local higher education provider. The accreditation was very
> important because it offered the opportunity for everyone to gain
> some form of qualification that would benefit them greatly in their
> applications now and in their future careers.

She describes how she gained a higher degree, 'something I believe I never would have been motivated to do if I had stayed in a normal school. Five others at least that I know of from that group have also obtained their Masters Degree qualification since and two or three others have diplomas'. She concludes that 'it is a tribute to the programme and above all the staff that the tutor describes the staff group as being one of the most enthusiastic that he had encountered. Thus we must have been well motivated in our circumstances!'

Similarly, Middlewood (1999) describes how school-based research-centred professional development programmes were found to produce a significant impact on staff morale. In one school due for closure, the maintaining of motivation was an actual stated aim of the programme. In the second school, the course was established in what was seen as a failing school, and then the news came of its intended closure. One of the school managers felt that the unifying aspect of the course was important in motivating them. Middlewood (1999, p. 94) concludes:

> The situations in these two schools offered evidence that, since
> the direct aim for school improvement could hardly be deemed
> to be relevant as the schools would no longer exist, the benefits

must lie in the process, firstly for maintaining and enhancing the motivation of teachers in potentially very demotivating circumstances and, secondly, enabling the schools' students to receive the best possible service during the schools' remaining time.

Providing individuals and teams with a sense of direction

Since motivation is focused on future action, the capacity of members of staff to be motivated will be greater if their organisation, their team and they themselves are able to see that future courses of action are clear and worthwhile. Organisations that 'wander' or 'meander' (Hopkins et al. 1994) or 'cruise' (Stoll and Fink 1998) have great difficulty in motivating staff either because there is complacency ('We're doing alright as we are') or because this new exhortation to work is just another initiative ('Here we go again').

Leaders who provide strategic direction also tend to provide ways of achieving strategic goals to aid motivation. A secondary head (Parker 1997) was fond of quoting the Koran: 'If you do not know where you are going, anywhere will do.' Even in the cases of the closing schools quoted above, a clear end was in view and some leaders used this to motivate colleagues. Howse and MacPherson (2001) showed how, in the development of New Zealand polytechnics, all motivation was lost by lecturing and support staff because they felt no educational focus and direction was being given by their senior managers. A focus on managerialism and financial planning by leaders meant that staff were not willing or able to see their increased workloads as being relevant to what they had believed to be the polytechnics' key purpose, i.e. student learning. Similar findings by Briggs (2002) in the further education sector in the UK reinforce that point.

The lesson for leaders is that staff want to work in a school or college that they feel is 'going somewhere' and this offers an opportunity for what leaders aspire to – the alignment of individual and organisational goals.

Giving as much recognition as possible

One of the key phrases in motivation is, according to Evans (1998), 'Nothing succeeds like success', and leaders need to take every opportunity to acknowledge and recognise both achievement and effort. Dwight's (1986) work on patterns of motivation showed how important it is to place emphasis on the *effort* people have put into their work and subsequent achievement, rather than on their ability. Hopefully, many employees will have both ability and effort but Dwight argued that the risk of overemphasis on ability may mean that when someone does not achieve, they may interpret it as not being as good as they thought and become demotivated, trying less hard next time.

As far as tangible recognition is concerned, especially in the form of payment, Lumby and Li (1998) show how it was possible for colleges in China, a country not known for its individual enterprise, to use funds generated by initiatives to provide a range of rewards and incentives. In England and Wales in 2002, the government awarded cash rewards to schools whose examination performance had improved significantly over three years. However, Baxter's (2003) study of how three secondary schools passed the money on within their schools showed the influence individual leaders had on staff motivation.

In School A, the head decided simply to divide the sum of money equally among every employee in the school at the time of the award. Thus, everyone (principal, teacher, secretary, caretaker, lunchtime supervisor) received the same sum. The resultant sum was not great, but it was proportionately (of salary) much higher for some than others, and the staff response was that 94 per cent of the employees found it 'very fair'.

In School B, a complex formula was developed to try to ensure that those who had contributed most directly to the improvement received most money, and others less so. Every employee received at least a token amount. Thirty-four per cent saw this distribution as being very fair.

In School C, the leadership allocated the money after a discussion among themselves, awarding most of the money to the school managers and heads of those departments that had improved significantly. Here, only 11 per cent of the staff saw this as very fair, a figure well below the numbers who had actually received awards!

Allowing as much employee ownership of work as possible

Fisher and Yuan's (1998) study showed that, in Russia and the USA, being kept informed and involved with decisions so these were not left to be passed down from 'on high' was seen as very important to employees. The literature of educational change (Hopkins et al. 1994; Fullan 1999) demonstrates that ownership of an initiative by those who are to implement it is crucial to success. Day et al. (1990) indicate ways in which staff may become demotivated if:

1   people are simply told that 'they must . . .'

2   people are put into a threatened position

3   it is felt that the plan is a 'gimmick' promoted by senior members of staff to further their own ends

4   people feel that the plan is mounted merely to satisfy higher authority

5   people feel alienated from the organisation or from whoever is responsible for the plan

6   the leader assumes the role of the 'expert' and there is a lack of opportunity for teachers to develop, or to exercise, responsibility (adapted from Day et al. 1990).

What kind of leadership is best for motivating staff?

There is increasing evidence (for example, Beatty 2007; Wong and Wong 2005; Lambert 2003) that educated leaders who are most likely to motivate staff are those with emotional intelligence. This quality includes motivation and empathy, as well as skills such as listening, problem-solving and negotiating. The ability of such leaders to form effective relationships with a significant number of staff is not in any way a 'soft' approach. As Middlewood (2010, p. 46) points out, 'the need to direct at times and prompt people to move out of personal comfort zones remains crucial'.

Conclusion

As the comment on emotional intelligence suggests, it seems that only leaders and managers who are themselves motivated will be successful in motivating others. Perhaps what motivates top-class leaders are specific behaviours such as self-control, self-confidence, an ability to win people over and a *strong motivation for achievement.* The lesson for those who wish to motivate others effectively appears to be, as so often in people management, begin with yourself!

References

Ball, S. (2001) 'Performativities and Fabrications in the Education Economy. Towards the Performative Society', in Gleeson, D. and Husband, C. (eds), 'The Performing School', London, RoutledgeFalmer.

Baxter, G (2003) 'A fair distribution of rewards?', Headship Matters, (25), 5–6, London, Optimus Publishing.

Beatty, B. (2007) 'Going through the emotions: Getting to the heart of school renewal', Australian Journal of Education, Special Issue, November.

Bezzina C. (2001) 'From administering to managing and leading: the case of Malta', in Pashiardis, P. (ed.), International Perspectives on Educational Leadership, Hong Kong, Commonwealth Council for Educational Administration and Management.

Bjerke, B. and Al-Meer, A. (1993) 'Culture's consequences: management in Saudi Arabia', Leadership and Organisation Development Journal, 14 (1), 30–35.

Blauner, S. (1964) Alienation and Freedom, Chicago, IL, University of Chicago Press.

Briggs, A. (2002) 'Facilitating the Role of Middle Manages in Further Education', Research in Post-Compulsory Education, 7 (1), 63–78.

Brookfield, S. (2005) The Power of Critical Theory: Liberating Adult Learning and Teaching, San Francisco, Jossey-Bass.

Butt, G. and Lance, A. (2005) 'Secondary Teacher Workload and Job Satisfaction. Do Successful Strategies for Change Exist?' Educational Management Administration & Leadership, 33 (4), 401–422.

Cerit, Y. (2009) 'The Effects of Servant Leadership Behaviours of School Principals on Teachers' Job Satisfaction', Educational Management Administration & Leadership, 37 (5), 600–623.

Coleman, M. (2002) Women Headteachers: Striking the Balance, Stoke-on-Trent, Trentham Books.

Day, C., Johnston, D. and Whitaker, P. (1990) Managing Primary Schools in the 1990s: A Professional Development Approach, London, Paul Chapman Publishing.

Day, C., Harris, A., Hadfield, M., Tolley, H. and Beresford, J. (2000) Leading Schools in Times of Change, Buckingham, Open University Press.

DfEE (1998) Teachers: meeting the challenge of change, Green Paper, London, DfEE.

Dwight, C. (1986) Patterns of Motivation, Oxford, Blackwell.

Erculj, J. (2001) 'Appraisal in Slovenia – the headteacher's burden?', in Middlewood, D. and Cardno, C. (eds), Managing Teacher Appraisal and Performance: A Comparative Approach, London, Paul Chapman Publishing.

Erikson, E. (1977) Childhood and Society, London, Triad/Granada.

Evans, L. (1998) Staff Motivation, Morale and Job Satisfaction, London, Paul Chapman Publishing.

Fisher, C. (1993) 'Boredom at work: a neglected concept', Human Relations, 46 (3), 395–417.

Fisher, C. and Yuan, A. (1998) 'What motivates employees? A comparison of US and Chinese responses', International Journal of Human Resource Management, 9 (3), 516–528.

Foskett, N. and Lumby, J. (2003) Leading and Management in Education: International Dimensions, London, Paul Chapman Publishing.

Fryer, M. (1996) Creative Teaching and Learning, London, Paul Chapman Publishing.

Fullan, M. (1999) *Change Forces: The Sequel*, London, Falmer Press.

Gleeson, D. and Gunter, H. (2001) 'The performing school and the modernisation of teachers,' in Gleeson, D. and Husbands, C. (eds), *The Performing School*, London, RoutledgeFalmer.

Handy, C. (1993) *Understanding Organisations*, Fourth Edition, Harmondsworth, Penguin.

Harrison, G. (1995) 'Satisfaction, tension and interpersonal relations: a cross-cultural comparison of managers in Singapore and Australia', *Journal of Managerial Psychology*, 10 (8), 13–19.

Herzberg, F. (1966) 'The motivation–hygiene theory', in Pugh, D. (ed.), *Organisation Theory: Selected Readings*, Harmondsworth, Penguin.

Hofstede, G. (1980) *Culture's consequences: international differences in work-related values*, Beverly Hills, CA, Sage.

Hopkins, D., Ainscow, M. and West, M. (1994) *School Improvement in an Era of Change*, London, Cassell.

Howse, J. and MacPherson, R. (2001) 'New Zealand's educational administration policies 1984–1994 and the strategic management of its polytechnics', in Pashiardis, P. (ed.), *International Perspectives on Educational Leadership*, Hong Kong, Commonwealth Council for Educational Administration and Management.

Hutchings, M., Mentor, I., Ross, A. and Thomson, D. (2000) *Teacher supply and retention in London 1998–99*, London, University of North London School of Education.

Ifanti, A. (1995) 'Policy making, politics and administration in education in Greece', *Educational Management and Administration*, 23 (4), 217–278.

Ingvarson, L. (2001) 'Developing standards and assessments for accomplished teaching: a responsibility of the profession', in Middlewood, D. and Cardno, C. (eds), *Managing Teacher Appraisal and Performance: A Comparative Approach*, London, Paul Chapman Publishing.

Johnson, M. (2003) 'From victims of change to agents of change', *Professional Development Today*, 6 (1), 63–68.

Kakabadse, A., Ludlow, R. and Vinnicombe, S. (1988) *Working in Organisations*, Harmondsworth, Penguin.

Kremer-Hayon, L. and Goldstein, Z. (1990) 'The inner world of Israeli secondary school teachers: work centrality, job satisfaction and stress', *Comparative Education*, 26, 285–289.

Ladebo, O. (2005) 'The effects of work-related attitudes on the intention to leave the profession: an examination of school teachers in Nigeria', *Educational Management Administration and Leadership*, 33 (3), 355–369.

Lainas, A. (2010) 'Local Directors of School Education in Greece, Their Role and Main Sources of Job Stress', *Educational Management Administration & Leadership*, 38 (4), 454–471.

Lambert, L. (2003) *Leadership capacity for Lasting School Improvement*, Alexandria, VA, Association for Supervisors and Curriculum Development.

Leithwood, K. (1990) 'The principal's role in teacher development', in Joyce, B. (ed.), *Changing School Culture through Staff Development*, Alexandria, Victoria, ASCD.

Lewis, C. (1995) *Educating Hearts and Minds: Reflections on Japanese Pre-School and Elementary Education*, New York, Cambridge University Press.

Lumby, J. (2003) 'Managing motivation', in Lumby, J., Middlewood, D. and

Kaabwe, S. (eds), *Managing human resources in South African Schools*, London, Commonwealth Secretariat.

Lumby, J. and Briggs, A. (2002) *Sixth Form Colleges: Policy, Purpose and Practice*, Leicester, University of Leicester and Nuffield Foundation.

Lumby, J. and Li, Y. (1998) 'Managing vocational education in China', *Compare*, 28 (2), 197–206.

Maslow, A. (1970) *Motivation and Personality*, New York, Harper and Row.

McGregor, D. (1960) *The Human Side of Enterprise*, New York, McGraw-Hill.

Mather, K. and Seifert, R. (2011) 'Teachers, Lecturers, and Labourers,' *Management In Education*, 25 (1), 26–31.

Middlewood, D. (1999) 'Some effects of multiple research projects on the host school staff and their relationships', in Middlewood, D., Coleman, M. and Lumby, J., *Practitioner Research in Education: Making a difference*, London, Paul Chapman Publishing.

Middlewood, D. (2001) 'The future of managing teacher performance and its appraisal', in Middlewood, D. and Cardno, C. (eds), *Managing Teacher Appraisal and Performance: A Comparative Approach*, London, Paul Chapman Publishing.

Middlewood, D. (2010) 'Managing People and Performance', in Bush, T., Bell, L. and Middlewood, D. (eds), *The principles of educational leadership and management*, London, Sage.

Middlewood, D. and Lumby, J. (1998) *Human Resource Management in Schools and Colleges*, London, Paul Chapman Publishing.

Müller, K., Alliata, R. and Benninghoff, F. (2009) 'Attracting and retaining teachers: a question of motivation', *Educational Management Administration and Leadership*, 37 (5), 574–599.

Mwanwenda, T. (1995) 'Job satisfaction among secondary school teachers in Transkei', *South African Journal of Education*, 19 (2), 84–87.

National Foundation for Educational Research (NFER) (2001) *The Quality of Teachers' Working Lives*, Slough, NFER.

Ozga, J. (1995) 'Deskilling a profession: professionalism, deprofessionalisation and the new managerialism', in Busher, H. and Saran, R. (eds), *Managing Teachers as Professionals in Schools*, London, Kogan Page.

Parker, R. (1997) 'Strategic planning and leadership', MBA dissertation (unpublished), University of Leicester.

Reece, I. and Walker, S. (2003) *Teaching, Training and Learning*, (School Education), Sunderland, Business Education Publishers Ltd.

Reynolds, D. and Farrell, S. (1996) *Worlds Apart: A Review of International Surveys of Educational Achievement including England*, London, HMSO.

Ryan, R. and Deci, E. (2000) 'Intrinsic and Extrinsic Motivation, Classic Definitions and New Directions,' *Contemporary Educational Psychology*, 25, 54–67.

Sabanci, A. (2008) 'School Principals' Assumption about Human Nature: Implications for Leadership in Turkey', *Educational Management Administration & Leadership*, 36 (4), 511–529.

Stoll, L. and Fink, D. (1998) 'The cruising school: the unidentified ineffective school', in Stoll, L. and Myers, K. (eds), *No Quick Fixes: Perspectives on Schools in Difficulty*, Basingstoke, Falmer.

Taylor, D. (2003) 'Managing within closing schools', *Headship Matters*, (23), 4–5, London, Optimus Publishing.

Whitaker, P. (1997) 'Changes in professional development; the personal dimension', in Kydd, L., Crawford, M. and Riches, C. (eds), *Professional Development for Educational Management*, Buckingham, Open University Press, pp.11–25.

Wong, P. and Wong, C. (2005) 'Promotion Criteria and Satisfaction of School Teachers in Hong Kong', *Educational Management Administration & Leadership*, 33 (4), 423–447.

Leading and managing through teams

Introduction: the rationale for teams

The notion of teamwork is widespread in schools and colleges in many countries. Teams are frequently advocated as an appropriate part of school and college structures. Katzenbach and Smith (1998) claim that teams are more effective than individuals:

> Teams outperform individuals acting alone or in larger groupings, especially when performance requires multiple skills, judgements, and experiences. Most people recognize the capabilities of teams; most have the common sense to make teams work . . . real teams are deeply committed to their purpose, goals and approach. High-performance team members are also very committed to one another. (p. 9)

Lashway (2003, p. 1) links teamwork to the wider focus on shared or distributed leadership. The task of transforming schools is too complex to expect one person to accomplish single-handedly. Accordingly, leadership should be distributed throughout the school rather than vested in one position.

Wallace (2001) elaborates on this view and advances five reasons for shared leadership:

- Shared leadership is morally just in a democratic country where individual rights are accorded high priority.

- Participating in shared leadership is a fulfilling experience for all involved.

- Team membership provides an opportunity for professional development.

- Co-operative relationships provide good models for children and students.

- Shared leadership is potentially more effective than principals acting alone, not least because staff 'own' the outcomes (adapted from Wallace 2001, pp. 153–154).

Woods et al. (2004) link distributed leadership to teams, stating that

the literature on teams, with its emphases on collaboration, multiple and complementary strengths and the need for all members to share a common view of both the purposes of the team and its means of working, has similarities to much of the discussion of distributed leadership. (p. 447)

Democratic participation provides the rationale for teamwork in South African schools.

The role of the senior management team is . . . to share the management tasks more widely in the school. This is necessary if the management of schools is to become more democratic, inclusive and participatory. (Department of Education 2000, p. 2)

Cardno (2002), drawing on experience in New Zealand, shows the importance of teamwork, and links it to the advent of site-based management:

Teams abound in schools because they are structured in ways that allow teachers to work together to make curriculum and management related decisions. In settings where the implementation of education reform has increased the complexity of school management through devolution, principals have embraced the opportunity to share new tasks and decision-making with teams. (p. 213)

It is evident that there is considerable support for the notion of teamwork in education. Indeed, the ubiquitous presence of teams in primary and secondary schools, a 'grass roots response' (Wallace 2002, p. 168), shows that they are widely believed to be an important feature of school organisation. However, such assumptions are by no means sufficient to ensure that teams are meaningful and effective. Developing successful teams can be problematic, as we shall see later in this chapter.

The composition of leadership and management teams

The shift in emphasis from 'management' to 'leadership' in education, noted in Chapter 1, is reflected in the language of teamwork, notably in English schools. The advent of the National College for School *Leadership*, and the introduction of a 'leadership' pay spine in England, have encouraged a change in nomenclature for the most senior teams in schools. Most now prefer to use the term 'senior leadership team (SLT)', rather than 'senior management team (SMT)'. Different terms are used in other countries; for example, 'school management teams' in South Africa.

Leadership teams are not statutory in most countries, so their composition is a matter of institutional choice. In South Africa, larger schools typically have a principal, one or two deputy principals, and several HoDs, who are responsible for learning areas and for certain whole-school activities. In most primary schools, there are no deputy principals and HoDs support the principal, as well as being responsible for different parts of the school (for example, foundation phase or intermediate phase) (Bush et al. 2010).

Rutherford (2002) refers to a 'lack of consistency' in the composition of SMTs in English primary schools. His research in the Catholic sector demonstrates some agreement but also a measure of diversity in his five one-form entry primary schools (see Table 8.1). Rutherford's case studies show that heads and deputies are generally included in SMTs in England but they vary in the number and roles of the other team members. Wallace (2001) confirms both the commonalities and the differences in structures, saying that SMTs in British primary schools typically 'consist of the head, deputy and other teachers with the most substantial management responsibility' (p. 153).

Table 8.1 Composition of SMTs in five English Catholic schools (adapted from Rutherford 2002, pp. 453–454)

	Headteacher	*Deputy head*	*School co-ordinators*
A	☞	☞	Religious education
B	☞	☞	Subject co-ordinators
C	☞	☞	Maths and English co-ordinators
D	☞	☞	Two key stage co-ordinators
E	☞	☞	None

Cardno (2002) shows that senior management teams are the most common permanent teams in New Zealand schools (see Table 8.2).

Table 8.2 Permanent teams in New Zealand schools (Cardno 2002)

Permanent teams	*Percentage of schools*
Senior management	81.8
Curriculum committee	63.8
Subject/department	61.4
Professional development	43.8
Student services	20.4

An important variable in teamwork is the number of members in the team. If the team is too large, it is difficult for individuals to make a meaningful contribution and meetings are likely to be dominated by the chair and other senior members. Equally, small teams may be ineffective because they do not have sufficient collective expertise. 'In smaller teams it is more difficult to bring together the range of skills and approaches that lead to the significant enhancement of problem solving, creativity and enthusiasm' (Chaudhry-Lawton et al. 1992, p. 137).

Belbin (1993) advocates a team of eight but the four primary schools studied by Wallace (2001) all had between four and seven SMT members. The smallest was at 'Winton' where the head wanted to promote sharing and debate and was concerned about the viability of large teams.

> I have always stuck out against a larger team because I couldn't see how I could make it workable on a regular basis. I couldn't imagine how I could have regular and meaningful meetings with seven or eight people . . . I don't think you can have genuine discussions in a group of that size. (quoted in Wallace 2001, p. 159)

Wallace's (2001) research illustrates the importance of meetings, both as 'symbols' of teamwork, and in providing a regular framework for their operation. SLTs in England typically meet on a weekly basis and thus have a regular presence in the school timetable. Meetings provide much of the *raison d'être* for teams and those which do not meet regularly are likely to wither and die.

Size also influences the number and type of teams in schools. In New Zealand, for example, 98.8 per cent of large primary schools have SMTs while only 75.6 per cent of small primary schools have them (Cardno 2002, p. 214).

A significant feature of leadership in high performing English schools is the large size of their SLTs. Two of the nine case study schools studied by Bush and Glover (2012a) have nine SLT members, while only the small primary schools have fewer than six. Two of the schools have dual SLT/SMT arrangements with the larger SLT addressing policy while the smaller SMT is responsible for operational matters (ibid.). The trend towards larger teams is confirmed by the NCSL (NCSL 2009). Bush and Glover (2012a) note that larger teams can handle more responsibilities.

Developing effective teams

Teamwork is increasingly advocated, as we noted earlier, but the acid test of their practical value is whether they operate effectively and contribute to the development of successful schools and colleges. Teams form part of an essentially normative framework for school leadership and management, with several overlapping assumptions:

- Principals should develop and communicate a distinctive vision for the school or college.

- Leadership should be transformational so that staff and the wider school community can be inspired to share, and to implement, the principal's vision.

- Professional staff are encouraged to participate in teams, ostensibly on an equal basis, despite the hierarchical structures within which they all work.

- Teamwork is likely to lead to 'better' and more widely accepted decisions.

The reality is often rather different from this 'harmony' model. In England, and many other countries, governments are transfixed by 'standards', evidenced by test and examination scores. Teamwork and distributed leadership receive a measure of support because they are thought likely to contribute to the standards agenda. Yet the government's policies compromise the distributed model, for several reasons:

- The school's distinctive vision is subordinate to the government's target driven approach.

- Accountability pressures have intensified, making it 'risky' for heads to share power with their colleagues.

- Teamwork may be limited to implementing external priorities instead of formulating ideas to meet the specific needs of the school and its pupils.

- Team processes may be perceived as valuable but they are vulnerable if they do not lead to the outcomes desired by government.

Wallace (2001) summarises the tension facing English heads operating in this climate:

> Headteachers are confronted by a heightened dilemma: their greater dependence on colleagues disposes them towards sharing leadership. In a context of unprecedented accountability, however, they may be inhibited from sharing because it could backfire should empowered colleagues act in ways that generate poor standards of pupil achievement, alienate parents and governors, attract negative media attention or incur inspectors' criticism. (p. 157)

These intensified external pressures have several implications for the nature of teamwork and for any assessment of its effectiveness. The extent and nature of teamwork and distributed leadership is a matter for the head, who has the power to increase, reduce or amend the level of shared decision-making. Glib assumptions of professional agreement, for example in South Africa where the Department of Education (2000, p. 2) claims that 'most SMTs work on the basis of consensus', have to give way to a more sober assessment of what is possible in a climate of enhanced accountability. Bush et al.'s (2010) study of teaching and learning in South Africa's Limpopo and Mpumalanga provinces shows that SMTs are often ineffective. In six of their eight case study schools, the SMTs either did not meet at all or they focused on routine matters, rather than the management of teaching and learning.

A survey of 180 Mpumalanga SMT members (Glover and Bush 2012), with a healthy 93 per cent response rate, showed that only a minority (32.8 per cent) of SMTs met at least weekly. Most met only once (24.4 per cent) or twice (29.2 per cent) a month, while a smaller number (12.5 per cent) met at most twice a term. Most (76 per cent) of these SMTs have written agendas and minutes but almost a quarter (24 per cent) have no formal record of the meetings.

Wallace (2002) points out that leadership and management impact on student learning but that the effect is indirect, or 'mediated', via classroom teaching. In smaller schools, where the principal is a full- or part-time teacher, there is the potential for direct effects but usually leadership exerts its influence on teachers who, in turn, seek to enhance pupil learning. Any single individual has a limited impact on outcomes but, if leadership is distributed widely, the potential effects are multiplied. 'It is as foolish to think that only principals provide leadership for school improvement as to believe that principals do not influence school effectiveness' (Hallinger and Heck 1999, p. 186).

The beneficial effects of teamwork are assumed to arise from the interaction between people motivated to collaborate in order to achieve desired outcomes. In this sense, the combined effects of the team are potentially greater than the sum of its individual parts. The team process produces positive effects that could not be achieved by individuals acting alone. Wallace (2002) describes this effect as 'synergy'. Referring to his research in English primary schools, he shows that:

> Effectiveness of teamwork was related to the degree of synergy – harnessing team members' energies to attain joint goals, whereby more could be achieved by working together than the aggregate of what individual members could achieve alone. (p. 169)

This example suggests that these schools had developed what Wallace (2001, p. 162) describes as a 'culture of teamwork' which 'was sophisticated enough for contradictory beliefs and values to coexist without conflict, mutually empowering all members'. Similarly, Bush and Glover (2012a) refer to 'cohesive teams' in their high performing English case study schools.

Although teams are well established in schools and colleges, there is only limited evidence of any systematic evaluation of their effectiveness, although this formed part of the Office for Standards in Education (Ofsted 2003) inspection framework for English schools. In the section of the framework devoted to leadership and management, inspectors were expected to assess 'how well the leadership team creates a climate for learning' (p. 45) and the extent to which 'leaders create effective teams' (p. 46). The 2012 framework does not specifically mention leadership teams, although it does refer to the need to develop leadership capacity (Ofsted 2012).

The 2003 Ofsted requirements suggest that school leaders should carry out regular assessments of the effectiveness of their teams. Middlewood and Lumby (1998, p. 49) identify three criteria for team effectiveness:

1   the extent to which the quantity and quality of specified outcomes for the team has been achieved
2   the extent to which the working of the team has enhanced its future capacity
3   the extent to which the capacity of individual team members has been enhanced.

The nine high performing English leadership teams share several key features which contribute to their effectiveness:

- developing shared values to underpin team work

- meeting regularly (at least weekly) to plan strategically and to hone the school's vision

- providing role clarity for all SLT members

- avoiding complacency by striving to improve their already high standards.

- stressing team unity and presenting a united front to other staff and stakeholders. (Bush and Glover 2012a)

In contrast, Bush et al.'s (2010) findings suggest that teams in South African schools require development if they are to become really effective. In particular, schools need to ensure that SMTs meet regularly, and focus on teaching and learning rather than on routine administration. The Mpumalanga survey data (Glover and Bush 2012) show that most SMTs are perceived to be effective (see Table 8.3).

Table 8.3 Perceptions of effectiveness in Mpumalanga (South Africa) schools

SMT effectiveness	Responses
Highly effective – no changes required	8%
Fairly effective – minor changes required	63%
Barely effective – some changes required	21%
Ineffective – major changes required	6%

Table 8.3 shows that most (71 per cent) respondents to Glover and Bush's (2012) survey regard their SMTs as highly or fairly effective. However, more than a quarter consider that their teams are 'barely effective' (21 per cent) or 'ineffective' (6 per cent). These figures should be interpreted with caution as they are based on self-reporting and respondents may wish to portray their schools in a favourable light.

Team development and learning

Team learning is linked to organisational learning (see Chapter 13). Leithwood (1998) claims that participatory decision-making is assumed in all forms of site-based management. This is generally achieved through 'the many task forces, groups, committees and teams that are responsible for enacting the bulk of non-classroom business in restructuring schools' (p. 204). He adds that team learning is an important ingredient of effective teamwork and has two main dimensions:

1   a shared understanding of the team's purposes
2   the actions permitted by the larger organisation for achieving those purposes.

These dimensions operate within a wider cultural framework which condition the ways in which teams function. The team's culture may be seen as a 'collective programming of the mind' (p. 209) and often involves tacit rather than conscious knowledge. This creates problems for new team members 'who may have difficulty understanding the shared meanings held by their team colleagues' (p. 209).

Leithwood (1998) adds that another learning challenge facing team members is 'what actions to take as individuals in order to contribute to the collective learning of the team' (p. 210). This may take the form of 'mutual adaptation', where individuals adapt their contributions in response to the specific requirements of new tasks and also as a reaction to the perceived changes by other team members.

Cardno's (2002) research suggests that there is a low emphasis on team training and development despite the pervasive influence of teams in New Zealand schools. She adds that 'teams have considerable capacity to learn because they are units of action' (p. 220) but such potential may be untapped because of certain barriers to learning. These barriers may involve an element of defensiveness:

> Defensiveness is evident in the kind of communication that
> takes place in organisations when issues surface that are likely to
> threaten or embarrass individuals or teams . . . For a team to learn
> (and to contribute to organisational learning) it must overcome
> the barriers to learning that are ingrained in both individual and
> collective behaviour. (p. 220)

Cardno (2002) also points to the need for strong leadership to promote team development and organisational learning. Such leadership could lead to productive rather than defensive communication and could release the 'unharnessed potential' of teams.

It is evident from this review that team learning is an important aspect of their effectiveness. Tuckman's (1965) classic model of team development assumes four stages of growth:

- forming
- storming
- norming
- performing.

Each of these stages has a potential learning dimension as members engage in mutual adaptation and the team moves from initial formation (or reformation in the case of changing membership) to successful operation or 'performance'. Cardno's (2002) point is that such learning should not be left to chance but should be built into the culture of teamwork, notably through leadership action. She reinforces this view in her later work (Cardno 2012, p. 153), where she stresses that the final stage of team development involves 'the capacity to perform their common task at a high level'.

The Mpumalanga provincial department of education in South Africa has chosen to register whole SMTs on the national Advanced Certificate in Education (ACE) leadership development programme, believing that this will enhance leadership density and ensure that all leaders understand reasons for change (Bush et al. 2011). However, the high performing English SLTs mostly preferred in-house development and largely eschewed formal leadership courses (Bush and Glover 2012a). This suggests that team development should be customised to the specific needs, and current position, of SLTs, rather than adopting a 'one size fits all' model.

Teamwork in action: co-principalship in New Zealand

One of the implicit assumptions of teamwork is that members operate as status equals. Their participation is assumed to be on the basis of specific expertise rather than formal positions in the school or college hierarchy. As we noted earlier, teams form part of a wider normative preference for collaborative work. However, the notion of *senior* leadership or management teams compromises this principle in that seniority is itself a qualification for membership. Given that shared leadership is in the gift of principals, there is always a balancing act between teamwork and hierarchy, as Wallace (2001, p. 159) notes in respect of English primary schools: 'The extent to which headteachers shared leadership depended on the balance they sought between expressing belief in the management hierarchy and in equal contribution of team members in the SMT's operation.'

This contradiction between hierarchy and collaboration is explored in Court's (2004) study of a co-principalship in New Zealand. The board of a small primary school with three teachers needed to appoint a new principal. Two of the three teachers submitted a proposal for a co-principalship. Their rationale was consistent with the team ethic:

> They believed that collaborative planning and decision-making contributed to the development of better teaching and learning programmes . . . they each thought that traditional management hierarchies were not the best model for school leadership . . . they wanted shared leadership practices and collective responsibility to evolve in ways that would best suit the school and people's strengths. (p. 180)

The school board was attracted to the proposal, and 'blown away' (p. 180) by the quality of the applications, but met resistance when they consulted state officials; 'they were told that this was illegal – it would blur accountability lines' (p. 174). Because New Zealand's schools are self-governing, the board was able to ignore this advice and made the collective appointment, beginning in 1993. The co-principals 'took a more inclusive, fluid and flexible approach to sharing the functions of leadership and management' (p. 186). They acknowledged the pressures for legal accountability but were also 'committed to working within deeper forms of professional and personal accountability' (p. 187).

Court (2004) concludes that the co-principalship contributed to a more democratic framework for school leadership and management, leading to genuine teamwork:

> The strength of the co-principal approach . . . is that its flat management structure was built on the prioritizing of open, honest communication and the sharing of information and decision-making both within the leadership team and between them and their support staff, board and parents in the school. (p. 193)

Teamwork in action: high performing leadership teams in England

The normative literature on teams (for example, Lashway 2003) assumes that teamwork is more effective than leaders acting alone. Bush and Glover's (2012a) study of high performing senior leadership teams, for the English NCSL, addresses whether, and to what extent, the operation of SLTs contributes to successful schools. The author's nine case study schools (four secondary, three primary and two special) were defined as 'high performing' because they received 'outstanding' Ofsted grades overall, and for leadership and management, in inspections conducted in 2008–2009.

Harris (2010, p. 55) defines distributed leadership as 'the expansion of leadership roles in schools, beyond those in formal leadership or administrative posts'. There is emerging evidence that distributing leadership may have a positive impact on school and student outcomes. Leithwood et al.'s (2006) widely cited paper presents 'seven strong claims' about successful school leadership. Two of these relate to distributed leadership:

- School leadership has a greater influence on schools and students when it is widely distributed.
- Some patterns of distribution are more effective than others.

SLTs can be regarded as an example of distributed leadership.

Bush and Glover (2012a) point to several distinctive features of their nine case study schools. One is the long service of most of their leadership team members. The implication is that effective team working takes time to develop, and that continuity is a requirement for high performance. 'These nine case studies collectively provide powerful evidence of the value of stability and continuity within SLTs, enabling the development, articulation, embedding and implementation of a clear vision, focused on student learning' (ibid., p. 26).

The nine case studies also support the notion that effective teams distribute leadership among SLT members in ways which give them a strong collective overview of teaching and learning, and of pastoral issues. As noted above, these schools reflect the trend towards larger and more diverse leadership teams, which can handle wider responsibilities. Most case study schools also devoted considerable time to team meetings. The teams appeared to be cohesive with a clear set of values, high levels of trust, and a purposeful approach to team leadership. Role clarity is also a key feature in many of these schools and the SLT is often regarded as 'the main decision-making focal point of the school' (HoD, school Y).

The participants were proud that their schools were rated 'high performing' but stressed the need to keep striving to raise standards and not to be complacent about their achievements. Most of the case study schools also appear to have given considerable attention to developing and maintaining good links with other staff, and to developing effective communication with staff and stakeholders.

This research suggests that unity is a signature feature of high performing teams and SLT members 'talk the same story' (head, school S) and adopt 'cabinet rules' (school B), meaning that full and frank discussion was acceptable among the SLT, but that a united front was to be presented to the school. However, there is unanimity that any differences that do arise should not become evident outside the SLT.

Leadership of SLTs provides a test for the normative shift away from solo leaders towards distributed leadership. The case study evidence shows that the heads retain a powerful role despite the rhetoric of distribution. This supports Gronn's (2010) concept of 'hybrid' leadership, combining solo and distributed elements.

The experience of the nine schools shows that distributed leadership is used in different ways, and to varying extents, reflecting the diverse complexity of school organisation and the nature of the relationships between heads and their colleagues, especially SLT members. Because school contexts vary significantly, it is not possible to present a 'blueprint' for effective distributed leadership, but the nine case studies all provide examples of how teamwork may contribute to high performance.

Advantages of teamwork

Teams have become widespread in schools and colleges in many different national contexts. This has occurred because leaders and staff feel that teamwork has advantages over individual activity. This is partly a normative position, a belief, rather than being grounded strongly in research evidence. The potential benefits are substantial but Coleman and Bush (1994, p. 280) warn that 'these are ambitious claims and are not likely to be achieved without excellent leadership and a high level of commitment from all team members'.

Johnson's (2003) research in four schools in three Australian states provides some evidence to support the view that teamwork confers benefits on individuals and organisations. He identifies three advantages on the basis of this research:

1   *Moral support*: 89.7 per cent of respondents claim that they receive moral support from their colleagues 'to some extent' or 'to a great extent'. 'Teachers in this study reported important emotional and psychological benefits associated with working closely with colleagues in teams' (p. 343).
2   *Morale*: collegial support within teams was perceived to have improved teacher morale and reduced absenteeism and stress. 'The positive approach has led to strong staff participation and morale. Absenteeism and excessive negative stress levels are low' (Teacher, school B, p. 343).
3   *Teacher learning*: teamwork provided teachers with opportunities to learn from each other; 81.6 per cent of respondents reported feeling 'to some extent' or 'to a great extent' part of a learning community. This included breaking down some of the traditional subject barriers 'which previously inhibited learning and sharing of expertise across subjects' (p. 344).

Such advantages do not accrue automatically as a result of teamwork. The school or college climate has a significant impact on whether teams succeed, as does the leadership of the team itself. Wallace (2002) argues that different levels of synergy are evident in teamwork. High SMT synergy is manifested in 'many ideas, willingness to compromise for consensus [and] outcomes acceptable to [the] head' (p. 182). Similarly, Bush and Glover's (2012a) study of English high performing leadership teams shows that successful teamwork depends on high levels of commitment from all SLT members, exemplified through regular meetings, a strong team ethic, continuity and team unity.

Disadvantages of teamwork

O'Neill (1997) identifies two fundamental limitations of teamwork in schools. First, teachers spend most of their working day physically isolated from their colleagues because teaching is overwhelmingly an individual or 'solitary' activity. Secondly, teachers value authority and the ability to exert control. In this view, teamwork is used as a means of organising the delivery of the curriculum within a framework of control. 'Mandated' team approaches do not produce teacher collaboration. Bolden et al. (2009) refer to a 'managerialist' top-down approach to the distribution of leadership in higher education, leading to difficulties in achieving ownership across the team.

Johnson (2003) refers to four disadvantages of team collaboration on the basis of his Australian research.

1   *Work intensification*: a sizeable minority of teachers (41.2 per cent) say that teamwork has not reduced their workload and many of these report added burdens, notably in attending team meetings. 'In many cases, the need to meet more frequently with colleagues to discuss and plan collaboratively placed an added work burden on teachers. Commenting on an "explosion of meeting commitments", one teacher at school B suggested that teachers needed "tenacity, stamina, and drive to work more in the same school time" . . . many teachers find that changing their work practices leads . . . to an intensification of their workloads' (Johnson 2003, pp. 346–347).

2   *Loss of autonomy*: 21 per cent of teachers reported feeling constrained when working collaboratively while a similar number felt pressured to conform with the team. This provides a different slant on O'Neill's (1997) point about teaching as an individual activity and shows that teachers value professional autonomy. 'The loss of independence and autonomy by these teachers was seen as an inevitable consequence of having to conform with the implicit norms and explicit decisions of their working team' (Johnson 2003, p. 347).

3   *Interpersonal conflict*: there was evidence of conflict between those who wanted to work collaboratively and teachers who preferred their autonomy. The former group were critical of these 'dissenters', 'resistors', 'back stabbers' and 'blockers'. 'The process of implementing collaborative practices in the four schools produced disputes between some staff' (p. 348).

4   *Factionalism*: team collaboration produced some divisive competition between teams. 'Different groups within a school

adopted different norms and set about defending them against the threat of other groups' (p. 348). This point is similar to the findings of Wallace and Hall's (1994) research on SMTs in English secondary schools. While the SMTs showed good internal coherence, they were perceived to be remote from other staff.

These limitations and disadvantages of teams show that even 'self evident "goods" like teacher collaboration' (Johnson 2003, p. 349) may lead to contradictions and paradoxes. In South Africa, for example, factionalism within SMTs inhibits effectiveness and can also damage learner outcomes (Bush and Glover 2012b).

Conclusion

Teams have become significant features of the organisation and structure of schools and colleges in many countries. They are valuable in providing an apparently professional means of responding to the pace of change, notably that imposed by external bodies. They provide one example of shared or distributed leadership, which is increasingly advocated, for example by the English NCSL (NCSL 2009). Teamwork can produce advantages in schools, for example in raising teacher morale and contributing to organisational learning (see Chapter 13). Yet, as we have seen, it may produce problems which can outweigh the benefits. 'Teams are not the solution to everyone's current and future organizational needs. They will not solve every problem . . . nor help top management address every performance challenge. Moreover, when misapplied, they can be both wasteful and disruptive' (Katzenbach and Smith 1998, p. 24).

Given the context-specific nature of school leadership and management, it is difficult and perhaps unwise to generalise about the factors most likely to lead to successful teamwork. This depends on the skills and attitudes of individual leaders and teachers more than the formal structures. Wallace (2001, p. 165) proposes three 'context-dependent' prescriptions based on his extensive research on English SMTs:

1   School leadership should be shared widely and equally to maximise the potential benefit for children's education and for teachers' job satisfaction and professional growth. This connects to Bush and Glover's (2012a) finding about the size of SLTs.
2   Headteachers have responsibility for promoting shared leadership but the right, because of their unique accountability for doing so, to delimit the boundaries of sharing and to have the final say

where there is disagreement over leadership decisions. This links to Gronn's (2010) notion of hybrid leadership.

3   Other teachers have the right to participate in school leadership but the responsibility, because of the headteacher's unique accountability for their work, to ensure that they operate within the boundaries set, including letting the headteacher have the final say where there is disagreement over leadership decisions.

This is consistent with Rutherford's (2002) research with Catholic primary schools in Birmingham, which led him to conclude that:

> The headteachers demonstrate a values-driven, contingent approach to their leadership that balances the advantages and risks of shared leadership with their personal accountability for the success of their schools. It is clear that they retain the responsibility for making a final decision when there are irreconcilable differences in opinion. (p. 457)

It is evident from these comments, based on empirical research, that teamwork has much to offer in dealing with school issues in a professional manner. However, teams mostly operate within what seems to be an inescapable hierarchical framework. Teams are valuable in coping with increasing workloads, and in promoting professional collaboration, but they can always be 'trumped' by the principal acting alone. Singular leadership remains more powerful than the collective leadership of teams.

References

Belbin, M. (1993) *Team Roles at Work*, London, Butterworth-Heinemann.

Bolden, R., Petrov, G. and Gosling, J. (2009) 'Distributing leadership in higher education: rhetoric and reality', *Educational Management, Administration and Leadership*, 37 (2), 257–277.

Bush, T. and Glover, D. (2012a) 'Distributed leadership in action: Leading high performing leadership teams in English schools', *School leadership and Management*, 32 (1), 21–36.

Bush, T. and Golver, D. (2012b) 'Leadership development and learner outcomes: Evidence from South Africa', *Journal of Educational Leadership, Policy and Practice*, 27 (2): 3-15.

Bush, T., Kiggundu, E. and Moorosi, P. (2011) 'Preparing new principals in South Africa: The ACE: School Leadership programme, *South African Journal of Education*, 31 (1), 31–43.

Bush, T., Joubert, R., Kiggundu, E. and Van Rooyen, J. (2010) 'Managing teaching and learning in South African schools', *International Journal of Educational Development*, 30 (2), 162–168.

Cardno, C. (2002) 'Team learning: opportunities and challenges for school leaders', *School Leadership and Management,* 22 (2), 211–223.

Cardno, C. (2012) *Managing Effective Relationships in Education*, London, Sage.

Chaudhry-Lawton, R., Murphy, K. and Terry, A. (1992) *Quality: Change through Teamwork*, London, Century Business.

Coleman, M. and Bush, T. (1994) 'Managing with teams', in Bush, T. and West-Burnham, J. (eds), *The Principles of Educational Management*, Harlow, Longman.

Court, M. (2004) 'Talking back to new public management versions of accountability in education: a co-principalship's practices of mutual accountability', *Educational Management, Administration and Leadership*, 32 (2), 173–195.

Department of Education (2000) *School Management Teams: Introductory Guide*, Pretoria, Department of Education.

Glover, D. and Bush, T. (2012) *School Management Teams: Organisation, Function and Development*, Johannesburg, Zenex Foundation.

Gronn, P. (2010) Where to next for educational leadership? in Bush, T., Bell, L. and Middlewood, D. (eds), *The Principles of Educational Leadership and Management, Second Edition*, London, Sage.

Hallinger, P. and Heck, R. (1999) 'Can leadership enhance school effectiveness?', in Bush, T., Bell, L., Bolam, R., Glatter, R. and Ribbins, P. (eds.), *Educational Management: Redefining Theory, Policy and Practice*, London, Paul Chapman Publishing.

Harris, A. (2010) 'Distributed leadership', in Bush, T., Bell, L. and Middlewood, D. (eds), *The Principles of Educational Leadership and Management, Second Edition*, London, Sage.

Johnson, B. (2003) 'Teacher collaboration: good for some, not so good for others', *Educational Studies*, 29 (4), 337–350.

Katzenbach, J. and Smith, D. (1998) *The Wisdom of Teams*, London, McGraw-Hill.

Lashway, L. (2003) 'Distributed leadership', *Research Roundup*, 19 (4), 1–2.

Leithwood, K. (1998) 'Team learning processes', in Leithwood, K. and Seashore Louis, K. (eds.), *Organizational Learning in Schools*, Lisse, Swets and Zeitlinger.

Leithwood, K., Day, C., Sammons, P., Harris, A. and Hopkins, D. (2006) *Seven Strong Claims about Successful School Leadership*, London, DfES.

Middlewood, D. and Lumby, J. (1998) *Human Resource Management in Schools and Colleges*, London, Paul Chapman Publishing.

National College for School Leadership (2009) *School Leadership Today*, Nottingham, NCSL.

Office for Standards in Education (Ofsted) (2003) *Framework 2003 – Inspecting Schools*, London, Ofsted.

Office for Standards in Education (Ofsted) (2012) *Framework for School Inspection*, London, Ofsted.

O'Neill, J. (1997) 'Managing through teams', in Bush, T. and Middlewood, D. (eds), *Managing People in Education*, London, Paul Chapman Publishing.

Rutherford, D. (2002) 'Changing times and changing roles: the perspectives of headteachers on their senior management teams', *Educational Management and Administration*, 30 (44), 447–460.

Tuckman, B. (1965) 'Developmental sequences in small groups', *Psychological Bulletin*, 63, 384–399.

Wallace, M. (2001) 'Sharing leadership of schools through teamwork: a justifiable risk?', *Educational Management and Administration*, 29 (2), 153–167.
Wallace, M. (2002) 'Modelling distributed leadership and management effectiveness: primary school management teams in England and Wales', *School Effectiveness and School Improvement*, 13 (2), 163–186.
Wallace, M. and Hall, V. (1994) *Inside the SMT: Teamwork in Secondary School Management*, London, Paul Chapman Publishing.
Woods, P., Bennett, N., Harvey, J. and Wise, C. (2004) 'Variabilities and dualities in distributed leadership: findings from a systematic literature review', *Educational Management, Administration and Leadership*, 32 (4), 439–457.

Part III

Key Processes

Recruitment and selection

Introduction

As this whole volume is based upon the assumption that it is people who are the most important resources in an effective school or college, it is axiomatic that having the best possible staff in place is highly desirable. In strictly chronological terms, recruiting and selecting effectively is therefore the highest priority. In reality, most leaders will take up their roles and manage the staff who are already in post. They will have occasion to arrange for some to depart and to appoint others. Whatever the numbers, the importance of getting recruitment and selection right is paramount. Certainly, a wrong appointment can be disastrous and costly.

The chapters in Part III examine some recent developments in key processes in teaching and managing in educational institutions. Developments in psychology continue to underline the point that eliminating subjectivity from processes such as selection or assessment of performance is impossible and, indeed, the importance of the values context within which staff are appointed may make this undesirable. However sophisticated various methods become, through psychometric testing for example, the uniqueness of leaders as fallible human beings means that some element of the personal viewpoint of the individual leader remains important in the process. This chapter outlines some key principles of effective recruitment and selection, and there is an argument for leaders maintaining these principles, even in periods of acute shortages in staff and considerable risks of abandoning them for short-term reasons. Since all selection is ultimately made on the potential of the appointee, there is a case for monitoring staff performance in employment, so that leaders and managers can review regularly their actual procedures for recruiting and selecting staff.

Strategic context

Recruitment and selection need to be considered not in the specific context of finding someone to do a particular job, but in the overall context of planning the human resource needs of the organisation, especially:

- how many and what types of people are needed
- which of these needs can be satisfied by transfer and development of existing staff and where staff need to be recruited externally.

This strategic view of the future needs of the organisation is best considered in the context of succession planning, which is dealt with in the final chapter of this volume.

Neglecting effective recruitment and selection in this strategic context, and simply reacting to an employee's departure by automatically replacing the person with another of the same type, can have risks which may not become immediately apparent. For example, poor recruitment and selection can raise the possibility of high staff turnover. This is not only damaging in terms of the constant process of obtaining new employees, but may lead to staff demotivation and low morale, and of course to 'client dissatisfaction'. This in turn leads to low levels of response to recruitment (Crossman and Harris 2006) and such a downward spiral can be difficult to halt.

In this context, recruitment, selection and the actual appointment are best perceived as one continuous process as far as their management is concerned, although each clearly involves a different stage:

- Recruitment is the process by which people are encouraged to apply for employment at the school or college.
- Selection is the process through which the best person for the particular post is chosen and offered employment.

- Appointment is the final agreement in which employer and employee commit themselves to the contract of employment.

Recruitment and selection in different contexts

The scope for leaders and managers at individual context level may be considerably constrained by the fact that staff are nominated or appointed to their organisations by education authorities. In China, for example, Washington's (1991, p. 4) research suggested that 'principals have no role in deciding who gets hired or fired'. Lewin et al. (1994) confirmed this but Bush et al. (1998, p. 190) found a school principal who claimed to have appointed at least 60 per cent of his staff.

In countries such as Cyprus (Pashiardis 2001) and Greece (Infanti, 1995), all qualified teachers are allocated to a particular area of the country, with a small amount of discretion given to local principals as to which particular schools they are employed in. In the Republic of South Africa, Thurlow (2003, p. 61) describes how recruitment typically is carried out 'centrally' through the provincial education departments. Schools notify the employing department of existing vacancies, together with some basic specification of the posts. In turn, the employing department is responsible for advertising all vacant posts in a gazette, bulletin or circular and prospective applicants apply directly to the department, using departmentally determined application forms and standard forms for curricula vitae. Furthermore, it is the employing department which handles the initial sifting of applicants for all posts in order to eliminate applications which do not comply with the basic requirements of the post(s) as stated in advertisements. Once this process, which is highly standardised, is completed, the employing department passes the remaining applications to schools, where the School Governing Board members are the key people responsible for final selections.

Some countries, such as Germany (Huber and Pashiardis 2008), operate a 'mixed' system of centralised and federal, where some decisions are taken at state level but are overseen by national bureaucracy.

In countries where responsibility for budget management has been passed to the individual schools or colleges (including the UK, New Zealand, Canada, Australia), decisions on recruiting and selecting staff are made by their leaders and governors. Each system has its own advantages and disadvantages, both for leaders and for potential applicants for posts. These are summarised in Tables 9.1 and 9.2.

Table 9.1 Possible advantages and disadvantages of centralised systems (from Middlewood 2010)

Possible advantages	Possible disadvantages
National policies can be closely adhered to	Decisions made with little awareness of institutional context
Records of staff applications maintained/monitored	Career progression not in applicant's control
Consistency of selection procedures more certain	National prejudices can be reinforced (e.g. in gender, race)
Staff only have to apply once	Individuals may be placed in places which they dislike
Greater objectivity in selection process	
Staff can be moved if situation requires it	Staff disruption – people moved if needed elsewhere
Staff mobility guaranteed – less chance of stagnation	Disruption to personal circumstances may be ignored

Table 9.2 Possible advantages and disadvantages of autonomous/ 'free-market' systems (from Middlewood 2010)

Possible advantages	Possible disadvantages
More of a genuine 'two-way process'; applicant can reject offer and apply elsewhere	Offers of appointments usually have to be made quickly
Institution knows its own local requirements best	If wrong appointment made, expensive and difficult to remove person
Selection process can involve local stakeholders	Selection process may differ from place to place
Individual organisational cultures can be considered	Applying for many different posts is laborious and time consuming
Applicants need only apply to places where they want to work	Unsuccessful applicants 'start from scratch' each time with new application
Potential employees can see actual site, meet colleagues, etc. where they may work	Merely competent/mediocre staff more likely to become complacent

Whether at national, federal or organisational level, there are aspects of the strategic context which need to be considered, such as the labour market, relevant legislation and the contextual conditions of the individual school or college.

Labour market

Clearly, the number of those available for work will be affected by a variety of factors such as:

- the general economic climate of the country

- the perceived status of jobs in education, compared with those in other areas of employment

- population and demographic trends, for example the number of people of a certain age available, the gender balance (the issue of low birth rates and ageing populations is considered in the next chapter, examining their impact on staff retention)

- the number of entrants into professions such as teaching and the numbers of those returning after career breaks of various kinds.

Legislation

Management of recruitment and selection has to be carried out within the framework of the relevant legislation. This can involve legislation concerning discrimination and the issue of applying equal opportunities in education, as discussed in Chapter 6. Another example might be legislation which deals with the holding of data about people who apply for posts, whether or not they are appointed. In the UK, the Data Protection Act means that those seeking to appoint staff can only hold data which is sufficient to allow the process of selection to be undertaken and that the data cannot be used for any other unrelated purpose. In practical terms, this means that all copies of application forms, references and other documents of unsuccessful applicants must be destroyed after the allowed brief period, as must any notes made by selectors after they have been retained for a period allowing for any legal appeal against their decision. Similarly, all employees must have clearance from the Criminal Records Bureau (CRB) before they can start work.

Local conditions

The particular circumstances of the school or college (Is it expanding or contracting? What is its local reputation?) and of its local environment will affect potential applicants in their decision as to whether to apply. The cost and availability of housing in the vicinity can be a key factor, as can the accessibility of the school or college by road or public transport, and the quality of such transport.

Effectiveness in recruitment

Within the strategic context described, managers of recruitment need to consider all possibilities before automatically deciding to appoint a new employee, for example:

- whether the post needs to be filled or whether the work can be reorganised, relocated or redistributed

- the nature of the job to be filled and the kind of person wanted

- whether someone should be recruited from inside the school or outside

- whether the incentives (for example, pay, promotion, support in post) are appropriate for the kind of person sought (from Hall 1997, p. 150).

Having made a decision that a new person should be appointed, effective leaders and managers are likely to have a clear picture overall of the kind of staff they wish to have in place to achieve their goals. This may involve a list of skills, capabilities and qualities that, ideally, employees should have, but the most important thing to be remembered here is that all appointments are primarily on the basis of *potential*. Until someone is actually doing the work involved in the post, the actuality is uncertain. Some organisations suggest the use of an 'exit interview' in which the person currently doing the job and due to leave is formally questioned about the reality of the work involved, rather than what is stated on paper.

In terms of the actual overall composition of the staff, leaders may need to examine carefully the current diversity of the staff personnel and, as discussed in Chapter 6, decide whether this maintaining or improving of staff diversity will be achieved by appointing a certain kind of person to the vacant post. International schools possibly represent one of the clearest examples of this:

> Staff should be carefully recruited so as to represent . . . the major culture areas of the world, and as many nationalities as possible . . . to give students a variety of racial, ethnic and national role models. (Blaney 1991, p. 74)

In reality, however idealistic the aspirations, leaders and managers have to deal with who actually applies. Hardman (2001) suggests that there were four categories of teachers applying for posts at international schools – local teachers, childless career professionals, career professionals with families and 'mavericks'. Each of these has different motives for applying, ranging from a genuine quest for new teaching opportunities to, in the case of some 'mavericks', a desire for global travel, exploration and a possible escape route from their own national system. As Cambridge (2000) points out, childless career professionals may be the easiest to employ because they are the cheapest to recruit, transport and provide accommodation for, further illustrating the difficulties for selectors in striving to appoint the best people for the jobs.

One of the issues in managing recruitment and selection in a highly centralised system is that the process involved is 'essentially bureaucratic' (Bush 2008, p. 62). This increases the chances of existing inequities in the system being confirmed, as indicated in Table 9.1. In Malta, for example (Bezzina 2002), it may be ageism, as the number of years' experience is seen as one of the most significant qualifications; it may be sexism (Blackmore et al. 2006), or lack of representation of certain groups as in South Africa (Bush and Moloi 2007) and the USA (Manuel and Slate 2003).

Bush (2008, p. 56) notes that in some countries where the political system itself has moved away from complete centralisation (such as in Eastern Europe), there is evidence of a 'loosening' of the rigid approaches to recruitment and selection that previously operated.

The recruitment process

Leaders and managers need to know the likely means of best attracting a range of suitable applicants based on their knowledge of the job and the qualities needed to perform it.

A job description and a person specification normally address these and, in constructing a job description, leaders and managers may need to ensure that it accurately reflects not only the nature of the job itself, but also the general approach to 'clients' taken by the organisation. Plachy (1987) neatly draws a distinction between 'duty-oriented' and 'results-oriented' job descriptions. Thus, a receptionist may:

- 'greet visitors and refer them to the appropriate person' (duty oriented)

- 'help visitors by greeting them and referring them to the appropriate person' (results oriented)

- 'answer visitors' questions and maintain an orderly reception area' (duty oriented)

- 'reassure visitors, by making them feel welcome, answering questions and maintaining an orderly reception area' (results oriented) (based on Plachy 1987).

The differences are subtle but significant, indicating to the possible employee something of the nature of the organisation and its overall approach to its work.

The task for those constructing the person specification is to identify the skills, knowledge, attitudes and values necessary to do the job effectively. Acknowledging the point made earlier about appointing on potential, Hackett (1992, p. 35) argues for a focus on the behaviour expected of the person when they are actually appointed:

A more direct approach to establishing just what you need to look for is to consider what the job-holder must be able to do – that is, what *abilities* he [sic] needs. If you can match these against the *demands* which the job will make, you are less likely to find that you have recruited someone who is incapable of performing to the required standard. If you also give some thought to the *rewards* which the job offers, in terms of pay and benefits, relationships and job satisfaction, you can then work out what individual *needs* these are likely to satisfy. If you recruit someone whose needs are met by the rewards the job offers, he [sic] is much more likely to stay and work hard.

Leaders and managers may wish to appoint people who will fit, both with the team within which they will be working and the culture and ethos of the organisation as a whole. Law and Glover (2000, p. 191) suggest that a tension exists

between traditional, reactive perspectives where staff are recruited to 'fit' existing plans (e.g. where recruitment is linked to an audit of forecast needs for specific skills, numbers and expertise) and a more proactive perspective where the (existing and potential) skills of current staff are recognised and developed, thus avoiding 'reactive' and potentially unstable recruitment strategies.

Their earlier research (Glover and Law 1996) found that too few schools were willing to analyse the institutional context closely enough 'perhaps because (of) taken-for-granted assumptions that skills and competencies are shared potentially by everyone' (p. 192). In the fast-changing context of educational organisations in the twenty-first century, it could well be argued that the 'proactive perspective' is highly desirable for effectiveness.

With new types of educational organisations emerging, and further new ones inevitable, the need for leaders to remain flexible and open-minded in their search for new staff is essential. With the growth of system leadership, federations of schools and the development of community or extended schools, applying methods of recruitment and selection which were appropriate to leading and managing a single institution is not a practical approach. In their research on extended schools in England (and similarly in Scotland and the US), Middlewood and Parker (2009) found that all members of staff needed to be aware, among many other conditions of service, that:

- conventional hours or holidays will not be the norm
- they may be answerable to more than one line manager
- flexibility of contracts will be a prerequisite of most job offers
- they will regularly be called upon to take on new roles
- all staff will be required to teach a variety of learners of all ages and abilities (Middlewood and Parker 2009, p. 63).

This led them to conclude that when a member of staff left, the temptation to consider a like for like appointment is to be resisted at all costs.

Who should be involved?

The perceptions of stakeholders other than professionals of what constitutes effectiveness in a person to be appointed, and of how the prevailing culture of the school or college is regarded, becomes important here. In any case, of course, the involvement of lay personnel in recruitment and selection of staff is statutory in several countries (for example, the UK, Australia, New Zealand), notably those where self-governance of schools and colleges has become a major feature of the education system. The main influence of lay personnel is that of parents, and of governors representing community, business and other interests; some of these are likely to have experience of recruitment and selection outside education. Research by Bush et al. (1993) into the first grant-maintained schools in England and Wales (i.e. funded directly by money from central government) showed that governors exerted a powerful influence in this area of school management.

There is a strong case for ensuring that those leading and managing recruitment and selection are trained to carry out this process. The key argument for training is the need for *consistency* both across all the people (a mixture of professional and lay) involved in appointing any individual and across the number of different occasions when appointments are to be made. Apart from the need for as much objectivity as possible, which consistency of approach will aid, it is a help to the school or college if a clearly understood operation comes into action each time a vacancy occurs, again saving unnecessary time and expense. Norris (1993, p. 27) indicates, for example, through research studies outside education, 'the interviewer bias was also found to be significantly reduced by using trained interviewers'.

In school staff procedures, parents can play a critical role. Principals such as Van Halen (1995, p. 15), having stated that it took him ten years – with 'significant' training – to feel confident about selecting teachers and middle managers, believed that training for parents involved in the process was essential.

> Parents on selection panels fall into one of three categories: those who leave the decisions to the professionals; a group that have their minds made up beforehand and do not come clean about the hidden agendas; and finally, the minority who are trained in the selection processes or who are open about the process and stay with the assessment criteria all along.

Morgan's (1997, p. 127) study of selection panels in action in England and Wales led him to examine the roles of professional and lay members and conclude that there can be a dilemma in relations between these roles. His recommendation was that the professional and lay roles should be visibly differentiated and be placed

> on a complementary rather than competitive basis in contexts where 'lay controllers' participate in the selection of staff, complementary roles would mean that heads or other 'professionals' would lead the systematic determination of the job criteria; deploy multiple means of deriving evidence on the key competency requirements; and assemble and accumulate the evidence of candidates' strengths and weaknesses in the form of complete profiles which would be used by the lay members for their final decision.

More contentious, perhaps, is the issue of whether pupils or students should be involved in the selection process. Parker (2011), in writing about 'student voice' in school improvement, describes one example where the students took some responsibility for managing the selection and appointment of a student learning manager, an appointment recommendation which was simply ratified by the school's governing body. Certainly, responding to a panel of student representatives during a selection process is by no means unusual in a number of schools and colleges. In Lithuania, Hardi (2002) notes that there is an actual entitlement for students to be involved in selection in all secondary schools.

Factors affecting selection management

Quality of applicants

As noted earlier, selectors can only make a choice from those who actually apply and it is at this stage that the care taken in job descriptions and person specifications will pay dividends. If none of the applicants reaches the minimum requirements, it is much easier and reassuring to be able to decide to re-advertise, rather than be tempted to 'have a look at what we've got anyway', running the real risk of choosing someone who does not meet the needs of the job. When the pressure is on to fill a post, this temptation can be significant, but the long-term consequences of appointing an employee who may turn out to be less than competent can be very damaging. Middlewood (1997) gives the example of a visibly pregnant interviewee competing for a post which urgently needs to be filled, when she will not be available immediately because of maternity leave. The best candidate should be appointed even though it means waiting.

Quality of selectors

The issue of personnel and training has already been discussed, but leaders and managers could consider the development of middle managers in this field by offering them involvement in the actual process, without them having any authority or responsibility in that specific appointment, for example observing at an interview (with candidates' permission), or reading applications.

Issues for selectors

Although some research studies (for example, Huber and Hiltmann 2009) have examined methods of selecting educational leaders, less attention is given to how these leaders select staff. However, some research, both inside and outside education, has indicated the large number of issues that can distort a selection process. These can include:

- basing judgements upon intuition rather than facts

- making 'snap' judgements

- insisting on a personal stereotype of what is a 'good' candidate

- comparing candidates with the previous post holder or with other candidates rather than the agreed criteria

- holding prejudices about which gender, for example, is more suitable for a post (Middlewood 1997).

The most human interactive part of the selection process, the interview, is particularly prone to these prejudices, and research by Norris (1993), Morgan (1997) and Grummel et al. (2009) among others, have shown shortcomings such as:

- Interviewers often make up their minds about a candidate within the first five minutes of the interview and – consciously or unconsciously – spend the rest of the interview trying to justify their judgement.

- Interviewers' judgement of candidates can be affected by their appearance, speech, gender and race either positively or negatively.

- Physically attractive candidates are more likely to be appointed.

- Interviewers who are impressed by one quality of an interviewee may transfer their approval automatically to other qualities (the 'halo' effect).

- Research on memory shows that we remember information we hear at the beginning and end of an interview and, thus, tend to forget vital details and facts given in the middle.

- It is impossible for the human brain to concentrate at the same level over a prolonged period; thus if you are interviewing several candidates on the same date, they may not receive equal amounts of your attention.

- An 'average' candidate who follows 'poor' ones is seen as 'good'.

For these reasons, the British Psychological Society reported that even well-conducted interviews were only 25 per cent better than choosing someone by sticking a pin in a list of candidates (Thomson 1993, p. 30)!

Perhaps the single most important factor in this process, where completely eliminating the subjective is impossible, is the 'similarity factor' (Byrne 1971). This is where selectors tend to be drawn towards choosing someone who has similar characteristics to themselves. Considerable research in sociology has shown that people are inevitably drawn to linking with those similar to themselves (Alexander et al. 2001), so that the impact of this similarity attraction paradigm on recruitment and selection decisions is hardly surprising. The NCSL in England, for example, found that school governors most often 'sought' an individual as similar as possible to the previous school leader instead of focusing on the future needs of the school (NCSL 2006, p. 7).

Also, Blackmore et al. (2006) and Grummel et al. (2009) all found that the homosociability of the selection process meant that objective criteria were often pushed aside as selectors sought 'safe' appointments and had firm ideas about the importance of the status and culture of the applicant's previous organisations, as did Roebken (2010) in an analysis of 'higher' education recruitment in Germany.

All these factors can point to the difficulties faced by applicants who are not part of the 'normal' groups so may not be as favourably considered, such as certain ethnic minority groups (Grummel et al. 2009).

However, the picture is not totally negative. Hinton (1993) points out that, despite errors occurring, these do not prove that people are necessarily inaccurate in their selections. Hinton (1993), Morgan (1997) and Blackmore et al. (2006), point to the large number of social, psychological and micropolitical factors at work during selection. Furthermore, Hinton warns that sometimes a group of people agreeing on a selection at the end of interviews will mistake the warm glow of relief and satisfaction of having agreed on *a* choice for the actually important one of agreeing that the correct choice has been made. Despite this, Hinton (1993, p. 137) concludes that the selection panel is significantly better than one person and 'despite differences in their judgements they could well perform their function successfully and select a suitable candidate for the job'.

Effective management of selection

With the need for consistency and relative objectivity being paramount, a structured approach to the process of managing the actual process of selection is advocated by Middlewood and Lumby (1998). They suggest that the key issues for leaders and managers to consider are:

1   Personnel: who will be involved – and the extent and nature of that involvement.

2   Criteria: against which standards will candidates be assessed?
3   Weighting: what should be the relative importance of the criteria?
4   Instruments: how will the candidates' performance be assessed?
5   Matching: making a decision on which person is best suited to the post.

Personnel

The involvement of both professional and lay people has already been discussed but further interesting issues and examples are developing. In South Africa, a teacher union representative is entitled to be present at the selection of all teachers and, in some schools and colleges in the USA and the UK, a representative of external stakeholders may be part of the selection process. Where the job involves greeting visitors, for example, a parent or 'client' representative may be used as they will be well placed to assess what is needed.

Criteria and weighting

Criteria are likely to include biographical data (especially qualifications and experience), skills, knowledge, attitudes and values (such as personal ambition or commitment). By analysing the job requirements and person specification, and thereby weighting the relative importance of the various criteria, a checklist can be made for all selectors to use consistently. Middlewood and Lumby (1998, p. 70) comment that the devising of weightings is 'difficult because of the need to rank elements of the work – it is easy to say that one task is more important than another but rather more difficult to give it a value. However, this is one way in which we can overcome some of the inconsistencies in the selection process'.

Instruments for assessing candidates

In several developed countries (the UK, the USA, Hong Kong, Singapore, Australia, Canada), methods of assessing candidates during a selection process have become increasingly sophisticated since the late 1980s. This is especially true at leadership level. In some countries, these are conducted centrally through assessment centres of various kinds, so that those who are successful can be nominated as having reached the required standard. Such assessment exercises can include, as well as psychometric tests:

- *In-tray exercise*: candidates are asked to sift and prioritise and decide upon action for a sample of documents.

- *Written report*: having been given certain information, candidates are asked to write a report for a particular audience.

- *Role play simulation*: candidates are asked to enact the job applied for in a particular situation.

- *Oral presentation*: candidates are asked to present formally to the interviewers a brief (usually five or ten minutes) synthesis of their views or approach to a particular issue. Usually, candidates may use visual aids in support of their oral presentation, for example slides or overhead projections.

- *Leaderless group discussion*: candidates are grouped together to discuss a topic or reach a decision on a question. Selectors are involved with the group's processes only as observers of individuals' performances. Situations in which the groups are placed are usually co-operative (for example, the group must come to a consensus on an issue), but operate within a competitive framework (adapted from Middlewood and Lumby 1998, p. 71).

All assessment processes still appear to involve a face-to-face interview and some of the potential inadequacies of interviews have already been referred to. Perhaps the most important thing for selectors to remember is that interviewing is a two-way process, enabling both interviewers and interviewees to be clear about whether they are suitable for the post. This approach reduces the risk of a situation which can be tense, stressful and even confrontational for candidates, which can blur the ability of selectors to see the true ability of the candidates. McPherson's (1999) study of the selection of secondary school principals in KwaZulu-Natal, South Africa, identified: 'The atmosphere in selection interviews is very tense and candidates are not made to feel at ease', among their problems, as well as bias of some committee members towards certain candidates, and the time allowed as being too short to enable candidates to do themselves justice (cited in Thurlow 2003, p. 66). Questioning is a specific skill in which interviewers can be trained, but in any case managers need to be clear about what it is they are trying to find out. Williams et al. (2001, p. 55) offer a case study of a school committed to appointing the best quality staff:

At all job interviews candidates are asked: 'Tell us about the worst day and the best day you have had in the classroom.' This is designed to explore their capacity to reflect on themselves, their classroom practice and their ability to learn from both success and failure. Staff are therefore encouraged to use their initiative, to risk failure and develop confidence in their own ability.

In another school, questions are asked 'designed to tease out the candidate's resilience and her/his capacity to deal with difficult situations in class' (Williams et al. 2001, p. 41).

It seems logical also to include observation in methods of assessing candidates' suitability for a post, since managers can see them actually carrying out a task which they are being appointed to do, albeit in a somewhat artificial situation (i.e. selected class, selected topic, etc.). Again, an example from Williams et al. (2001, p. 41) is typical:

> All short-listed candidates are asked to teach 'their best lesson' to a particular class, and they are observed by the head, the senior teacher responsible for staff development and a governor. Questions are then asked at the interview about the lesson.

Although less common than with teachers, examples also occur of classroom assistants being observed working with pupils with SEN (Lorenz 1999) and receptionist/clerical staff being observed while working in the office for a period (Williams et al. 2001).

Matching

The crucial point in managing the final part of the recruitment and selection process is that *all* the evidence available needs to be reviewed by those selecting. The weakness of many processes has been the overemphasis placed on the interview, which is almost always the final part of the process (Morgan 1997; Blackmore et al. 2006). The whole evidence should include the original applications, the references (where applicable), feedback from panels, observations, other assessment methods *and* the interview. Southworth (1990) stresses the importance of applying three criteria to the total evidence:

- adequacy (i.e. how sufficient it is)

- integrity (i.e. how truthful and reliable it is)

- appropriateness (i.e. how relevant it is).

It is worth noting that where some selectors, especially lay people such as governors or parents, are brought into the process only at the final stage of the interview, it would be difficult for leaders and managers to criticise them for seeing the interview as the most important part of the whole selection process.

Monitoring the effectiveness of recruitment and selection processes

Ultimately, the test of how effectively the recruitment and selection processes have been managed lies in the quality and performance of the staff appointed. Performance and its review is discussed in full in Chapter 12 but making a link between an employee's subsequent performance and the way that person performs during selection is acknowledged as being difficult (Middlewood 1997; Morgan 1997). Miles (2000) carried out research on this topic in three secondary schools in England and found there was not a single case where school leaders, when dealing with ineffective or only adequate performance of staff, had even considered whether the way those staff had been selected had any bearing on this. The leaders tended to hold the view that as the selection process had resulted in some good performers, it was not worth changing it – a view that they probably would not have found acceptable in other parts of their management! Huber and Pashiardis (2008), in summarising a review of international research into recruitment and selection processes, conclude that any evaluation of selection methods was a research vacuum and 'no information about the reliability and validity is available' (ibid., p. 196). This lack of proper research-based evidence may point to an underlining of the fact that leaders are more prone to use personal assessment in this field than in most other areas of their work.

Conclusion

It is perhaps surprising that, in an area of staff leadership and management that underpins every aspect of this field, there is relatively little research. Considering that getting the right persons into the employment of the institution is the crucial requisite to all that follows, there is clearly a need for a rigorous and effective approach to recruitment and selection. While many successful appointments are made, one error in selection can be both expensive and also particularly damaging in statutory education where those receiving poor teaching have in effect only one chance. Although this chapter has acknowledged that subjectivity cannot, and perhaps should not, be excluded from the process, there are considerable risks that fallible human judgement is likely to affect it.

As Lumby with Coleman (2007, p. 111) pointed out, humans can see the need for change in others more easily that in themselves: 'Leaders assume that because they do not intend discrimination, others do not experience it.'

It follows that leaders 'who can recognise the prejudices they themselves hold and who have a willingness to face them will have a better chance of minimising their impact on decisions based on impressions made on them' (Middlewood, 2010, p. 135). With this self-awareness comes the need for leaders to be flexible, take a strategic view of the future of the institution, and ensure that each appointment is a 'contextual fit' (Huber and Pashiardis 2008, p. 156) for the post that needs to be filled.

References

Alexander, J., Giesen, B. and Mast, J. (2006) *Social Performance*, Cambridge, Cambridge University Press.

Bezzina, D. (2002) 'The Making of Secondary School Principals: Some Perspectives from Malta', *International Studies in Educational Administration*, 30 (2), 2–16.

Blackmore, J., Thomson, P. and Barty, K. (2006) 'Principal Selection, Homosociability, the Search for Security and the Production of Normalised Identities', *Educational Management Administration and Leadership*, 34 (3), 297–317.

Blaney, J. (1991) 'The international school system', in Janietz, P. and Harris, D. (eds), *World Year Book of Education 1991: International Schools and International Education*, London, Kogan Page.

Bush, T. (2008) *Leadership and Management Development in Education*, London, Sage.

Bush, T. and Moloi, K. (2007) 'Race, racism and discrimination in school leadership: evidence from England and South Africa', *International Studies in Educational Administration*, 25 (1), 41–59.

Bush, T., Coleman, M. and Glover, D. (1993) *Managing Autonomous Schools: The Grant-Maintained Experience*, London, Paul Chapman Publishing.

Bush, T., Coleman, M. and Xiaohong, S. (1998) 'Managing secondary schools in China', *Compare*, 28 (2), 183–195.

Byrne, D., (1971) *The Attraction Paradigm*, New York, The Academic Press.

Cambridge, J. (2000) 'International schools, globalization and the seven cultures of capitalism', in Kayden, M. and Thompson, J. (eds), *International Schools and International Education*, London, Kogan Page.

Crossman, A. and Harris, P. (2006) 'Job Satisfaction of Secondary School Teachers', *Educational Management Administration and Leadership*, 34 (1), 29–46.

Glover, D. and Law, S. (1996) *Managing Professional Development in Education*, London, Kogan Page.

Grummel, B., Devine, D. and Lynch, K. (2009) 'Appointing Senior Managers in Education – Homsociability, Local Logics and Authenticity in the Selection Process', *Educational Management Administration and Leadership*, 37 (3), 229–349.

Hackett, P. (1992) *Success in Management: Personnel, Third Edition*, London, John Murray.

Hall, V. (1997) 'Managing staff', in Fidler, B., Russell, S. and Simkins, T. (eds), *Choices for Self-Managing Schools*, London, Paul Chapman Publishing.

Hardi, S. (2002) 'Students and teachers: mutual assessment', paper presented to International Education Conference, Athens.

Hardman, J. (2001) 'Improving recruitment and retention of quality overseas teachers', in Blandford, S. and Shaw, M. (eds), *Managing International Schools*, London, RoutledgeFalmer.

Hinton, P. (1993) *The Psychology of Interpersonal Perception*, London, Routledge.

Huber, S. and Hiltmann, M. (2009) 'The recruitment and selection of school leaders – first findings of an international comparison', in Huber, S. (ed.), *School Leadership – International Prospectus'*, New York, Peter Lang.

Huber, S. and Pashiardis, R. (2008) 'The recruitment and selection of school leaders', in Lumby, I., Crow, G. and Pashiardis, P. (eds), *International Handbook on the Preparation and Development of School Leaders*, London, Routledge.

Ifanti, A. (1995) 'Policy making, politics and administration in education in Greece', *Educational Management and Administration*, 23 (4), 271–278.

Law, S. and Glover, D. (2000) *Educational Leadership and Learning*, Buckingham, Open University Press.

Lewin, K., Xu, H., Little, A. and Zheng, J. (1994) *Educational Innovation in China: Tracing the Impact of the 1985 Reforms*, Harlow, Longman.

Lorenz, S. (1999) *Effective In-Class Support: The Management of Support Staff in Mainstream and Special Schools*, London, David Fulton.

Lumby, J. with Coleman, M. (2007) 'Leadership and Diversity: Challenging Theory and Practice in Education', London, Sage.

Manuel, M. and Slate, J. (2003) *Hispanic superintendents in America*, PhD dissertation, El Paso, University of Texas.

McPherson, J. (1999) *Selection of schools principals*, unpublished dissertation for M.Ed. in Educational Management, University of Natal.

Middlewood, D. (1997) 'Managing recruitment and selection', in Bush, T. and Middlewood, D. (eds), *Managing People in Education*, London, Paul Chapman Publishing.

Middlewood, D. (2010) 'Managing People and Performance', in Bush, T., Bell, I. and Middlewood, D. (eds), *The Principles of Educational Leadership and Management*, London, Sage.

Middlewood, D. and Lumby, J. (1998) *Human Resource Management in Schools and Colleges*, London, Paul Chapman Publishing.

Middlewood, D. and Parker, R. (2009) *Leading and Managing Extended Schools*, London, Sage.

Miles, E. (2000) 'Selection and performance', unpublished MBA dissertation, University of Leicester.

Morgan, C. (1997) 'Selection: predicting effective performance', in Kydd, L.,

Crawford, M. and Riches, C. (eds), *Professional Development for Educational Management*, Buckingham, Open University Press.

National College for School Leadership (2006) *Go for it! Reasons to become a headteacher*, Nottingham, NCSL.

Norris, K. (1993) 'Avoidable inequalities?', *Management in Education*, 7 (2), 27–30.

Parker, R. (2011) 'The impact on school culture', in Middlewood, D., Parker, R. and Piper-Gale, J. (eds), *Learning through research*, Leicester, Beauchamp College.

Pashiardis, P. (2001) 'Secondary Principals in Cyprus: views of the principals versus the views of the teachers: a case study', *International Studies in Educational Administration*, 29 (3), 1–23.

Plachy, R. (1987) 'Writing job descriptions that get results', *Personnel*, 64 (10), New York, American Management Association.

Roebken, H. (2010) 'Similarity Attracts: An Analysis of Recruitment Decisions in Academia', *Educational Management Administration and Leadership*, 38 (4), 472–486.

Southworth, G. (1990) *Staff Selection in the Primary School*, London, Blackwell.

Strathern, M. (2000) 'The tyranny of transparency', *British Educational Research Journal*, 26 (3), 309–321.

Thomson, R. (1993) *Managing People*, London, Butterworth-Heinemann.

Thurlow, M. (2003) 'Recruitment and selection', in Lumby, J., Middlewood, D. and Kaabwe, S. (eds), *Managing Human Resources in South African Schools*, London, Commonwealth Secretariat.

Van Halen, B. (1995) 'We can do it better', *Principal Matters*, 7 (3), 14–15.

Washington, K. (1991) 'School administration in China: a look at the principal's role', *International Journal of Educational Management*, 5, 4–5.

Williams, S., MacAlpine, A. and McCall, C. (2001) *Leading and Managing Staff through Challenging Times*, London, The Stationery Office.

10

Induction and retention

Introduction

Effective leaders and managers of people in individual schools and colleges need to ensure that their employees' potential is maximised at all stages of their development during their time at the institution. This obviously covers the period from the moment they are appointed and take up their posts to the time they leave, either for another post elsewhere or because they retire from their professional careers. If staff depart too readily from the organisation before full potential – at whatever level – is realised, this can be a serious loss to the organisation's performance capacity and can also be very cost ineffective.

This chapter links two important aspects of this leadership and management issue. It explores the importance of induction for all employees as the crucial first phase of employment, and discusses how effective induction can make a significant difference to a new member of staff's performance.

While many of the issues concerning induction have remained relatively unchanged since the previous edition of this book, there have been significant developments which have affected the leadership and management of retention. In developed countries such as Australia, New Zealand and the USA (Thomson 2009) and most especially in Europe, the impact of an ageing population and a falling birthrate on the economies of these countries, particularly in terms of pension entitlement, has meant a radical reconsideration of retirement ages and thereby the length of people's working lives and careers. New legislation concerning pension entitlement and retirement ages has been enacted in several European countries. In education, therefore, as well as in many other occupational areas, there are fewer teachers and other staff to replace retiring older ones. The additional retention issue for educational leaders is thus how to encourage older staff to stay on and defer retirement, or even in some cases, return from retirement. This aspect of retention is therefore considered in this chapter, as well as the more conventional question of how to retain key staff who have much to contribute to a school or college, when it seems likely or possible that they are planning to leave the institution or, indeed, the profession.

Links between induction and retention

It is difficult to ascertain whether there is a causal link between an effective induction process and the consequent ability of the organisation to retain the employee's services, but it is probably easier to suggest the opposite, i.e. if a person is given a poor start in a school or college, there may be a very good chance that the person will not stay very long. Hicks and Tilby (2004) surveyed eleven teachers who had left three schools in Hertfordshire, England, after only one year. Eight out of the eleven felt they had 'not been made to feel welcome' or 'not felt supported' when they began at the schools. Tilby (2007) followed up her initial research by interviewing ten of those eleven teachers more than two years later. Of these ten, two had left teaching altogether; two had moved twice more since their first post; and six were developing successfully in the schools to which they had moved initially. Eight of the ten still vividly recalled the poor induction they felt they had received in their first schools. 'It is difficult not to conclude that the two who had moved several times in four years could hardly blame poor induction programmes for their professional instability. However, it seems clear that the eight (of ten) who were now successfully developing, including two outside of education, had been able to achieve stability and professional competence when they had been given a supportive induction.' (Tilby 2007, p. 68). Both of those working outside of education commented that, rightly or wrongly, they felt they had never really 'recovered' from the poor start made in their first job in the profession.

While there is limited evidence linking the quality of induction with the wish of teachers to remain in the profession, Ladebo's research in Nigeria led him to conclude that 'a programme of socialisation could be mounted for new entrants into the teaching service, to help align the individual's values and expectations with those of the teaching service and (they) would be less willing to consider leaving the profession' (2005, p. 367).

Common sense would suggest that the favourable impressions about their new school or college formed by new members of staff would have an influence on how long they wished to continue working there. In the Department of Education and Science (DES 1992) guidance on probationary teachers, it was suggested that only in the third year of a post did newly qualified teachers (NQTs) begin to give back to the school more than they were taking from it. In times of staff shortages, it becomes even more important to retain effective employees, thus increasing the significance of effective management of induction. Middlewood and Parker (2009) found that an in-depth induction into the multi-faceted aspects of working in a full service extended school did have an impact on employees' attitudes towards how likely they were to remain at the school.

What is induction?

Induction is formally seen as important in the effective management of staff in many countries. The Commonwealth Secretariat and World Bank (1992) included 'agreed procedures on induction' in its framework for effective management of staff within educational organisations and recognised it as a practice which was very much the business of site-based leaders and managers. The main purposes of induction may be seen as:

- socialisation – enabling new employees to become part of the organisation
- achieving competent performance – enabling new employees to contribute to the organisation through the way they carry out their job
- understanding the organisational culture – enabling new colleagues to appreciate the core values and beliefs of the institution.

Socialisation

Schein (1978, pp. 36–37) identifies five elements in this process of inductees being assimilated into the organisation:

1   accepting the reality of the organisation (i.e. the constraints governing individual behaviour)

2   dealing with resistance to change (i.e. the problems involved in getting personal views and ideas accepted by others)

3   learning how to work realistically in the new job in terms of coping with too much or too little organisation and too much or too little job definition (i.e. the amount of autonomy and feedback available)

4   dealing with the boss and understanding the reward system (i.e. the amount of independence given and what the organisation defines as high performance)

5   locating their place in the organisation and developing an identity (i.e. understanding how an individual fits into the organisation).

The first four of Schein's elements all contain reference to, or an assumption about, induction including coming to terms with what the *real* job is like in the organisation. No matter how thorough the process of recruitment and selection has been, it is only when the actual work begins that the realities of the nature of the work, the responsibilities and the organisation are fully recognised. What was allowable and even encouraged in a previous place of work may be frowned upon in the new place. Routines may be different and require considerable adjustment.

Crow (2006) suggests that there are two kinds of socialisation: professional (preparation to undertake the role) and organisational (adapting to the new school's or college's context). Since each institution and each context is unique, the importance of enabling new post holders, at whatever level, to have the opportunity for structured familiarisation with their new post and surroundings appears incontestable.

The notion of establishing their place in the school or college for more junior staff is also something that takes time. A post may have *status* on paper, but it is possible for the inductee holding the post to discover that others have more *stature* and that colleagues go to them automatically instead of to the inductee, for example, for decisions. Similarly, new post holders may be told to get on with the job, but when they do so they are asked why they did not check first, simply because the degree of autonomy is different from that experienced elsewhere.

Achieving competent performance

Although leaders and managers will always want their new appointees to perform very effectively from the first day, it is likely that those in their first posts in particular will take a little time to achieve this. Kakabadse et al. (1987, p. 8) suggest there may be three stages to reaching high performance:

1 *getting used to the place*, i.e. overcoming the initial shock of the new organisation and job demands

2 *relearning*, i.e. recognising that new skills have to be learned or how learned skills have to be reapplied

3 *becoming effective*, i.e. consolidating their position in the organisation by applying new behaviours and skills or integrating newly formed attitudes with ones held from the past.

This suggests that the key element for the inductees is learning, both about themselves and the organisation.

Understanding organisation culture

This may be seen as enabling new employees to assimilate the values of the new organisation, so that ideally their loyalty will be part of their commitment to it. Culture is fully described and discussed in Chapter 4.

Whom is induction for?

In England and Wales, the School Management Task Force (1990) recommended that all new members of staff in schools should have an entitlement to induction but this remains an aspiration in many schools and colleges. In developed countries, there is considerable emphasis on the need for effective induction for teachers beginning their professional careers and, since the 1990s, for new principals/headteachers. In developing countries, 'there has been little educational research regarding the entry-year needs and critical skills for beginning principals' (Kitan and Van der Westhuizen 1997, p. 127). Bush (2008, p. 65) confirms this in his overview of leadership preparation, suggesting that the literature 'often gives little attention to induction'. He points out, however, that countries such as Finland, Sweden, some German states and New South Wales, Australia, have established formal structured induction programmes for new principals, and that several other countries had this under consideration.

As far as other staff in schools and colleges are concerned, the situation is weaker. Much less emphasis has been given to the needs of middle managers (Blandford 2000) and Thomson (1993, p. 110) suggests that temporary and part-time staff can often be ignored in induction processes 'in the misguided belief that they will not care much about the organisation and that they are just there to do the job'. Similarly, as noted in Chapter 3, support staff are often put in the position of having to organise their own induction (Balshaw and Farrell 2002), because school leaders simply do not provide it.

Finally, it can be argued that even when someone takes up a new post within the same organisation, for example, through internal promotion, some form of induction is needed for that person. Dean (2001) reflects how, on being promoted from deputy to head within the same school, it was assumed that he knew all there was to know about the school and the post, whereas when he had been appointed as deputy, he had been inducted carefully.

What is involved in effective induction?

Whatever form the induction process takes, the central issue is that it should 'meet the needs both of the inductee and the organisation' (Blandford 2000, p. 178). Managing the induction of newly appointed staff may well include the following:

- arranging preparatory visits to the school or college prior to starting

- giving information about the organisation

- offering guidance and support over personal (for example, accommodation) issues related to taking up the new appointment

- (in larger institutions) arranging off-site programmes for all new employees together

- allocating a specific person as mentor to support the new employee during induction (this is an important and widely used practice and is dealt with fully in Chapter 11).

It is easy for leaders and managers to devise lists, especially of the information that they feel inductees need. These lists can be formidable, covering everything from the physical layout of the site, through every organisation policy, to details of individual students. However, such lists, if presented merely as lists, can be daunting, especially for people in their very first posts.

Induction programmes

One of the commonest ways in which leaders and managers support new members of staff is by devising a formal induction programme. In addition to the preparatory visits mentioned earlier, these normally consist of a series of meetings, seminars or workshops which familiarise the inductee with the school or college and its personnel, and usually include the opportunity to raise queries or problems found in the earlier stages of employment in the new post. Sometimes such programmes are arranged exclusively for NQTs, sometimes for all those newly appointed to the organisation. It should be noted that such programmes often exclude:

- part-timers
- support staff
- those internally promoted or transferred to another post.

In community or extended schools, the issue of including support staff is often effectively managed, because of recognition of the multi-role nature of many staff working there. Thus in the full service extended schools mentioned above, induction programmes were provided for office staff and even voluntary workers (Middlewood and Parker 2009).

Emphasising the importance of induction

There is evidence that, unless leaders and managers show their belief in the importance of induction, it may be ineffective. In the vocational post-compulsory sector of education, many so-called 'technical teachers' felt that their qualification was in their former occupation and felt no need for induction (Holloway 1994), the consequence being in many cases 'an alienating experience for the students' (p. 47). The organisation's leaders and managers need to show an active interest in the induction process, however removed they might be in a larger school or college from the day-to-day management of it. Andrews (1998, pp. 79–85) identifies five different paradigms of teacher induction:

- the laissez-faire
- the collegial
- the formalised mentor–protégé
- the statutory competency based
- the self-directing professional.

and there are elements in all but the first of these which the manager may feel are relevant for all induction. The leader may feel the need to get directly involved sometimes simply to demonstrate the organisation's care for its employees and also its insistence on high standards. Middlewood (2003) refers to the following example from South Africa: The principal of a primary school near Pietermaritzberg related how he had appointed a new teacher who lived a long way from the school. After a few weeks he began to arrive late and as he did this began to become unpopular with other staff. The principal discussed the reasons for his lateness with him and was convinced that the alleged transport problems were not the real reason. The principal then drove to the teacher's house each morning although it was forty miles out of his way, to bring the teacher in. This meant the teacher had to be up even earlier as the principal was in school by 7.15am, whereas the teacher was not expected until 8.00am. After just over a week, the teacher declined the lift and began to arrive at school regularly on time. As he became accepted as a loyal member of staff, he became contented and lateness was no longer a problem. The problem had been identified and solved at an early stage. The drives in together, although only for a week, also enabled the principal to develop a helpful relationship with the teacher, facilitating the induction period.

Effectiveness in induction

It is suggested that induction is most likely to be effective where both managers and inductees see the process as something to which they *both* contribute, a principle common in people management. Newly appointed members of staff can be at their most vulnerable in the early period and can easily feel isolated when everyone else seems comfortable, for example with routines and procedures. Although it is a period for reflection for newcomers, those early days can make this difficult (see Hall 1997, p. 172).

One of the values of the notion of an induction programme for *all* new employees is of course that it decreases this sense of isolation and vulnerability. Such feelings can be especially likely in a school or college in very disadvantaged circumstances, working with difficult or disengaged students. Here, the need to know the specific community context of the institution may be crucial to understanding the students' home lives and circumstances. One headteacher of a large secondary school in a London borough of extreme deprivation describes a part of that school's induction process:

> We take all new staff on a full day – half day at least – round our area in a mini-bus. The vehicle has the school name on the side so there's nothing covert – the staff will find out how the school

is perceived. At least two current staff accompany them, ones who live in the area, one teacher, one assistant. The bus goes down every street. Where it can't get through, they get out and walk for a while. The trip includes a stop for a snack at a local fast food or even 'greasy spoon' place! It's a sensible balance – if they (especially the NQTs) are not to be voyeurs – they're there to see something of the conditions that our students and their parents live in. They hear a range of languages, including some ripe stuff! They also can meet police, wardens, shopkeepers, etc. I've never had one person come back saying 'I don't want to work here.' They don't pontificate about weak parents either.

I ought to do it more for existing staff because conditions do change over time. (quoted in Middlewood et al. 2005, p. 164)

This example is a development of Crow's (2006) 'organisational socialisation' and, as such, helps new staff into a clearer awareness of the many factors affecting the way they will be expected to do their work.

Induction therefore needs to involve a significant element of being self-directed and, as far as managers are concerned, to be viewed as a two-way process. Induction programmes and the whole induction process require this perception. There would be a great danger for managers in assuming all was going well with a new member of staff when this was not the case, since a simple matter such as the difference in status deterred the beginner from being outspoken.

Research carried out by Sehlare et al. (1994) in high schools in the former Bophuthatswana found several discrepancies between the views of principals and those of 'beginner' teachers regarding the induction process for the latter. (There were also, it should be noted, several areas of agreement.) Differences in perception of the support being given to the teacher were found in the following areas:

- classroom organisation and management
- the referral system in the school
- the teaching load of beginner teachers
- interaction with parents
- feedback from the principal
- effectiveness of formal meetings in the school.

Clarifying the aims and objectives of the school is an important aspect of early experience in the school community if newcomers are to integrate their own practice and values, and 100 per cent of principals felt they did this for the beginner teacher 'always' or 'often'. In contrast, almost exactly half (50.7 per cent) of the teachers in the same school felt their principals did this 'always' or 'often'. In fact, 32.5 per cent said it was done 'sometimes' and 16.2 per cent said 'never'! It is the manager, of course, who has the responsibility, and if beginner teachers have the perception that they are not being helped enough in dealings with parents, then it *is* an issue.

Careful monitoring of the induction process could lead to feedback on an aspect so apparently quantifiable as the teaching load of beginner teachers. In the above research, 43.5 per cent of teachers felt their teaching load was too heavy a burden, whereas 78 per cent of principals were satisfied that they did not put too much pressure in this way on their beginners.

The researchers drew conclusions from their work that many of the differences could be ascribed to communication problems between the two partners. They believed this was affected by, on the one hand, a lack of confidence of beginner teachers to communicate freely with the principal and on the other the failure of the principal to be proactive in helping teachers in formal situations such as in-school meetings or meeting parents. They identified time and a conducive atmosphere as being the key elements in narrowing 'the gap between what the principal thinks he is doing to help, and what the beginner teacher actually experiences' (Sehlare et al. 1994, p. 77).

In short, although induction is for the new provided by the experienced, the induction process will be most effective where the experienced acknowledge that they have things to learn from it also. In both senses, therefore, any resources for induction 'should be seen as an investment' (Jones and Stammers 1997, p. 82).

The importance of retention of staff

There is a reasonable amount of evidence (NCE 1996; Mortimore and MacBeath 2003) to suggest that an effective school or college is most likely to have a staff which has a 'balanced mix' of younger and newer employees, those who have significant professional experience and those who are mature people in the later years of their careers. Common sense would suggest that this is likely to be the case, offering in theory a mixture of enthusiasm and new ideas, confidence in practice and wisdom of long experience. It must be stressed of course that these qualities by no means necessarily relate to the implied age groups, but it does indicate to leaders and managers the importance of retaining the services of a reasonable proportion of staff so that the organisations can benefit from their knowledge of the place of employment, its culture and practices. Of course, it is important that good quality staff do leave, moving on to a promotion elsewhere for example, when the time is right, but if too many staff leave, especially after only a year or two in post, the age and experience profile of the staff becomes unbalanced. Moreover, a momentum of staff exodus can be started and a high turnover rate of staff is often a key element in failing or poorly performing schools (Stoll and Myers 1998).

Career cycles

If induction, as mentioned earlier, is ideally managed as a 'bridge' between the very early stages in post and the subsequent development of a professional career, then the issue of retention may not arise until later in a person's career. If we examine models of life and career cycles, it can be helpful for analysing when retention may become an issue. Leithwood (1992) and Ribbins (2008) suggest four key career stages for teachers/leaders:

1   discovering the ability to teach and manage classrooms (initiation phase)
2   developing professional confidence and flexibility (development phase)
3   developing leadership and responsibility (autonomy phase)
4   plateau ('winding down' phase).

This final phase can be positive or negative – 'moving on' or 'moving out' (Ribbins 2008)

Writers such as Day (1996, p. 124), suggest that teachers need to be led and managed with a focus on their development as 'whole persons throughout their careers . . . recognising that teachers are not technicians but that teaching is bound up with their lives, their histories, the kind of persons they have been and have become'.

In such contexts, leaders and managers need to recognise not only the skills levels reached by staff and the responsibilities they are capable of taking on, but also the attitudes, aspirations and personal relationships developed which can all influence decisions about whether they should leave or remain at a school or college. Each of the stages described has its own specific issues for leaders in terms of managing retention.

A particularly challenging stage for leaders and managers to retain effective employees is the one which follows the induction, the settling in or 'coming to terms with reality' stage. Since the school or college will have given much to developing these staff, much will be lost if they leave at that point, just when, it can be argued, a positive return is being made for the organisation's investment. In England, a worrying feature for the teaching profession has been the exodus of 16 per cent of teachers after three or four years' experience (Johnson 2003).

Draper's (2002) research into teachers' career plans in Scotland found that they could be divided into four categories:

- stayers – those who plan to stay in the classroom

- starters – those who will be applying for promotion

- stoppers – those who have sought promotion but do not intend to do so in the future

- movers – those who have sought and will continue to seek promotion.

She concludes that leaders and managers of staff need to be constantly aware of staff's career plans; ignoring them is a 'risky strategy' which could have a serious impact on retention.

Each of the first three phases described above will have its own challenge for the leaders in individual institutions involving possible opportunities for internal promotion and similar strategies, discussed later. However, the final phase of a teacher's professional career, as mentioned in the introduction to this chapter, is now one which is having to be given serious consideration in terms of retention because of changing external circumstances.

Populations of most developed nations are now falling; Japan's, for example, is expected to fall by 30 per cent by 2060, Hong Kong's by 20 per cent, and virtually all European nations by 15 per cent. It is the effect of declining birthrates, with the new longevity of lives in the developed world, which is causing huge challenges. Not only does it cause problems in terms of pensions, retirement ages and public expenditure on services such as education, but for many professional occupations it means that there is a decreasing pool of younger workers to draw on as the older employees retire. In this context, schools and colleges need to consider ways in which older teachers may be encouraged to remain in the organisation beyond the time of normal departure. This new context of retention is, according to Hedge et al. (2006), likely to be most felt in Asia and Latin America because most developing economies will have but one generation to manage this change, as their shift from predominantly young to predominantly old societies will take only about 25 years.

Despite the fact that European nations, for example, have known these trends for a long time, the ever-changing nature of educational leadership has allowed little time for strategic approaches to this aspect of teacher retention.

Research by Müller et al. (2009) in Switzerland identified the three positive reasons for entering teaching as the same as those for leaving the profession when these issues changed, i.e. job characteristics, working conditions and image of the profession. In the Netherlands, Bal and Visser (2011) identified organisational support and negotiated changes in work role as possible retention management strategies. Such studies advocate 'bridge retirement' where teachers are able to continue working beyond the statutory age but with changed conditions. Table 10.1 suggests a possible model for retention strategies which may be considered at organisational level.

Table 10:1 Possible leadership retention strategies at career stages of teachers

Phase	Possible reasons for leaving at phase end	Possible reasons for staying at phase end	Possible retention strategies
Initiation phase	Desire for promotion Dissatisfaction with school/college Dissatisfaction with teaching	Failure to get new job Domestic needs	Internal promotion Negotiate new role(s) Additional payments
Development phase	Desire for promotion Need for a change	Failure to get new job Acceptance of status quo Domestic needs	Internal promotion Job swap Internal re-development
Autonomy phase	Promotion Need for a change	Failure to get new job Changes in contextual circumstances	Personalised CPD Job swap/retention
Final phase	Retirement	Loyalty to school/college Need for staff society Financial needs Fear of idleness/boredom	Negotiate new work role Negotiate flexible working hours Reduce workload Retrain/personalised CPD

Retention at a national level

Some aspects of retention relate to the whole issue of whether employees wish to remain in the education profession anyway, and are therefore to some extent beyond the influence of individual leaders and managers. For example, in some developed countries, a benign economic climate can make retention difficult. As Hallgarten (2001) points out, in England 'The creative industries have flourished and many barriers to female graduate employment have been eroded (leading to) . . . teaching too often being compared unfavourably with the growing range of alternative careers' (p. 15). He goes on to report how the number of teachers who left the profession for employment outside education rose by about 30 per cent between 1998 and 1999, and the number of returners continued to decline.

Conversely, in a number of developing countries, as economies improve, education becomes more important, pay rises and fewer people are likely to leave the profession (Foskett and Lumby 2003). In developing countries, especially in centralised systems, teachers leaving the profession, for example in Nigeria (Ladebo 2005) and the Seychelles (Nourice 2008), identified a key factor as the way the government of a small island state constantly moved teachers from school to school, regardless of qualifications or context.

As discussed in Chapter 7, when morale and motivation are low because of national factors, leaders and managers have extra pressures on them to retain good quality staff who may be dispirited and beginning to consider alternative career options. The irony here is that during difficult economic times, jobs outside the profession are likely to be fewer anyway.

While 'retention' is the key issue for leaders and managers at institutional level, Bush (2002) makes a useful distinction between three terms:

- Retention means keeping teachers within the profession or in a particular school.

- Attrition means loss of teachers from the profession.

- Turnover relates to the movement of teachers from a particular school. This involves people moving to other schools as well as those leaving the profession (p. 1).

Retention during periods of shortage

Apart from those regions or countries where staff movement is managed centrally, i.e. people are allocated to different schools after a fixed period of years, the issue of retaining effective staff is particularly challenging during periods of labour shortages in the education profession. In such circumstances, individual schools and colleges may become even more conscious of the need to hold on to the staff they have for fear of there being no replacements available, or only very inferior ones.

In such times of acute staff recruitment difficulties, leaders at all levels sometimes adopt specific strategies to hold on to key staff (these examples are all drawn from England where a shortage of teachers has existed since at least 2001).

Golden handcuffs

At national level in England, the government has offered cash incentives of specific sums to those entrants who guarantee to remain in the profession for at least three years, with mention of a further cash bonus if a further two years of service are given.

At district level, one local education authority which was reorganising all its school system (from first, middle and upper schools to primary and secondary schools) feared that many teachers would leave the area because of the turbulence and the enforced changes to jobs and schools. It offered in 2003 and 2004 'golden handcuffs' of lump sums to those who would guarantee to stay at least three years in their new post. In a number of recent national initiatives in the USA, and England and Wales, financial incentives have been offered to new recruits to the teaching profession, as long as they commit themselves to at least three years in teaching. Charity sponsored initiatives, such as Teach First, Teaching Leaders and Future Leaders provide significant additional payments to recruits with just such a proviso.

At individual school level, Hicks and Tilby (2004) found three headteachers of large secondary schools – in three separate areas – who stated that they had negotiated individual one-year contractual 'deals' with key staff (all were heads of subject departments) which involved special 'cash bonuses' or 'incentives to remain' for a further year at their schools. These staff were seen as highly effective, hard to replace and needed in their schools and departments at a crucial time. One head commented that the cost of recruiting, appointing and training a new head of department would cost almost as much as the 'handcuff' payment, so he considered it well worth the money, especially as he was not guaranteed to get a replacement at all. These deals were not secret in the schools and appeared to be readily accepted by other staff. Although they were technically linked with achievement targets, all three headteachers admitted that they were the same targets that would have been set anyway, regardless of the additional money.

Internal promotions

Hicks and Tilby's (2004) research showed that the commonest strategy used by school leaders to retain key staff was to offer them promotion within the school. In one school, out of a teaching staff of 82, 17 were offered and accepted a promotion in 2002, 14 of whom had been actively considering applying for a post elsewhere. Three of these admitted that they had specifically approached the headteacher 'to see what might be offered' even though they had not been anxious to leave!

All the promotions involved additional responsibilities, some of which were felt to be genuine, others more contrived. Eight of the 14 felt that the promotion and additional money attached would retain them for only a year at the most and several of the 17 believed that other staff were 'wary' of the strategy.

As far as support staff in the same schools were concerned, the strategy did not apply as the headteachers made it clear that these were easy to replace, because of a plentiful supply, and promotion would be earned in the normal way.

The weakness of both of the above strategies is that they are essentially short-term, retaining staff for a year or two at most. This is not likely to be a sufficient period for the supply of replacements to have improved significantly. There is also the risk of an even bigger exodus at the end of the short-term period, leaving the staff in an even more exposed staffing position. They may be effective, however, in helping an organisation through a period of turbulence or pressure where staff stability is deemed essential. The other risk is that when staff have differential salary rates, as Hardman (2001) found in international schools, inequalities in pay and conditions of service can lead to feelings of resentment.

Other strategies

Because of concern about teachers leaving urban areas, Chicago established a Teacher Retention Unit. Its main features are:

- regular meetings with teachers and principals
- commissioning research on the teacher retention issue
- investigating the reasons why teachers leave teaching
- conducting exit interviews with departing teachers
- assisting teachers to find new positions within Chicago
- facilitating networking to support Chicago teachers (Chicago Public Schools Retention Unit 2002).

Retaining temporary and part-time staff

There is a particular irony that during periods of staff shortage schools and colleges need to call upon the services of many temporary, agency or supply staff as replacements, and also make more use of part-time staff. The quality of these staff is critical to ensuring continuity of effective learning and therefore retaining the best of these temporary staff is a key requirement of leaders and managers. In further education colleges, especially in vocational areas, a traditional reliance on part-time and temporary staff has often meant their neglect in terms of effective management (Lumby 2001). In mainstream schools, given disruption because of failure to fill a vacancy, leaders and managers need to develop strategies to ensure that the best of the temporary staff wish to return to their schools. Cole (2001, p. 7) points out that 'supply teachers are a unique and valuable group without whom a school could not function effectively'. She focuses on the need for the students to understand that constant new faces in the classroom means little progress is made and that they should understand that 'disrespectful behaviour at the expense of the supply teacher simply means they will not return, and another new face will appear the next day' (p. 7).

Cole's research (2001) showed that supply teachers valued most of all 'friendly and supportive staff' as by far the main reason why they were willing to return to a school. 'Good information' and 'student discipline support' were also important but the emphasis on the staff relationships was clear, helping them 'feel a sense of security and belonging during their time at the school' (p. 7), thus motivating them to return.

Retention: long-term strategies

The following strategies are more qualitative in nature than the short-term more quantitative measures described above.

Offering high-quality professional development

A school or college's commitment to provision of effective professional development on site which meets the individual and career needs of staff can have a powerful influence on their own willingness to commit themselves to that organisation. Taylor's (2003) study of a college-based Masters degree programme showed that the majority of those undertaking the programme were determined to stay until they completed the whole course and obtained their qualifications. She quotes the principal as saying: 'It has become a conscious ploy of mine to get key staff on the programme so that they will feel committed to completing it, thus keeping them here for at least three years' (p. 94). Taylor further points out that these staff would not apply for posts elsewhere which did not offer a comparable opportunity.

Writers such as Bell and Bolam (2010) and Gray (2005) acknowledge the way in which regular opportunities for professional development play a part in retaining high-quality staff. The staff concerned see these opportunities not only as developing their skills, but also as enhancing their career profiles, thus enabling them to make better decisions about the correct timing of a move to another institution, helping them as it does to be at the right stage for a different or more senior post. Even in situations involving, say, potential redundancies, the strategic planning of continuing professional development (CPD) is invaluable. As Scott (1997, p. 25) comments: 'A potential re-development of a teacher trained in one particular area needs to be predicted years ahead.'

Developing a positive culture

Although culture is written about in more detail in Chapter 4, there are some actions which leaders and managers may note are of significance in encouraging employees to feel that theirs is a place in which they wish to continue to work.

Praise and recognition

- A brief, informal note to an employee.

- Taking time in regular meetings or informal gatherings to recognise the work of employees.

- Providing positive feedback in the presence of more senior staff.

- Utilising the performance management process to comment on good performance.

- Presenting employees with plaques, certificates, formal letters or the like.

- Running an employee or team of the month programme, say, in the in-house magazine.

Career opportunities

- Providing formal or informal training opportunities.

- Supporting an individual or team to take on new initiatives or additional responsibilities.

- Allowing valued employees greater autonomy in their work.

- Providing opportunities to attend external or overseas training programmes, seminars or conferences.

- Instigating career breaks or sabbaticals to recognise key contributors to the organisation.

- Offering valued employees the opportunity to rotate in higher positions or to lead key projects in the organisation (based on Mercer 2001).

Sensitivity on the part of leaders and managers is essential. Praise and recognition are effective aspects of management style but the praise and opportunities need to be individualised. For instance, in a department where teamwork is encouraged, recognition for any one individual while ignoring the team may provoke dissatisfaction, embarrassment and one-upmanship. Individual preferences need to be kept in mind. The opportunity to attend an overseas conference may prove to be more of an inconvenience than a benefit to an employee with a dependent child. Instead, a management development programme at a local institute might be more welcome.

Conclusion

The more seamless the whole process of induction, following on from appointment, and the associated programme of support and development, the more likely it is that valued employees will stay at the school or college. The time will come for many when it is appropriate for them to leave, but the nature and quality of leadership and management may make them feel that they wish to remain until that appropriate time arrives. They may also be willing to support their organisation through any difficult times that may occur in the meantime.

References

Andrews, I. (1998) 'The mentor and beginning teacher's differing relationships within five paradigms', in Gray, W. and Gray, M. (eds), *Mentoring: Aid to Excellence in Education, the Family and the Community*, Vancouver, International Association for Mentoring.

Bal, M. and Visser, M. (2011) 'When are teachers motivated to work beyond retirement age? The importance of support, change of work role and money', *Educational Management Administration and Leadership*, 39 (5), 590–602.

Balshaw, M. and Farrell, P. (2002) *Teaching Assistants: Practical Strategies for Effective Classroom Support*, London, David Fulton.

Bell, L. and Bolam, R. (2010) 'Teacher professionalism and continuing professional development: contested concepts and their implications for school leaders', in Bush, T., Bell, L. and Middlewood, D. (eds), *The Principles of Educational Leadership and Management*, London, Sage.

Blandford, S. (2000) *Managing Professional Development in Schools*, London, Routledge.

Bush, T. (2002) 'Teacher retention: research evidence,' paper for Education and Lifelong Learning Scrutiny Panel, London Borough of Greenwich.

Bush, T. (2008) *Leadership and Management Development in Education*, London, Sage.

Chicago Public Schools Retention Unit (2002) *What Is the Teacher Retention Unit?*, Chicago, Chicago Public Schools Retention Unit.

Cole, O. (2001) 'Motivating and retaining your supply staff', *Headship Matters*, (13), 5–7, London, Optimus Publishing.

Commonwealth Secretariat and World Bank (1992) *Priorities for Improving Teacher Management and Support in Sub-Saharan Africa*, London, Commonwealth Secretariat.

Crow, G. (2006) 'Complexity and the beginning principal in the US: perspectives on socialisation', *Journal of Educational Administration*, 44 (4), 310–335.

Day, C. (1996) 'Leadership and Professional Development: developing reflective practice', in Busher, H. and Saran, R. (eds), *Managing Teachers as Professionals in Schools*, London, Kogan Page.

Dean, C. (2001) 'Internal promotion to headship', *Headship Matters*, (11), London, Optimus Publishing.

Department of Education and Science (DES) (1992) *The Induction and Probation of New Teachers*, London, HMSO.

Draper, J. (2002) 'Should I stay or should I go?', *Primary Headship*, (2), London, Optimus Publishing.

Foskett, N. and Lumby, J. (2003) *Leading and Managing Education: International Dimensions*, London, Paul Chapman Publishing.

Gray, S. (2005) *An Enquiry into Continuing Professional Development for Teachers*, Cambridge, Esmée Fairbairn Foundation and Villiers Park Educational Trust.

Hall, D. (1997) 'Professional development portfolios', in Kydd, L., Crawford, M. and Riches, C. (eds), *Professional Development for Educational Management*, Buckingham, Open University Press.

Hallgarten, J. (2001) 'Making teacher supply boom-proof', *School Leadership*, (3), 9–11.

Hardman, J. (2001) 'Improving recruitment and retention of quality overseas teachers', in Blandford, S. and Shaw, M. (eds), *Managing International Schools*, London, RoutledgeFalmer.

Hedge, J., Borman, W. and Lammlein, S. (2006) *The ageing workforce: realities, myths and implications for organisations*, Washington DC, American Psychological Association.

Hicks, G. and Tilby, J. (2004) 'Holding on to key staff', *Headship Matters*, (25), 7–8, London, Optimus Publishing.

Holloway, D. (1994) 'Further education teachers' development: a post-technocratic model', *Journal of Teacher Development*, 3 (1), 46–57.

Johnson, M. (2003) 'From victims of change to agents of change', *Professional Development Today*, 6 (1), 63–68.

Jones, K. and Stammers, P. (1997) 'The early years of the teacher's career', in Tomlinson, H. (ed.), *Managing Continuous Professional Development in Schools*, London, Paul Chapman Publishing.

Kakabadse, A., Ludlow, R. and Vinnicombe, S. (1987) *Working in Organisations*, Aldershot, Gower Press.

Kitan, M. and Van der Westhuizen, P. (1997) 'Critical skills for beginning principals in developing countries: a case from Kenya', *International Studies in Educational Administration*, 25 (2), 126–137.

Ladebo, O. (2005) 'The effects of work-related attitudes on the intention to leave the profession: an examination of school teachers in Nigeria', *Educational Management Administration and Leadership*, 33 (3), 355–369.

Leithwood, K. (1992) *Teacher Development and Educational Change*, Lewes, Falmer Press.

Lumby, J. (2001) *Managing Further Education: Learning Enterprise*, London, Paul Chapman Publishing.

Lumby, J. (2003) 'Managing motivation', in Lumby, J., Middlewood, D. and Kaabwe, S. (eds), *Managing Human Resources in South African Schools*, London, Commonwealth Secretariat.

Mercer, W. (2001) *Retaining your Star Performers*, Birmingham, Headstart.

Middlewood, D. (2003) 'Managing induction', in Lumby, J., Middlewood, D. and Kaabwe, S. (eds), *Human Resource Management in South African Schools*, London, Commonwealth Secretariat.

Middlewood, D. and Parker, R. (2009) *Leading and Managing Extended Schools*, London, Sage.

Middlewood, D., Parker, R. and Beere, J. (2005) *Creating a Learning School*, London, Paul Chapman Publishing.

Mortimore, P. and MacBeath, J. (2003) 'School effectiveness and improvement: the story so far', in Preedy, M., Glatter, R. and Wise, C. (eds), *Strategic Leadership and Educational Improvement*, London, Paul Chapman Publishing.

Müller, K., Alliata, R. and Benninghoff, F. (2009) 'Attracting and retaining teachers: A question of motivation', *Educational Management Administration and Leadership*, 37 (5), 574–599.

National Commission for Education (NCE) (1996) *Success Against the Odds*, London, Routledge.

Nourice, T. (2008) 'Issues in the retention of teachers in the Seychelles', MA dissertation (unpublished), University of Warwick.

Ribbins, P. (2008) 'A Life and Career-Based Framework for the Study of Leaders in Education', in Lumby, J., Crow, G. and Pashiardis, P. (eds), *International Handbook on the Preparation and Development of School Leaders*, London, Routledge.

Schein, E. (1978) *Career Dynamics*, New York, Addison-Wesley.

School Management Task Force (1990) *School management: the way ahead*, London, HMSO.

Scott, W. (1997) 'The Positive Side of Redundancy', *Management in Education*, II (3), 25.

Sehlare, B., Mentz, P. and Mentz, E. (1994) 'Differences in perceptions of principals and beginner teachers on the induction of the latter', *South Africa Journal of Education*, 14 (2), 73–77.

Stoll, L. and Myers, K. (1998) *No Quick Fixes: Perspectives on Schools in Difficulty*, London, Falmer Press.

Taylor, J. (2003) 'The impact of a college-based Masters programme on school culture and its effectiveness', unpublished MBA dissertation, University of Leicester.

Thomson, P. (2009) *School Leadership: Heads on the Block?* London, Routledge.

Thomson, R. (1993) *Managing People*, Oxford, Butterworth-Heinemann.

Tilby, J. (2007) 'The Retention of Key Staff in Secondary Schools', MBA dissertation, University of Leicester (unpublished).

11

Mentoring and coaching

Introduction: what do we mean by mentoring?

Mentoring has become increasingly significant as a mode of professional development in many countries, including Australia, England, Wales, Hong Kong, Singapore, South Africa and the USA. It is regarded as an important dimension in the preparation and ongoing development of teachers and leaders. It is also a significant part of the socialisation process for educators learning a new role. Crow (2001) distinguishes between two forms of socialisation:

- professional – preparing to take on an occupational role, such as teacher or principal
- organisational – focusing on the specific context where the role is being performed.

Socialisation includes three types of new learning (p. 3):

- skills to perform the job, for example classroom observations
- adjustment to the specific work environment, for example who to trust for information
- internalisation of values, for example the importance of collaboration and collegiality.

187

Adjustment to the school or college context may be eased by an effective induction programme (see Chapter 10). Support and development are important in the leadership and management of all staff, not just those new in post, and mentoring and coaching are two of several approaches used to facilitate socialisation. Educational leaders are adults and need to be involved in determining their own learning needs. This suggests that there should be scope for differing learning styles and for consideration of individualised learning. Mentoring is one important example of individualisation.

Mentoring refers to a process where one person provides individual support and challenge to another professional. The mentor may be a more experienced leader or the process may be peer mentoring. Daresh (1995, p. 8), in reviewing the literature from an American perspective, points to 'the experienced professional as a mentor, serving as a wise guide to a younger protégé'. While this model is common, Crow (2001) also refers to co-mentoring where the process is mutual. This peer-mentoring model may be regarded as being akin to critical friendship in that neither party is seen to have more expertise or experience than the other.

Research with headteachers in England concluded that the most appropriate mode was that of peer-mentoring. Unlike new teachers, principals are all senior professionals with substantial experience, leading to the view that mentors and mentees have 'equal standing'. This perspective was adopted by all mentors in the research although some mentees favoured an 'expert–novice' model, recognising the mentor's greater experience of the headship role (Bush et al. 1996, pp. 135–136).

The nature of mentoring is inevitably influenced by the context in which the process takes place. While it is often regarded as a Western concept, Leung and Bush (2003) suggest that it has a long history within Chinese culture:

> Lifelong mentoring, which is embedded in the Chinese culture and heritage, is the passing of the ancestor's knowledge, values, attitudes and ethics to the successive generation . . . the best relationship between a mentor and a mentee is like water, a natural element that ultimately changes the shape of whatever it touches. (p. 263)

Mentoring and coaching

Rajan's (1996) study of leadership in 500 organisations showed that 'coaching and mentoring' were ranked as the most valuable means of promoting leadership development. Bassett (2001) distinguishes coaching from mentoring by stressing the skills development dimension of the former:

> Mentoring has more to do with career and life development and cannot be successfully entered into between a learner and their manager or assessor. Whereas coaching is considered to be about enabling the individual to improve their performance in their chosen field and is commonly used in the sports and skills development arena. (p. 3)

West and Milan (2001, pp. 7–8), writing from a general leadership perspective, differentiate coaching for development from skills and performance coaching:

> The development coaching task is to create the conditions for reflective learning. A coach does this by first creating a psychological space, which allows the executive to stand back from the workplace, and then providing a supportive, yet challenging, relationship and dialogue in which the executive can gain perspective on his or her experiences and self, and on his or her leadership task within the organization.

They claim that development coaching has three dimensions:

- professionalism: maintaining neutrality and explicit standards of conduct, guaranteeing confidentiality, committed to ongoing personal and professional development

- purpose: helping the individual to adapt congruently and therefore creatively and innovatively to the challenges involved

- the relationship: a collaboration between two people with the goal of a growth in self-awareness and functioning of the client; power is equal.

These authors regard coaching as a marriage between consulting and counselling (see Table 11.1).

Table 11.1 The coaching continuum (West and Milan 2001, p. 70)

Consulting	Counselling
Hard	Soft
Head	Heart
Cerebral	Emotional
Analytical	Experiential

Mentoring may also include an element of counselling. This view received some empirical support from research in the English East Midlands:

> Mentoring does have elements of counselling, notably in listening and empathising with the mentee (mentor).
>
> The mentor's work is like that of a counsellor, she listens and makes me reflect (new principal). (Bush 1995, p. 11)

West and Milan (2001, p. 191) conclude that coaching has much to offer in developing leaders:

> Professional coaching for leadership development has a substantial contribution to make to business and, in particular, to the leaders running businesses. Through providing a partnership of equals, development coaches can support leaders in addressing the challenges they face. Development coaching can assist leaders to learn by standing back from their context; it can help them develop leadership competence for that context: and, finally, it can help them to achieve balance in their often unbalanced lives.

Mentoring and coaching were among the processes used in the NCSL's New Visions programme for early headship. The evaluation of the programme (Bush and Glover 2005) shows that coaching, 'peer coaching', and mentoring have been used effectively in some of the regional groups but less so in others, and not utilised at all in some groups. Where used, mentoring was often informal and involved either group leaders mentoring the new heads or a co-mentoring model where the new heads provided mutual support and challenge. Coaching and 'peer coaching' were successful aspects of the New Visions programme, involving leaders coaching participants or co-coaching between the new heads themselves.

Coaching is in the ascendancy as a mode of development in NCSL programmes (Bush et al. 2007). Simkins et al. (2006), looking at NCSL approaches, conclude that three important issues affect the coaching experience: coach skills and commitment, the time devoted to the process, and the place of coaching within broader school leadership development strategies. This connects with Leask and Terrell's (1997) advocacy of coaching as a development mode for middle managers.

Coaching is often regarded as an effective learning mode within leadership development programmes. Coaching, and mentoring and other forms of peer support, appear to work best when training is thorough and specific, when there is careful matching of coach and coachee, and when it is integral to the wider learning process (Bush et al. 2007).

Mentoring in practice

Bush et al. (2007) note that mentoring is becoming more person centred with an increased awareness of the need to match mentor and mentee, to ensure that mentors are properly trained and that there is time, support and understanding of the reflective process. Hobson and Sharp's (2005) systematic review of the literature found that all major studies of formal mentoring programmes for new heads reported that such programmes have been effective, and that the mentoring of new heads can result in a range of perceived benefits for both mentees and mentors. Pocklington and Weindling (1996, p. 189) argue that 'mentoring offers a way of speeding up the process of transition to headship'.

Mathews (2003) argues that mentoring roles may be diverse, including those of guide, teacher, adviser, friend, tutor, catalyst, coach, consultant, role model and advocate. He concludes with cautions about the time required to make the process effective, and notes that mentoring relationships, particularly those which are cross-gender, may not be satisfactory.

Harrison et al. (2006) argue for a greater element of critical reflection for mentoring to be successful. Hawkey (2006) extends the argument for a new approach to mentoring through the use of appropriate language and understanding of emotional intelligence, so that there is empathy between mentor and mentee. Achinstein and Athanases (2006) suggest that mentoring fails where it is over-prescriptive and directive with only one right solution (p. 167). It is more likely to be successful where it is collaborative, investigative and transformative in nature.

Underhill (2006) examined mentoring research over the past 25 years to assess its effectiveness and concluded that 'the overall mean effect size of mentoring' was significant, indicating that mentoring does improve career outcomes for individuals. However, informal mentoring is shown to be more effective than formal programmes, echoing Herbohn's (2004, p. 393) finding that 'informal mentoring relationships benefit the protégé, the mentor and the employing organisation'.

There is only limited evidence of the use of mentoring in Europe. Watson's (2003) overview of provision in 24 European countries concludes that:

> Very few systems appear to be giving careful and systematic thought to how headteachers can be supported in their work in a way which leads to, rather than diminishes, professional skills, confidence and attitudes. It is in these contexts that peer support and mentoring can be of great importance to those involved. (p. 9)

The mentoring process is used in many countries and for several different groups of education professionals. This section provides an overview of some of these categories.

Student mentoring in Hong Kong

Mentoring for students in Hong Kong is motivated by concern about attrition rates, not least because student numbers partly determine university funding levels. Two universities have adopted mentoring so that 'student retention can be increased and academic achievement can be promoted' (Leung and Bush 2003, p. 264). The Hong Kong Baptist University has a formal and compulsory programme which deliberately matches mentors (academic staff) and mentees (students). The objectives of this programme are:

1   to help students to adjust to the changes during their transition to the university setting
2   to help students understand the field of study
3   to share experiences and views on different issues
4   to assist students to achieve their own goals by providing information, opportunities, guidance and suggestions in problem solving and learning techniques (Leung and Bush 2003, p. 265).

Large-scale research with mentors and students shows that there were several problems in implementing this programme:

- There were too few women staff to meet the demand for same-sex mentoring.

- Mentoring is not regarded as a formal part of staff workload so it tended to be conducted whenever there was 'spare time'.

- There was no training for mentors.

- Mentoring was not part of the reward system of the university so it often had a low priority (Leung and Bush 2003, pp. 267 and 269).

A mentoring programme for students is valuable to help them to adjust to the organisation, and to help in developing positive learning outcomes. Leaders and managers should consider introducing mentoring for students, as well as staff.

Mentoring for school leaders in South Africa

The South African Department of Basic Education (DBE) piloted a national leadership development programme for school principals and aspiring principals from 2007. This ACE (School Leadership) is a two-year part-time programme, delivered by universities, with a common curriculum, comprising five core modules and 'foundation' modules on ICT and language (see Chapter 14). This section draws on the longitudinal evaluation of the programme (Bush et al. 2009; Bush et al. 2011). The evaluation comprised baseline and impact surveys of all 420 pilot participants and case studies of 27 of them.

Mentoring is a distinctive and central feature of the ACE programme, designed to facilitate the transfer of learning to candidates and to school practice. Mentors are appointed by the university and/or the provincial education department, and work with participants for the duration of the programme. Bush (2008, p. 43) says that 'mentoring refers to a process where one person provides *individual* support and challenge to another professional' but, within the ACE programme, mentoring usually relates to groups, not individuals.

Selection of mentors

The matching process between mentor and mentee is critical to its effectiveness. This also links to the selection procedure. Some universities employ people who have worked with the higher education institution (HEI) on other similar programmes. These are often retired principals, whose professional experience is seen as directly relevant to their role.

In some provinces, notably in Eastern Cape, KwaZulu Natal and Gauteng, the mentors are representative of the student population in terms of race, gender and their experience of similar school contexts, providing the potential for appropriate matching of mentors and mentees. This is not the case in Limpopo and Mpumalanga, where mentors are predominantly male, overwhelmingly white and with leadership experience in well-resourced City schools, not in the township and rural schools where the great majority of candidates are employed.

Mentoring practice

Mentoring is widely regarded as a key dimension of the programme, providing the potential for personal engagement with candidates and their schools. Mentors can also be the conduit between HEI theory and school-level practice. In many provinces, including Eastern Cape, Limpopo and Mpumalanga, there is a two-stage process:

- group 'facilitation' as part of, or separate from, the formal teaching sessions at the university

- visits to candidates' schools to provide on-site support.

Mentors are responsible for a number of candidates, ranging from nine in Eastern Cape to 38 for some in the Western Cape. The facilitation sessions take place in groups and do not match the generally accepted definition of mentoring, which assumes a one-to-one relationship. In Gauteng, the mentors do not visit candidates' schools so any 'mentoring' takes place during cohort sessions and through telephone conversations.

Where visits do take place, the candidates often praise the help and support provided by the mentors. There were good and 'supportive' relationships in Eastern Cape but here, and in Limpopo and Mpumalanga, the researchers' observations suggest that candidates are 'over-dependent' on the mentors, who adopt 'a tightly focused teacher–student relationship', which is not likely to lead to innovative leadership practice.

In KwaZulu Natal, the researcher reports a confused picture with mentoring apparently not yet in place in some districts. Only two of the six candidates had an 'effective mentoring experience' while the others said that their mentors 'did not seem to know what they were supposed to do' and did not 'enhance their management'. In contrast, mentoring in the Western Cape was reported to be the 'best part' of the ACE programme.

The evaluation concludes that there is a need for a review of mentoring practice within provinces, HEIs and the DBE. The authors note that there are two major constraints on effective practice: the cost of providing one-on-one mentoring, and the limited availability of well-trained and motivated professionals, with good experience of leading township and rural schools, who are also free to visit candidates' schools during the working day. Ideally, mentors would be selected from successful principals, be subject to specific training and be employed centrally to provide expert mentoring in candidates' schools (Bush et al. 2009; Bush et al. 2011).

Mentoring for aspiring principals in Singapore

Training for prospective school principals in Singapore was introduced as early as 1984, well ahead of most other countries. The Ministry of Education and the National Institute of Education (NIE) collaborated to develop the Diploma in Educational Administration (DEA) which had an annual intake of 50 vice-principals from primary and secondary schools. The programme was full-time for one year and participants were selected by the Ministry.

Mentoring was an integral part of the training programme and occurred largely when participants were attached to a mentor principal's school on a full-time basis for eight weeks. Mentees practised a range of leadership skills negotiated with their mentors. Participants were coached, reinforcing the links between mentoring and coaching noted earlier, and given feedback on how they had handled their tasks. Mentors also modelled leadership behaviour through their own daily work. The mentoring pairs were supported by an NIE facilitator whose role was to ensure that learning objectives were clearly understood and pursued. Bush and Chew (1999, p. 46) conclude that 'the Singapore model of mentoring is . . . working reasonably well, judging by . . . feedback obtained from yearly cohorts of DEA participants, many of whom have assumed principalships after their training'.

The DEA was replaced by the Leaders in Education programme in 2002 and this also includes a mentoring component. Participants are allocated to schools for workplace learning, supported by the 'steward principal'. Chong et al. (2003, p. 169) say that this is intended to produce a 'profound learning experience for the participant'.

Mentoring for school leaders in the USA

Daresh (2004) reports that, in the USA, 32 states have enacted laws and policies that call for mandated support programmes to assist new school principals. Earlier, he reviewed the American research on mentoring for school leaders and reached the following broad conclusions:

- The main rationale for mentoring is that 'the role of the leader is a lonely effort, and that having the ability to relate to peers concerning personal and professional concerns is a way to reduce that sense of isolation'.

- Mentoring enhances university-based programmes by linking participants with colleagues in the real world who can provide practical solutions to problems faced in the field.

- There is a lack of clarity about the purposes and definitions of mentoring.

- Both participants *and* mentors appear to benefit from mentoring (Daresh 1995, p. 14).

Barnett and O'Mahony (2008, p. 239) argue that the most effective US programmes contain the following elements:

- organisational support from the superintendent and other key decision-makers

- clearly defined outcomes that provide information on the knowledge and skills to be attained

- a clear process for screening, selecting and matching mentors and protégés

- training for mentors and protégés

- a learning-centred focus which addresses the needs of the protégé.

Mentoring and coaching within NCSL programmes in England

Mentoring became a significant part of headship development in England from 1991 following the work of the School Management Task Force. This initiative was introduced at a time when there was no formal requirement for heads to be trained for their management role. Bush (1995, p. 3) described this in-service model of professional development 'as a substitute for training rather than forming part of it'.

Since the opening of the NCSL in 2000, mentoring and coaching have been important elements of most college programmes. Bush et al.'s (2007) overview of 35 NCSL evaluations found that coaching appears to have taken over from mentoring as the main descriptor of support and challenge for English school leaders. For example, the former Leading from the Middle (LftM) programme used coaching in two ways: coaching triads and in-school coaches. Coaching triads required participants to play three roles; coach, coachee and observer. The programme evaluation shows that participants were very positive about this, describing it as a 'highlight'. In-school coaches are generally heads or senior staff in participants' schools. The coaching received mixed reviews. While its potential was widely recognised, there were a number of perceived problems including lack of clarity about the coaching role, that some coaches were too passive and that coaches were well meaning but too busy. Despite these problems, the programme clearly helped in the development of coaching capacity in schools.

Coaching was also a central part of the Working Together for Success (WTfS) programme, designed for senior leadership teams, but it was criticised as very poor, too theoretical and over the heads of middle managers. Despite this, the report adds that some schools had used coaching successfully with other staff.

The London Challenge Coaching and Mentoring course was well received and some schools were well on the way to developing a coaching and mentoring culture. However, the evaluation adds that there was concern that some 'coaching' activity was superficial and anecdotal. It states that coaches need appropriate personal qualities and the knowledge and skills to coach in subtle and effective ways. Training is regarded as the key to developing these attributes.

Coaching has superseded mentoring as the main descriptor of personalised support for school leaders, although there is some evidence of semantic confusion. Coaching plays an important part in many NCSL programmes and is often regarded as an effective learning mode. Coaching, and mentoring and other forms of peer support, appear to work best when training is thorough and specific, when there is careful matching of coach and coachee, and when it is integral to the wider learning process (Bush et al. 2007).

The benefits of mentoring

The literature points to the importance of adults being co-constructors of their learning. This is even more significant for school leaders, who are well educated senior professionals with a highly developed sense of their own learning needs. Mentoring has the potential to produce significant benefits for mentees, mentors and the education system. 'Mentoring needs to produce benefits for both mentor and protégé if it is to be a mutually rewarding experience and provide motivation for both partners. Ideally, these benefits should extend to the schools involved in the relationship' (Bush 1995, p. 7). Luck's (2003) research for the NCSL shows that the process had a positive impact on both mentors and mentees.

Benefits for mentees

Mentoring programmes have been widely welcomed as a contribution to the professional development of staff at entry points to new or promoted posts. Hobson (2003, p. 2), for example, states that 'all major studies of formal mentoring programmes for new headteachers have concluded that such mentoring work was effective'. The main benefits for headteachers are perceived to be:

- peer support, notably in mentoring for new headteachers and principals

- enabling heads to gain in confidence in their new role

- a reduction in the isolation experienced by many heads through the 'sounding board' provided by mentors

- developing their expertise in a range of areas, including staff management and motivation, and conflict resolution (Luck 2003).

Some of these benefits also apply to NQTs. Bush et al. (1996, p. 127) refer to four main gains for this group of mentees. Participants welcome mentors who:

- listen and act as a sounding-board

- offer guidance and reassurance

- are non-judgmental

- can admit that they are also fallible.

Mentoring may not always form part of a formal scheme and there can be benefits from informal support. Petzko et al. (2002) surveyed 1,400 middle school principals in the USA. When asked to identify the person who influenced them most during their first year as principal, 44 per cent indicated another principal while 22 per cent said it was a central office administrator. These respondents advocate the provision of trained mentors for new principals.

Training is an important dimension of successful mentoring programmes and the quality of the mentoring experience for participants is likely to vary according to the level and nature of training provided for mentors. Playko (1995), drawing on extensive experience of mentoring for school leaders in the USA, stresses that experience as a principal is not sufficient to ensure quality mentoring processes. Specialised training is also required.

Benefits for mentors

There is significant evidence from a range of contexts about the many benefits for mentors. Research on student mentoring in Hong Kong (Leung and Bush 2003) found that most of the mentors enjoyed the process, as one respondent illustrates:

> I got great satisfaction mentoring students. We talked about many things, his studies, his social life and what he wants to do in his career. Although there were many difficulties, we have developed understanding and [a] close relationship after one year. (p. 268)

Mentors of NQTs also derived benefits from the process, describing it as 'a learning partnership', 'a two way interaction', 'for mutual support' and 'of benefit to both of us' (Bush et al. 1996, p. 128). Luck's (2003, p. 31) research confirms these benefits: 'The data clearly show that mentors benefited from the experience as well as mentees, thereby achieving a double whammy for professional development'.

Barnett and O'Mahony's (2008, p. 241) overview of mentoring and coaching shows several benefits for mentors and coaches. These include networking, professional development, increased self-esteem and the facilitation of communities of learning.

The benefits for mentors might be regarded as one of the unintended consequences of a process which is designed to produce gains for participants. Similar advantages were evident in the NCSL's former New Visions programme for early headship, where the consultant heads report many benefits for themselves and their schools (Bush and Glover 2005).

Benefits for schools and the education system

Mentoring has been encouraged or sponsored by governments because of its perceived benefits for the education system. In South Africa, for example, mentoring has been identified as a key process in developing principals and in contributing to improvement in schools and throughout the education system (Bush et al. 2011). Research in Singapore (Chong et al. 2003) and England (Bush et al. 2007) points to two main system gains:

- The relationship provides a steady supply of trained teachers and leaders.

- The process helps teachers and leaders to become effective more quickly, thus developing schools and the wider system, as well as the individuals concerned.

Limitations of mentoring

Crow (2001), in a detailed review of internship and mentoring, stresses four potential pitfalls:

- Mentors may have their own agendas.

- Mentoring can create dependency.

- Some mentors attempt to clone mentees.

- Mentoring runs the risk of perpetuating the status quo (p. 13).

Research in England and Singapore (Bush and Chew 1999, p. 50) confirms these problems and adds that there is a risk of an inappropriate 'match' between mentor and mentee. Roberts (2000) and Samier (2000) both point to the importance of the 'chemistry' between mentor and mentee.

The gender aspects of matching may be particularly problematic. Most of the students at Hong Kong Baptist University preferred same-sex mentoring but this was not possible for many female students because of the under-representation of women staff. Only 95 out of 310 female students (30.6 per cent) had women mentors. This had negative consequences for mentees, mentors and the quality of the programme:

> Some female students had complained that they were embarrassed to talk to their male mentors about their personal problems (female mentor).

> The reason that I prefer to have a mentee of the same sex is to avoid destructive gossip and discrediting innuendoes (male mentor). (Leung and Bush 2003, pp. 267–268)

Research in South Africa illustrates the problem of dependency identified by Crow (2001) above. Mentoring is a central element in the national ACE (School Leadership) programme for current and aspiring principals. While this dimension is widely applauded, the evaluation report notes that most mentors promoted dependency by offering 'solutions' rather than developing mentees' independence. When the mentoring programme ended, following course completion, many participants had not developed the skills to operate effectively without mentors' 'prescriptions' (Bush et al. 2009, Bush et al. 2011).

Barnett and O'Mahony (2008, p. 241) note that mentoring has been proclaimed as the 'saviour' of leadership development but they caution that it is only one form of professional learning. They comment that lack of time to devote to the relationship is the most commonly cited problem in the literature.

Despite these potential problems, research in several countries (Barnett and O'Mahony 2008; Bush et al. 2011, Hobson and Sharp 2005) shows that they are outweighed by the advantages and that mentoring is often highly successful in promoting the development of students, teachers, and practising and aspiring leaders. However, the limitations provide helpful cautions for school and college leaders planning to introduce, or to develop, mentoring or coaching programmes.

Conclusion: towards a model of mentoring

There is little doubt that mentoring has the potential to foster the development of participants, whether these are students, new teachers or school leaders. Hobson and Sharp's (2005) systematic review of the literature found that all major studies of formal mentoring programmes for new heads reported that such programmes have been effective, and that mentoring can result in a range of perceived benefits for both mentees and mentors.

Hobson and Sharp (2005) also discuss the relationship between mentoring and coaching, and say that the inclusion of coaching within mentoring programmes is 'contentious'. A large proportion of mentors associated with one English programme argue that the term 'coaching' was not appropriate in describing the mentoring of new headteachers (p. 39). The latter term may be appropriate where specific skills are being developed but the need is often for someone to mentor by promoting reflection on skills, attitudes and behaviours (Bush et al. 2007). Hankey (2004) makes a similar point, suggesting a shift from the 'apprenticeship' model of mentoring to one focusing on reflection and professional discourse.

Carroll (2005) suggests that there needs to be a new approach to mentoring involving an inquiry perspective through:

- re-stating: repeating an idea to invite additional attention or concurrence

- re-cycling: re-introducing an idea from earlier in the session to position it in relation to a current observation

- re-conceptualizing: developing or broadening an example into a more general idea

- re-contextualizing: shifting the perspectives brought to bear on it

- making a warranted inference: making an inference based on the previous speaker's comment and implicitly inviting concurrence or disagreement (p. 465).

Whatever the 'label' used to describe the relationship, the key requirements are to ensure that mentors/coaches are selected carefully, matched with appropriate mentees/coachees and, above all, trained to work towards the objectives of the specific scheme to which they are contributing. If these desiderata are met, mentoring and coaching can continue to make a powerful contribution to the learning of students, teachers and leaders. Mentoring and coaching are key aspects of leadership development (see Chapter 14).

References

Achinstein, B. and Athanases, S. (2006) *Mentors in the Making: Developing New Leaders for New Teachers*, New York, Teachers' College Press.

Barnett, B. and O'Mahony, G. (2008) 'Mentoring and coaching programs for the professional development of school leaders', in Lumby, J., Crow, G. and Pashiardis, P. (eds), *International Handbook on the Preparation and Development of School Leaders*, New York, Routledge.

Bassett, S. (2001) 'The use of phenomenology in management research: an exploration of the learners' experience of coach-mentoring in the workplace', paper presented at the Qualitative Evidence-Based Practice Conference, Coventry, May.

Bush, T. (1995) 'Mentoring for principals: pre-service and in-service models', *Singapore Journal of Education*, 15 (1), 1–13.

Bush, T. (2008) *Leadership and Management Development in Education*, London, Sage.

Bush, T. and Chew, J. (1999) 'Developing human capital: training and mentoring for principals', *Compare*, 29 (1), 41–52.

Bush, T. and Glover, D. (2005) 'Leadership development for early headship: the New Visions experience', *School Leadership and Management*, 25 (3), 217–239.

Bush, T., Glover, D. and Harris, A. (2007) *Review of School Leadership Development*, Nottingham, NCSL.

Bush, T., Kiggundu, E. and Moorosi, P. (2011) 'Preparing new principals in South Africa: the ACE: School Leadership Programme', *South African Journal of Education*, 31 (1), 31–43.

Bush, T., Coleman, M., Wall, D. and West-Burnham, J. (1996) 'Mentoring and continuing professional development', in McIntyre, D. and Hagger, H. (eds), *Mentors in Schools: Developing the Profession of Teaching*, London, David Fulton.

Bush, T., Duku, N., Glover, D., Kiggundu, E., Kola, S., Msila, V., and Moorosi, P. (2009) *The Zenex ACE: School Leadership Research: Final Report*, Johannesburg, Department of Basic Education.

Carroll, D. (2005) 'Learning through interactive talk: a school-based mentor teacher study group as a context for professional learning', *Teaching and Teacher Education*, 21 (5), 457–473.

Chong, K.C., Stott, K. and Low, G.T. (2003) 'Developing Singapore school leaders for a learning nation', in Hallinger, P. (ed.), *Reshaping the Landscape of School Leadership Development: A Global Perspective*, Lisse, Swets and Zeitlinger.

Crow, G. (2001) *School leader preparation: a short review of the knowledge base*, Nottingham, NCSL.

Daresh, J. (1995) 'Research base on mentoring for educational leaders: what do we know?', *Journal of Educational Administration*, 33 (5), 7–16.

Daresh, J. (2004) 'Mentoring school leaders: Professional promise or predictable problems?', *Educational Administration Quarterly*, 40 (4), 495–517.

Hankey, J. (2004) 'The good, the bad and other considerations: reflections on mentoring trainee teachers in post-compulsory education', *Research In Post-Compulsory Education*, 9 (3), 389–400.

Harrison, J., Dymoke, S. and Pell, T. (2006) 'Mentoring beginning teachers in secondary schools: An analysis of practice', *Teaching and Teacher Education*, 22 (8), 1055–1067.

Hawkey, K. (2006) 'Emotional intelligence and mentoring in pre-service teacher education: a literature review', *Mentoring and Tutoring*, 14 (2), 137–147.

Herbohn, K. (2004) 'Informal mentoring relationships and the career processes of public accountants', *The British Accounting Review*, 36 (4), 369–393.

Hobson, A. (2003) *Mentoring and Coaching for New Leaders*, Nottingham, NCSL.

Hobson, A. and Sharp, C. (2005) 'Head-to-head: a systematic review of the research evidence on mentoring new head teachers', *School Leadership and Management*, 25 (1), 25–42.

Leask, M. and Terrell, I. (1997) *Development Planning and School Improvement for Middle Managers*, London, Kogan Page.

Leung, M.L. and Bush, T. (2003) 'Student mentoring in higher education: Hong Kong Baptist University', *Mentoring and Tutoring*, 11 (3), 263–272.

Luck, C. (2003) *It's Good to Talk: An Enquiry into the Value of Mentoring as an Aspect of Professional Development for New Headteachers*, Nottingham, NCSL.

Mathews, P. (2003) 'Academic mentoring: enhancing the use of scarce resources', *Educational Management and Administration*, 31 (3), 313–334.

Petzko, V., Clark, D., Valentine, G., Hackmann, D., Nori, J. and Lucas, S. (2002) 'Leaders and leadership in middle level schools', *NASSP Bulletin*, 86, 631.

Playko, M. (1995) 'Mentoring for educational leaders: a practitioner's perspective', *Journal of Educational Administration*, 33 (5), 84–92.

Pocklington, K. and Weindling, D. (1996) 'Promoting reflection on headship through the mentoring mirror', *Educational Management and Administration*, 24 (2), 175–191.

Rajan, A. (1996) *Leading People*, Tunbridge Wells, CREATE.

Roberts, A. (2000) 'Mentoring revisited: a phenomenological reading of the literature', *Mentoring and Tutoring*, 8 (2), 146–169.

Samier, E. (2000) 'Public administration mentorship: conceptual and pragmatic considerations', *Journal of Educational Administration*, 38 (1), 83–101.

Simkins, T., Coldwell, M., Caillau, I., Finlayson, H. and Morgan, A. (2006) 'Coaching as a school leadership development strategy: Experiences from "Leading from the Middle"', *Journal of In-Service Education*, 32 (3), 339–354.

Underhill, C. (2006) 'The effectiveness of mentoring programs in corporate settings: a meta-analytical review of the literature', *Journal of Vocational Behaviour*, 68 (2), 292–307.

Watson, K. (2003) *Selecting and Developing Heads of Schools: Twenty-three European Perspectives*, Sheffield, European Forum on Educational Administration.

West, L. and Milan, M. (2001) *The Reflecting Glass: Professional Coaching for Leadership Development*, London, Palgrave MacMillan.

12

Leading and managing for performance

Introduction

The educational performance of institutions, teachers and learners in many countries has been increasingly significant as economic prosperity has been perceived to be closely linked to the quality of an educated and skilled workforce. Regularly published international tables of comparative attainments, usually test results at certain ages, clearly indicate this emphasis on the importance of educational attainment. Recognition that leaders who see 'developing people' (Leithwood and Riehl 2005, pp. 19–22) as a core practice leads to the acknowledgement that those who engage *directly* with learners are the key agents for improving performance. This chapter is concerned with how the leaders and managers in individual schools and colleges enable their staff to perform as effectively as possible. Only through that will the educational goals of the organisation be achieved.

This chapter discusses what we mean by 'performance' and how the purposes and implications of performance management schemes may be perceived according to their different contexts. It considers the implications of these for changing notions of professionalism, and then examines some key principles underpinning the leadership and management of effective performance and its review at institutional level, including the significance of related issues, such as performance related pay (PRP). It proposes that managing performance is not a separate process for leaders but an integral part of employee leadership and management as a whole, and central to the success of the organisation. Only this kind of approach is likely to be effective in a fast-changing world where notions of effectiveness in learning are evolving rapidly.

What is meant by performance management?

Performance itself is a concept which involves the behaviour and actions which lead to results, and also includes the use of the skills and knowledge required to achieve these (Forrester 2011). The term and process, 'performance management', developed in business and industry where Townley (1989) suggested that as the production line approach disappeared, there was seen to be a need for closer monitoring of employees' increased autonomy. In the late 1980s and the 1990s, it was applied to public services as a 'process that links people and jobs to the strategy and objectives of the organisation' (Murlis 1992, p. 65) through a systematic approach to setting goals, measuring progress, giving feedback and recognising success. In England, by the beginning of the twenty-first century, Mahoney and Hextall (2001, p. 175) could write that 'we now find that there are performance management systems at work in almost all areas of the public service, for example, health, housing, tax collection, employment services, local authority provision, etc.'

In education, the need of national governments of developed countries, in particular for accountability for the large resources expended in education, led them to develop ways of appraising teachers' performance. In the late 1980s and early- to mid-1990s, there were various attempts to introduce performance appraisal for teachers and headteachers, for example in England and Wales. There, because of its essentially 'added-on' nature, it became a low priority and was eventually described as 'discredited' (Middlewood 2001a). By the end of the 1990s, 'appraisal' had been seen as tending to look back, and performance management, which was purported to be more forward looking, had absorbed assessment of teachers' performance within it. Appraisal is considered later in this chapter, but we now consider how different perceptions of the purpose of performance management can influence its effectiveness.

Purposes and perceptions of purpose

Accountability

As people working in a public sector financed by taxpayers, there can be little argument that teachers, lecturers and others need to be held accountable for their performance, whether this is at an organisational or individual level. For those working in the private sector of education – and this is a considerable proportion in some countries, such as the Netherlands and Greece – the need for accountability is equally important, albeit to a different authority. Even those proposing models of staff assessment which encourage team and organisational learning through feedback recognise the need for the institution to be demonstrating to those outside that such procedures are 'robust as well as reflective and can submit readily to scrutiny from external frameworks' (Middlewood et al. 2005, p. 13).

As accountability is one of the 'Seven Principles of Public Life' (Nolan 1996), and some of the others include integrity, honesty and selflessness, it clearly has an ethical dimension. Some of the most relevant kinds of accountability include:

- political

- market

- moral

- professional.

Perhaps in education, the key question is 'Accountability to whom?'. Moreland's (2009) research found that the teachers said they felt most accountable to 'pupils and parents – also to the department team' (ibid., p. 747). If this professional accountability is the crucial one for teachers and lecturers, it is the task and duty of leaders and managers to ensure institutional accountability and operate a management of performance process which enables this. As schools and colleges, not only in developed countries but increasingly in developing ones, gain increased autonomy, the issue of whether to apply a national scheme of performance management or to develop a scheme specific to an individual type of institution becomes crucial for leaders. As Baroness O'Neill, philosopher and Principal of Newnham College (in 2006), said: 'I am not against accountability per se, only against stupid forms of accountability', referring to what she saw as the obsession by the national government with the minutiae of test scores and similar quantitative assessments.

Development

In terms of assessing teacher performance, earlier models tended towards either an accountability *or* developmental scheme, as suggested in Middlewood's (2002) continuum. Common sense dictates that, in any framework of assessing performance, 'we need to ensure that all teachers are given appropriate development opportunities' (Moreland 2009, p. 757). We see development here as incorporating improvements both in skills (for example, in classroom practice) and in self-confidence and motivation in, for example, team membership and learning from and with others.

Control

However, the emphasis on business style practices mentioned above in education has led a number of writers and researchers to conclude that the real purpose of performance management is that of control (Forrester 2011). The application of standards, targets, benchmarks, audits, etc. to the educational world has led to what is commonly referred to as the 'performativity culture', where the focus is almost exclusively on the measurement of outcomes, especially in test or examination results or scores. After 11 years as a headteacher, Arrowsmith (2001, p. 21), wrote that 'I struggle to recall a piece of legislation which, when implemented, would have increased children's enjoyment of education and made them want to come to school more.'

Schools have been forced to play the 'standards game' (Gleeson and Gunter 2001, p. 145) due to the 'technicist, managerialist and mechanistic emphasis of national policies' (ibid., p. 151). The development of this culture may be because of confusion 'of structure with purpose, measurement with accomplishment, means with ends, compliance with commitment' (Stoll et al. 2003, p. 185) or more sinister political reasons. 'Coercion is replaced by self-steering – the appearance of autonomy' (Ball 2003, p. 54).

Whatever the reason, the impact on the notions of what constitutes a professional employee in educational institutions has been profound. If self-regulation and ownership are seen as the cornerstones of professionalism, the impact of performance management on educational employees such as teachers and lecturers has been, in many people's views, to replace these with an attitude which sees them as functionaries (Ozga 1995) or, more extremely, 'wage slaves' (Mather and Seifert 2011, p. 30).

Concerns about control have been expressed in the UK, New Zealand

(Fitzgerald et al. 2003), Australia (Smyth and Shacklock 1998) and South Africa (Thurlow 2001). Several of these countries continue to use the term 'appraisal' for assessment of performance.

All the above differences in perceptions of the purpose of performance management or performance reviews can clearly lead to irreconcilable differences between managers and 'managed'. For example, in Israel, Gaziel (2008) found that the difference in belief about the purpose of performance assessment was the most important factor in presenting it being 'shallow and inconsistent and a waste of time' (ibid., p. 348).

South Africa provides a clear example of the mistrust of the purposes of appraisal and teacher performance, as Thurlow (2001) makes clear. Prior to the removal of apartheid, the conviction held by most teachers in South Africa was that the performance management and appraisal system was secretive, top-down and for the purposes of control, especially of non-white teachers. By 1996 in the post-apartheid republic, Jantjes (1996, p. 53) was still able to point to a 'lack of common understanding between teachers and administration as to the real purposes of teacher appraisal' and suggested that it would continue to be 'regarded with mistrust', until this was rectified.

This 'legacy of mistrust coming from previous experience is the biggest obstacle for the school manager to overcome in developing some form of effective performance management' (Middlewood 2002, p. 131), and whichever model evolves in South Africa, there is an attempt in the public documentation to be open and clear about purposes (Mokgalene et al. 1997).

Basic purposes

Perhaps, for leaders and managers, there is a need to return to what we believe to be the basic purpose of managing performance, which is that, to work effectively, employees need:

- to know what it is they have to do
- to receive help, support, advice, etc. when they need it
- to get regular feedback on how they are performing
- to receive recognition for what they have done.

We now turn to considering factors which impact on the effectiveness of any scheme for managing performance.

The importance of context for performance management

The performance of employees in education, as in other employment areas, is deeply influenced by the culture within which the employee operates. The intensity of the focus upon the teacher, for example, is strongly affected by the attitude taken towards teachers in a particular society or culture. Furukawa (1989, p. 54) suggests that 'Japan's strong tradition of group importance' would not allow a heavy emphasis on assessment of the individual, a view supported by Hampden-Turner and Trompenaars (1997) who see the way that Western managers can be competitive, individualistic and concerned with achieved status as being alien to the Japanese outlook. In Islam, the teacher is respected 'like one's father' (Shah 1998), so that duties and respect owed to the father are transferred to the professional site, making a detailed or challenging assessment of performance not only difficult and unlikely, but possibly anti-Islamic. In Pakistan Madrasas (i.e. educational institutions with religious affiliations), religious discourse dominates all human resource management (HRM) functions so that all judgements of teaching are of a higher authority.

Hampden-Turner and Trompenaars (2003, p. 51) support the view that, in many Asian countries, the 'teacher is life-time father', turning the whole context for examining teacher performance on its head, 'performance' here being perceived in an entirely different context from in the West. In China, Bush et al. (1998, p. 191) describe the process of teacher performance evaluation as complex.

Given frequent peer observation and joint preparation, Chinese teachers are well informed about the teaching quality of their colleagues in the whole school and able to make comments on colleagues' teaching style, subject knowledge level, capacity for managing class discipline, strength and weakness in teaching, and reputation among students. As a result of this familiarity, teachers are evaluated by a committee of their peers as well as by the principal (Washington 1991). This process is frequent and iterative rather than occasional and 'top-down'.

According to Child (1994, p. 81) Western approaches to performance 'touch sensitive fields in China, and Western functionalism is farthest removed from the collective norms of Chinese traditions and socialist ideology'.

The influence of aspects of religious belief upon reviewing performance is not confined to Asian or Eastern contexts. In some Church schools in Western countries, the leaders are clear that the values expressed through the faith must be fully integrated and indeed dominate the process of performance management. Thus the Diocese of Sheffield (2000) quotes 'challenge, evaluation, consolidation, celebration and *prayerful* reflection will be important characteristics to our approach in this school and will be an accepted part of the process' (quoted in Sikes 2001, p. 96). Robertson (2001) describes how actual performance objectives of staff need to reflect closely what a Church school exists for in its provision for pupils and employees, including greater insight into their spiritual being.

The importance of contexts illustrates how closely attitudes to, and the effectiveness of, performance management are allied to what intrinsic view and value of education exists in the particular context within which performance management is implemented. The performativity culture discussed above, for example, is widely seen as encouraging a view of learning which is narrow and essentially utilitarian.

Problems associated with assessing performance of educational staff

Implementation

As with various leadership initiatives, the manner in which a scheme is introduced can have significant impact on how successful it may be. Any resentment at a perceived ill-judged imposition will often last beyond the initial introduction. National schemes of performance management therefore are often perceived to be imposed in a top-down way, with little ownership by the staff affected. In a study in New Zealand, Piggot-Irvine (2010, p. 230) describes an attempt to overcome 'reluctant and mistrusting participants in the appraisal process, considering it a managerial inspection'. Even in a study where the findings were mainly positive (Jennings and Lomas 2003), the biggest negativities came from resentment about the imposition of the scheme.

Difficulty of measuring outcomes

As Preedy (2001, p. 94) has explained, outcomes in education can be 'multidimensional, complex and long term'. While defining what to count as an outcome is difficult enough 'finding indices which adequately capture these outcomes is yet more difficult, and developing devices with which to appraise achievement of these outcomes is of yet another order' (Mahoney and Hextall 2001, p. 184). This relates to the extreme difficulty of making comparisons between those who will need to operate in one way in one context and others operating in a different way in a quite different context. Thrupp's (1999) comparison of teachers' effectiveness in prosperous and deprived schools in New Zealand illustrates the quite different notions of effectiveness that emerge.

A further factor is the issue of attribution. There is a problem in attempting to identify the particular contribution made to a learner's performance by any individual teacher, rather than by a whole history of teachers and 'there are also real issues about the significance of external factors which are quite literally beyond the control of any school or teacher' (Mahoney and Hextall 2001, p. 184).

Another criticism of the focus on assessing performance of individual staff is that it encourages the idea that achieving outcomes is the only desirable aim for staff and this is at the expense of reflection, an essential part of the development process.

This 'anti-reflection' aspect of, for example, the England and Wales performance management scheme may in itself be a reflection of the work culture of Northern European nations where staff in general work the longest hours. Senge (1993) describes the Japanese manager who, when he is sitting quietly at his desk, will not be interrupted by his staff as they know he is working hardest then. When he moves around his office, they know it is safe to disturb him. He contrasts this with the Western notion of the exact opposite being the case. Humphreys and Oxtoby (1995) also point out that the notion of a thrusting, energetic middle manager is alien to Egyptian colleges, whereas the quiet person who gets on with his job is seen as the ideal. In such contexts, notions of performance and therefore of assessing outcomes are completely different, as discussed earlier.

The issue of rewards

Whatever the format of performance management, there is an acknowledgement that recognition or rewards are an important part of the process. While material rewards are eschewed as alien in some cultures, in Western countries there is debate about the merits of value pay schemes or what is commonly known as performance related pay (PRP). Motivation was explored in detail in Chapter 7, but various national governments appear convinced that additional money for those who have performed well is a valuable means of extrinsic motivation of educational professionals.

According to the Effort Reward Imbalance Model (ERIM), there are basically three systems of reward distribution:

- money

- esteem

- career opportunities and development (Siegrist 1996).

The evidence from outside education that PRP can work is not encouraging. Evans (2001, p. 110) points out that, while recognition is a motivator, it is only so by being repeated regularly, whereas PRP is concerned with one-off rewards. Moreover, she argues that, if PRP does bring about change in some professionals' practice, it would be merely in the functionalist area of development. PRP is seen as one half of the reward and punishment aspect of performance management (Forrester 2011) or carrot and stick (Mather and Seifert 2011).

One of the biggest concerns about PRP in education is its potential divisiveness. Middlewood's (2001, p. 137) research found 'the importance attached by the teachers to a team ethos, a sense of unity and recognition that teachers work most effectively in a strong, mutually supportive framework', all of which would be threatened by schemes to pay some teachers at the expense of others. Bassey (1999, p. 22) draws on comparisons with other public sector employees to point out that 'individual performance related pay is perceived as rarely helping teamwork'. Farrell and Morris (2004, p. 108) found that it 'undermines team ethos,' while Forrester (2011) suggests it induces division among staff and impairs teachers' capacity to organise collectively as teams. This potential dilemma is illustrated in the key question of 'what about the attitude of those who achieve reasonably well, but are *not* rewarded?' Wragg et al. (2004) found in their research into the application of PRP to teachers in England and Wales that there was bitter resentment from those teachers who had not received awards, as well as complaints about bureaucracy and form-filling. Similar findings came from Mather et al.'s (2009) study in the further education sector in England.

One of the biggest arguments in favour of PRP is that its very existence indicates to its employees that the organisation does value performance highly, and the absence of it may show the opposite (Murphy and Cleveland 1995). Furthermore, proponents of PRP, such as Tomlinson (2000), argue that it is a definite *dis*incentive to effective staff in education when they see moderate colleagues who achieve less than themselves receiving the same payment. He sees pay as one of the means of 'positive reinforcement' for effective professionals, and suggests that however collegial an educational organisation is, the differences (i.e. improvements) are ultimately 'made by the individual teacher in the individual classroom' (p. 12). However, other research (for example, Farrell and Morris 2004) found that PRP was seen as having little impact on what was done in the classroom and little effect on motivation or teacher recruitment or retention.

It should be noted, however, that some other forms of incentivisation have also been seen to fail. For example, the introduction of a threshold scheme in teachers' pay in England and Wales followed the same route as a similar scheme in Australia, and, as forecast by Ingvarsson (2001), 95 per cent passed the threshold and the progression quickly became automatic, thus showing no significant reward for the most effective teachers.

In countries where there appears to be a secure and inevitable progression through the years of a career in education, with progression by increment payment, it is unsurprising that critics look to some form of reward to enable differentiation. Looking at the dissatisfaction of teachers in Hong Kong with the rigidity in the system blocking paths to promotion, Wong and Wong (2005, p. 444) specifically recommend 'a more diversified reward system such as introducing some forms of pay-for-performance system . . .' It seems likely that the issue of PRP in education will continue to remain debatable in the future.

Managing performance at individual site level

Schemes often fail because either they are:

- imposed in a top-down way with little ownership by the staff affected, or
- transferred from one setting to another where there may be significant differences in approaches and cultures.

The positive aspect of all this is that there is considerable scope for leaders and managers at individual school or college level to develop schemes which are customised to the specific organisation. Knowledge and understanding of the staff, what motivates them, and the organisation's own vision and goals, give leaders and managers opportunities for this. Although good organisation of any scheme is essential, the emphasis for leaders and managers is also on the broader context of commitment and development within which the performance occurs. Without these, any scheme, however well organised and intentioned, can become a ritualistic version to satisfy national requirements, or a kind of tokenistic rating of performance, such as found in Egyptian schools (Humphreys and Oxtoby 1995) or as described by Middlewood (2001b) in Greece.

Features of performance management schemes

Whatever the scheme, leaders and managers need to address particular issues and manage them in the way most appropriate to their school or college. Moreland (2011, p. 23) suggests that by focusing on the learning experience, we can be reminded constantly that performance management will be about improving education, not browbeating teachers. Leaders and managers need to consider therefore:

- what data should be collected
- from what sources it should be collected
- how it should be collected.

What data should be collected?

The crucial point here is that the information collected should be both quantitative and qualitative. As performance management in education followed that in business and industry, it was ironic to find since the 1990s a huge emphasis on assessing educational employee performance on quantitative data (primarily test and examination results) at a time when what Eccles (1995) describes as a 'revolution' had taken place in industry, i.e. the realisation of the prime importance of qualitative data in a 'new philosophy of performance measurement' (p. 14). The increasing and more sophisticated use of ICT makes compiling the data easier, especially quantitative data, but it also increases the risk of simply collecting too much data, adding complication to any scheme.

To decrease the emphasis on test results and scores, data representing feedback from stakeholders on the teachers' or lecturers' performance is valuable. Such data are

> more sensitive to the complexities of connecting . . . processes
> causally to outcomes. These would include elements of self,
> peer, student and parent evaluation, in addition to support from
> external agencies . . . These indicators of effectiveness become
> things to be empirically verified, refined and discovered in
> particular contexts of practice. (Elliott 2001, p. 208)

From what sources should data be collected?

Feedback from students and parents seem, eventually, to be certain to become an essential source of data, in addition to colleagues, line managers and others so often seen as the automatic assessors of performance. Advocates of what is known as '360 degree feedback' support this notion of an increasing range of relevant sources. Tomlinson (2000, p. 94) describes it as a way of genuinely evaluating individual performance and supporting development, and points to the time needed between collection and action required, reducing the pressure for hasty action and allowing reflection.

However, the leaders' and managers' knowledge of the sources, and their relationships to and within the community of the institution, is crucial if trust is to be developed and maintained. In South Africa, the involvement of the people from local villages in the committees for new arrangements for performance appraisal, although laudable in its democratic intentions, led to women feeling threatened and dis-empowered by the male dominance in those communities (Sebakwane-Mahlare 1994), thereby undoing the positive professional benefits that the women may have felt through being in educational employment at all. In New Zealand, minority ethnic men and women are questioning the male white dominance of the system, according to Foskett and Lumby (2003, p. 81). Leaders and managers need to consider how those who are to supply evidence are chosen, whether these have been agreed with the employee, or whom to negotiate with if there is disagreement over this.

How should data be collected?

Since teacher appraisal, lesson observations are now well established as a contribution to assessing performance, although this is by no means true in all countries. In 2012, in England and Wales, there was disagreement between the Secretary of State and the three main teachers' unions about the Secretary of State's proposals for the observation protocol in the light of the number of actual observations. Clearly, documentation exists in terms of reports and ratings also. A contrasting approach operates in some parts of India where teachers need to keep diaries in which they record their achievements as well as occasions when they fall short of targets (Rajpu and Walia 1998).

For leaders and managers in each individual school or college, the issue is again one of sensitivity, it being necessary to agree not only the source but also the suitability of the method of collection for its intended purpose. For example, a questionnaire to parents (which needs to be constructed carefully anyway) may only elicit responses from those who are enthusiastic about the employee, or indeed hostile, and these responses are likely to be based on limited experience.

Discussion between manager and employee

At the heart of any performance management process lies the discussion (variously called 'interview', 'dialogue', 'review meeting') between members of staff and the manager responsible for their performance. This part of the process has been seen as valuable even when other parts have been discredited and Moreland (2009) reports that these were highly valued, even where negativity existed about many aspects of performance management, often providing the main opportunity for some members of staff to sit down and review their development with a senior colleague. It is here that the reports from whatever sources are reviewed, importantly including self-appraisal, and agreement about further goals and opportunities are negotiated. Some form of report of what has been agreed is also necessary and the balance between a degree of confidentiality and openness needs to be struck. The confidentiality of information about an employee revealed at the discussion must be respected but this has to be balanced with the need to have an overview of the employee's performance and future, so that it can be seen as allied to the organisation's vision and goals.

Dealing with underperformance

This remains one of the most difficult and least pleasant areas of performance management for leaders and managers. Too often, the rhetoric is concerned with very poor or unsatisfactory teachers or lecturers and focuses on the difficulty of getting rid of them. Politicians have found this is a fruitful area for headlines perhaps but much more difficult to legislate for. For example, in England, a licensee scheme was proposed in 2009, so that every five years teachers would need their licence to teach renewed – or not! However, the proposal was seen as both costly and hugely bureaucratic and was indefinitely postponed. In 2012, the Secretary of State for Education expressed concern about the difficulty of removing poorly performing teachers. The new preferred model in appraisal and capability for England suggests a timescale as short as four weeks for a teacher to demonstrate improvement and avoid procedures leading to dismissal. Previously, capability issues had been seen as separate from assessment/appraisal processes.

However, this focus on the incompetent should not distract from the need for leaders and managers to deal with those who are underperforming. As in all aspects of performance, the need is to identify precise criteria by which a person can be judged to be failing. The two words most widely used in various countries are 'incapability' and/or 'incompetence' and clear evidence against any criteria is essential. Poor time-keeping, failure to keep records and failure to mark students' work are examples of the tasks which are the easiest to note, whereas, for example, regular poor attendance by learners at a teacher's or lecturer's class could be attributable to a variety of factors. Foreman (1997, pp. 210–212) usefully summarised for leaders and managers the reasons for underperformance into three broad categories:

- shortcomings of the manager

- outside influences (both job related and non-job related)

- shortcomings of the teacher/lecturer.

Only when the first two have been carefully examined, should the leader focus on the third, when the first questions are:

- 'Can this person improve with appropriate support?'

- 'What is the appropriate support in this case?'

When the support has proved ineffective after an appropriate time, then the relevant disciplinary procedures may need to be initiated.

Issues facing leaders and managers in managing performance

There is a potential tension for leaders between ensuring staff have the opportunity to improve their skills for the benefit of pupils or students and the need to avoid processes that are too mechanistic processes when encouraging development of the people they lead and manage. At the same time as encouraging a more creative approach to teaching and learning, the intense focus on measurable outcomes (especially in terms of test and exam results) forces leaders to ensure the school or college as a whole *is seen* to be performing well. Part of the leader's task is to develop an appropriate culture (see Chapter 4) with a clear focus on learning (see Chapter 13).

Principles for developing effective managing of performance

Considering all the above, if it is possible to suggest some key principles which leaders and managers may need to place at the heart of their managing of performance, perhaps the criteria for an ideal effective process at national level would include that it:

- accepts that it takes different forms in different contexts

- allows specific institutions – or types of institution – to develop schemes appropriate to them

- includes a significant amount of self-evaluation

- includes a significant amount of qualitative as well as quantitative data

- is flexible enough to adapt to changing circumstances (adapted from Middlewood and Parker 2009).

While this is challenging, there are those who argue that 'there is some evidence that richer – and more extended – forms of accountability might be achievable' (Bottery 2004, p. 93). As he suggests, it will be the mark of a confident society when 'it is capable of knowing when to trust and when to demand an audited account' (ibid.).

The principles for leaders and managers at school or college level could include:

- Customise any national guidelines to fit the specific school or college.

- Consider the use of 360 degree feedback. Leaders and managers would be well advised to begin this process with their own performance, as is happening in England and Wales, New Zealand and some states of Australia.

- Consider the idea of assessing performance of teams rather than the relentless focus on individuals. Individual action plans can be developed within this process. In researching evaluation and accountability in extended or community schools and centres, Middlewood and Parker (2009) found examples of such practice. They describe one team (ibid., pp. 80–81) where members included teachers, support assistants and care staff. All team members received feedback from all the others. Following both self-assessment and qualitative data analysis, both team and individual targets were set and opportunity still existed for confidential discussions if needed. Such processes seem appropriate for a collegial context such as a school or college.

Conclusion

The performance of staff in educational organisations will continue to be of the utmost importance and therefore for leaders and managers the task of ensuring the best possible performance from everyone will remain crucial. The development of an ethos of trust could be a critical factor and the values embodied in this will need to exist in all related processes, including the way in which performance is assessed. This assessment will of course include dealing with unsatisfactory performers as well as highly successful ones. Above all, the management of performance is very unlikely to be effective if treated as an 'add-on' but rather needs to be central to overall leadership and management at institutional level. Given that this is an area under considerable scrutiny by all those involved as well as by external stakeholders, it clearly represents one of the biggest challenges to leaders and managers, both now and in the future.

References

Arrowsmith, R. (2001) 'A right performance', in Gleeson, D. and Husbands, C. (eds), *The Performing School*, London, RoutledgeFalmer.

Ball, S. (2003) 'The teacher's soul and the terrors of performativity', *Journal of Education Policy*, 18 (2), 215–228.

Bassey, M. (1999) 'Performance related pay for teachers: research is needed', *Professional Development Today*, 2 (3), 15–28.

Bottery, M. (2004) *The Challenges of Educational Leadership*, London, Paul Chapman Publishing.

Bush, T., Coleman, M. and Ziaohong, S. (1998) 'Managing secondary schools in China', *Compare*, 28 (2), 83–195.

Child, J. (1994) *Management in China during the Age of Reform*, Cambridge, Cambridge University Press.

Diocese of Sheffield (2000) *Model Policy for Performance Management for Roman Catholic Schools in Hallam and Church of England Schools in Diocese of Sheffield*, Sheffield, Sheffield Hallam Pastoral Centre.

Eccles, R. (1995) 'The performance measurement manifesto', in Holloway, J., Lewis, J. and Mallory, G. (eds), *Performance Measurement and Evaluation*, Milton Keynes, Open University Press.

Elliott, J. (2001) 'Characteristics of performative cultures', in Gleeson, D. and Husbands, G. (eds), *The Performing School*, London, RoutledgeFalmer.

Evans, L. (2001) 'Developing teachers in a performing culture. Is PRP the answer?', in Gleeson, D. and Husbands, C. (eds), *The Performing School*, London, RoutledgeFalmer.

Farrell, C. and Morris, J. (2004) 'Teacher attitudes towards performance-related pay in schools', *Educational Management Administration and Leadership*, 32 (1), 81–104.

Fitzgerald, T., Yangs, H. and Grootenbauer, P. (2003) 'Bureaucratic control or professional autonomy: performance management in New Zealand schools', *School Leadership and Management*, 2 (1), 74–80.

Foreman, K. (1997) 'Managing Performance', in Bush, T. and Middlewood, D. (eds), *Managing People in Education*, London, Paul Chapman Publishing.

Forrester, G. (2011) 'Performance management in education: milestone or millstone?', *Management in Education*, 25 (1), pp. 5–9.

Foskett, N. and Lumby, J. (2003) *Leading and Managing Education: International Dimensions*, London, Paul Chapman Publishing.

Furukawa, H. (1989) 'Motivation to work', in Riches, C. and Morgan, C. (eds), *Human Resource Management in Education*, Milton Keynes, Open University Press.

Gaziel, H. (2008) 'Principals' Performance Assessment: Empirical Evidence from an Israeli Case Study,' *Educational Management Administration and Leadership*, 36 (2), pp. 337–382.

Gleeson, D. and Gunter, H. (2001) 'The performing school and the modernisation of teachers', in Gleeson, D. and Husbands, C. (eds), *The Performing School*, London, RoutledgeFalmer.

Hampden-Turner, C. and Trompenaars, F. (1997) *Mastering the Infinite Game: How East Asian Values Are Transforming Business Practices*, Oxford, Capstone.

Hampden-Turner, C. and Trompenaars, F. (2003) 'A mirror-image of the world: doing business in Asia', in Warren, C. and Jaynt, E. (eds), *Doing Business With New Markets*, London, Nicholas Brealey.

Humphreys, M. and Oxtoby, R. (1995) 'Improving technical education in Egypt: management development, international assistance and cultural values', *The Vocational Aspect of Education*, 47 (3), 274–287.

Ingvarsson, L. (2001) 'Developing standards and assessments for the teaching profession', in Middlewood, D. and Cardno, C. (eds), *Managing Teacher Appraisal and Performance*, London, Routledge.

Jantjes, E. (1996) 'Performance based teacher appraisal: from judgement to development', *South African Journal in Education*, 16 (1), 50–57.

Jennings, K. and Lomas, L. (2003) 'Implementing performance management for headteachers in English secondary schools: a case study', *Educational Management Administration and Leadership*, 31 (4), 369–383.

Leithwood, K. and Riehl, C. (2005) 'What do we already know about educational leadership?', in Firestone, W. and Riehl, C. (eds), *A new agenda for research in educational leadership*, New York, Teachers College Press.

Mahoney, P. and Hextall, I. (2001) 'Performing and conforming', in Gleeson, D. and Husbands, C. (eds), *The Performing School*, London RoutledgeFalmer.

Mather, K. and Seifert, R. (2011) 'Teacher, Lecturer or Labourer', *Management in Education*, 25 (1), 26–31.

Mather, K., Worsall, I. and Seifert, R. (2009) 'The changing focus of workplace control in the English FE sector', *Employee Relations*, 31 (2), 139–157.

Middlewood, D. (2001a) 'Appraisal and performance in the UK', in Middlewood, D. and Cardno, C. (eds), *Managing Teacher Appraisal and Performance: A Comparative Approach*, London, RoutledgeFalmer.

Middlewood, D. (2001b) 'The future of teacher appraisal and its management' in Middlewood, D. and Cardno, C. (eds), *Managing Teacher Appraisal and Performance: A Comparative Approach*, London, RoutledgeFalmer.

Middlewood, D. (2002) 'Managing appraisal and performance,' in Bush, T. and Bell, L. (eds), *The Principles of Educational Management*, London, Sage.

Middlewood, D. and Parker, R. (2009) *Leading and Managing Extended Schools*, London, Sage.

Middlewood, D., Parker, R. and Beere, J. (2005) *Creating a Learning School*, London, Paul Chapman.

Mokgalene, E., Carrim, N., Gardiner, M. and Chisholm, L. (1997) 'National Teacher Appraisal Pilot Project Report', Johannesburg, University of Witterand.

Moreland, J. (2009) 'Investigating Secondary School Leaders', *Educational Management Administration and Leadership*, 37 (6), 735–765.

Moreland, J. (2011) 'Managing Performance for Effective Classrooms', *Management in Education*, 25 (1), 21–25.

Murlis, H. (1992) 'Performance related pay in the context of performance management', in Tomlinson, H. (ed.), *Performance-Related Pay in Education*, London, Routledge.

Murphy, K. and Cleveland, J. (1995) *Understanding Performance Appraisal*, London, Sage Publications.

Nolan, A. (1996) *Spending Public Money: Governance and Audit Issues*, London, HMSO.

O'Neill, O. (2006) Speech at Launch of Cambridge Assessment Network, Cambridge.

Ozga, J. (1995) 'Deskilling as a profession: professionalism, deprofessionalism and the new managerialism', in Busher, H. and Saran, R. (eds), *Managing Teachers as Professionals in Schools*, London, Kogan Page.

Piggot-Irvine, E. (2010) 'One school's approach to overcoming resistance and improving appraisal: organisational learning in action', *Educational Management, Administration and Leadership*, 38 (2), 224–245.

Preedy, M. (2001) 'Evaluation: measuring what we value', in Middlewood, D. and Burton, N. (eds), *Managing the Curriculum*, London, Paul Chapman Publishing.

Rajpu, J. and Walia, K. (1998) 'Assessing teacher effectiveness in India: overview and critical appraisal', *Prospects*, 28 (1), 137–150.

Robertson, M. (2001) 'Performance management and performance objectives in church schools', *Education Today*, 51 (1), 41–44.

Sebakwane-Mahlare, S. (1994) 'Women teachers and community control in Lebowa secondary schools', *Multicultural Teaching*, 12 (3), 31–41.

Senge, P. (1993) *The Fifth Discipline*, London, Century Business.

Shah, S. (1998) 'Gender perspectives on principalship in Pakistan', unpublished PhD thesis, University of Nottingham.

Siegrist, J. (1996) 'Adverse health effect of high effort/low-reward conditions', *Journal of Occupational Health Psychology*, 1, 27–47.

Sikes, P. (2001) 'Teachers' lives and teaching performance', in Gleeson, D. and Husbands, C. (eds), *The Performing School*, London, RoutledgeFalmer.

Smyth, J. and Shacklock, G. (1998) *Re-making Teaching: Ideology, Policy and Practice*, London, Routledge.

Stoll, L., Fink, D. and Earl, L. (2003) *It's About Learning (and it's About Time)*, London, RoutledgeFalmer.

Thrupp, M. (1999) *Schools making a difference: let's be realistic!*, Buckingham, Open University Press.

Thurlow, M. with Ramnarain, S. (2001) 'Transforming educator appraisal in South Africa', in Middlewood, D. and Cardno, C. (eds), *Managing Teacher Appraisal and Performance: A comparative approach*, London, RoutledgeFalmer.

Tomlinson, H. (2000) '360 Degree feedback – how does it work?', *Professional Development Today*, 5 (2), 93–98.

Townley, B. (1989) 'Selection and appraisal: reconsidering social relations', in Storey, J. (ed.), *New Perspectives on Human Resource Management*, London, Routledge.

Washington, K. (1991) 'School administration in China: a look at the principal's role', *International Journal of Educational Management*, 5, 4–5.

Wong, P. and Wong, C. (2005) 'Promotion criteria and satisfaction of school teachers in Hong Kong', *Educational Management Administration and Leadership*, 33 (4), 423–447.

Wragg, E., Haynes, G., Wragg, C. and Chamberlain, R. (2004) *Performance Pay for Teachers*, London, Routledge.

13

Organisational learning and professional development

Introduction

This chapter examines the way in which professional development within a school or college is more likely to be effective when it takes place within the context of an institution which in itself is a 'learning organisation'. The development and learning of the people and the organisation, ideally, become inextricably integrated. It is argued that this commitment to continuous learning is fundamental to the school or college achieving its aims through a shared vision or mission. In this chapter, the features and requirements of a learning school or college are explored, and the various types of, and contexts for, professional learning and development are examined. The crucial role of leaders and managers in developing such schools and colleges through collaborative learning so that professional learning communities can emerge is emphasised.

A focus on learning

Educational organisations, whether they be nurseries, kindergartens, schools, colleges or universities, exist to facilitate learning in one form or another. The people who are employed to work in them have learning as their key purpose, however removed some of their daily tasks may seem to be from this. The people who clean and maintain buildings, playgrounds or fields, and those who prepare and serve meals, do this so that the pupils or students can learn effectively in the best possible environment, and in the best possible condition. *In the same way*, the clerical staff's ultimate focus in dealing with paperwork is for the same purpose – the systems they administer have the same function. As we noted in Chapter 3, it is crucial that *all* these staff understand this fundamental principle and that they all have the opportunity to develop themselves in their particular roles and therefore become continuous learners.

The staff for whom this is most obviously and visibly true are the teachers and lecturers, although increasingly, as also noted in Chapter 3, numbers of support staff work directly with pupils or students in facilitating their learning. Much educational literature and research substantiate the view that the most effective teachers are those who themselves are good learners, and who continue to learn (Blandford 2000; Stoll et al. 2003; Earley and Bubb 2004; Middlewood et al. 2005). Therefore, a school or college which is able to encourage its teachers, support staff and, ideally, all its employees to share a commitment to their own learning and development, should be the one that is most effective in facilitating pupil or student learning. This is an apparently simple premise, but its simplicity disguises a number of issues which are likely to affect the realisation of such a learning organisation.

In many developing countries, where resources are scarce, the focus in staff development remains firmly on more conventional training and development of teachers. In the study by Dalin (1994) of educational improvement projects in Ethiopia, Bangladesh and Colombia, high priorities included reducing the large number of unqualified and untrained teachers in schools through training and staff development which focused on basic classroom skills, writing and updating schemes of work for pupils and making resources for their pupils' use. As both Coleman (2003) and Middlewood (2003) point out in research on South African schools, the struggle to put in place an appropriate culture of learning and teaching depends first and foremost on establishing the idea that learning is important. In those contexts, it is easy to understand that a leader's first priority may be to get attendance and punctuality (of both teachers and pupils) to a reasonable standard (Chisholm and Vally 1996).

In developed countries, where scarcity of resources is less of an issue, assumptions cannot be made that teachers are necessarily effective learners. Since the 1990s, the emphasis in many of these countries on quantitative outcomes, more tests and examinations, and assessment of performance in such terms has narrowed the focus in schools and colleges towards achievement of set targets rather than the 'double-loop' learning which is a form of questioning and reconsidering the actual aims of the learning itself (Cardno 2012). However, it is suggested that a focus on organisational learning through the development of all those who work in a school or college may well be the most effective way to raise pupil or student performance, as well as laying the foundations for lifelong learning.

In research on Extended Schools in England, where reciprocal learning links with local communities involving a wide range of stakeholders were developed (Middlewood and Parker 2009) and in the evaluation of Cummings et al. (2007), it was found that the performance of those schools involved had risen and that the achievement gap between advantaged and disadvantaged pupils had narrowed. Such Extended Schools, as with Community Schools in the USA (Dryfoos et al. 2005) and in Scotland (Sammons et al. 2003), challenged most assumptions about conventional schooling and the way in which external stakeholders influenced learning.

Features of a learning school or college

The concept of a 'learning organisation' originated in the business world: Revans (1982) proposes the equation that the rate of learning in an organisation must be equal to, or greater than, the rate of change. As educational organisations also became aware of the need for constant change, and that relying on current principles and processes would lead to stagnation, so the importance of committing all those in the school or college to continuous learning and development has necessarily become for many of them the key to continuing success.

Essentially, the main features of such schools or colleges are that they:

- focus their energies and activities on learning, recognising that learning may come in many different forms as appropriate to a wide range of learners

- establish and develop an ethos and ethic of enquiry

- recognise that learning can come from many sources – not just from formal teaching; external networks and stakeholders such as parents also contribute to learning

- accept that learning is a lifelong process and that the organisation's role is in making a contribution to this process

- are in a continuous transformational state.

As this list suggests, such schools or colleges will not be quiet and peaceful places in which to work! Since the organisation advances by constant challenging of assumptions and behaviour, there is a continuous quest for 'new and better ways of doing business' (Holyoke et al. 2012, p. 437)

A learning organisation may be seen more realistically by leaders and managers as an aspiration; working towards which will help a school or college achieve the outcomes that it desires for all its people. For this to happen, the organisation clearly needs to have a common sense of purpose. In research on school innovation, McCharen et al. (2011, p. 689) found that this 'sense of shared purpose is a noticeable aspect of a learning organisation' and that this commonality had its basis in 'shared commitment to values, such as the integrity of teaching or the need for social justice'. This sense of shared purpose is what drives the school or college forward, enabling it to continuously develop and adapt to changing circumstances, secure in its ability to use the learning of its people.

The process of learning itself takes various forms; ideally, a learning school or college will be facilitating:

- learning as a means to an end

- learning as a process, learning how to learn

- learning which provides knowledge which is worth pursuing for its own sake.

Learning as a means to an end is learning that is perceived by the learner as being worthwhile, because it leads to something specific and tangible. Often this will mean acquiring a skill which enables the learner to perform a new task, or, most commonly in formal education, a qualification or certification which leads to better employment prospects and thereby a better standard of living. This, inevitably, is a view of learning taken by many people in many developing countries where educational attainment is seen as the 'passport' to economic success, for example in South Africa to build youths' self-confidence, teach them basic skills and prepare them for employment (Jansen and Middlewood 2003). This is not restricted to such contexts, however. Sugimine (1998, p. 121) describes the desperate competition in Japan to get children into the right streams so that 'schools have become fact-grinding and knowledge based institutions even at elementary level', all to try to ensure entry to schools and colleges which would 'guarantee' success in the 'prosperity stakes'. In some European countries, such as Greece (Middlewood 2001), extra classes are seen as essential for children to pass examinations for the same reason. In England and Wales since the 1990s, great concern has been expressed about the emphasis placed on learning merely to gain certification at the expense of creativity and deeper thinking (Ball 2003; Strain 2007).

A perception of learning as a process, a journey rather than a destination (Middlewood et al. 2005), enables learners to take from formal education into life beyond an understanding of themselves as a learner which they can apply effectively in future contexts. Learning to gain knowledge for its own sake embraces the intellectual curiosity which is enjoyed by those who learn a particular topic and are fascinated and feel enriched by what they learn in, say, history or science. Those who suggest that effective teachers are passionate about *what* they teach (the subject) would see this kind of learning as an essential component in the learning school or college.

All these kinds of learning need to exist because all are essential to the development of people as a whole, although the emphasis on one kind at the expense of another will inevitably occur over time and according to place or national policies. Similarly, it is suggested that there are different levels of learning (such as 'shallow' or 'deep'), so learning at each of these levels will exist in the organisation, because they all exist as part of everyday life and learning. However, a school or college which focuses on one type of learning at the expense of another will not be a true learning organisation because it will be insufficiently adaptable for meeting new circumstances. Overemphasis on 'shallow' learning will encourage it to be tempted by 'quick-fix' or short-term solutions, whereas only 'deep' learning can really provide the knowledge that will enable meaningful change to occur. As Bush and Glover (2003, p. 17) explain:

> Deep learning is centred on the creation of personal understanding through reflection (individual and shared) which results in the creation of knowledge, which can then be transformed into action.

The range of types and levels of learning fits well with the developing notions of multiple intelligences (Gardner 1983), the understanding of the importance of emotional intelligence (Golman 1996) and awareness of the huge number of factors which affect individuals' capacity to learn (Middlewood and Parker 2009). *However*, it is the overall or collective capacities that an organisation has which makes it a learning school or college. These capacities are those of the learners within the school or college and will depend upon how they are enabled and encouraged to learn and develop.

Staff professional development

Any organisation where the staff are neglected as adult learners will reduce its potential to be effective for those who attend it. The words 'training and development' are the most commonly used ones in the context of staff learning but learning by training has the connotations 'of highly specific, content-driven and targeted programmes geared to knowledge acquisition and information-giving' (Law and Glover 2000, p. 247). As such, it relates very much to a functionalist view of education, one which sees it essentially as a means to an end.

The word 'development', on the other hand, implies concern for the staff *as people* in their learning, either professional or personal or both. 'Professional' originally implied certain qualities inherent in the occupation (especially a degree of autonomy). As such, professional learning and development implies that employees will have a degree of ownership in determining what training is needed for them to improve. In that context, it is closely linked with personal development, because the engagement of the feelings, attitudes and motivation of the individual are seen as essential if they are to improve. Several writers on teacher development, such as Day (1999) and Ribbins (2008), argue that development relates to individual history as well as present circumstance, that the work that educational staff do 'is bound up with their lives, their histories, the kind of person they have been, and have become' (Day 1999, p. 124).

However, even in an apparently successful school or college, many 'staff and administrators are often isolated and view themselves more as independent contributors rather than an integral part of a larger organisation' (Freed 2001, p. 18). It is when staff collectively demonstrate a commitment to longer-term, 'deep' development rather than a 'surface or quick-fix short-term training approach' (Piggot-Irvine 2010, p. 242) that significant learning and change is likely to occur.

Effectiveness in professional development

For leaders and managers to enable staff professional development to be effective, they need to be aware of several factors.

Recognising what is involved in effective adult learning

Although it would be an error to classify all adults of a certain chronological age as adults in terms of their learning capacity, the following may be seen as generally true:

- Adults' own experiences are a rich resource for learning.

- Adults tend to be specific in their learning needs, according to what is seen as relevant to their requirements.

- Adults may feel anxiety about a perceived attack on their competence.

- Adults tend to be self-directing as they develop (based on Brookfield 2005; Knowles 1980).

However, Brookfield (2005) suggests that the use of the word 'mature' is more appropriate for those learners who become more self-directing as they develop, and that this is a more complicated notion than 'the imparting of skills and knowledge to individuals who have attained a certain chronological age' (ibid., p. 93).

Furthermore, adult learning, which has been described by Merriam (2001) as an 'ever changing mosaic', is constantly being re-explored and the recognition of informal and incidental learning is now widely acknowledged. Beatty (2008, p. 146) suggests that 'our understandings of adult learning and development are particularly relevant to leadership preparation and development'. Thus, it can be argued that no effective professional development can be carried out unless careful consideration has been given to the way in which it is both presented and likely to be accepted. For those working in education such as teachers and lecturers, the need to access the deeper purposes in new practices, the theory underpinning a new process, may be important. Those in education generally constitute a well-qualified and intelligent workforce who are able to 'work through the lenses of social, economic and political identities' (Beatty 2008, p. 153). While some teachers in England and Wales came to see CPD as about conforming to governmental regulations (Neil and Morgan 2003) and in Scotland as about accountability and performance (Purdon 2004), there needs to be a recognition that educational staff should have the opportunity to challenge and reflect when developing the practices they believe to be feasible and in the best interest of their learners.

Ensuring relevance to the institutional context

Each school or college has its own specific context, both in place and in time. Just as national contexts differ widely, from those where attendance at school is the main concern to those with an overzealous focus on test results, so do contexts within many countries. The urban, inner-city, rural and suburban contexts all have their special features and these may be reflected in the specific workforce that the institution has. It may be, for example, very stable or highly mobile, have a focus on very young staff or a majority of very experienced members of staff. For the CPD to be effective, it has to pay attention to the needs of that specific context and workforce. While key principles will remain the same, and the role of the leader will also be the same (as discussed later), it should be remembered that whereas all staff members are individuals and engaged in personal learning, what they have in common is the same group of pupils or students. Research (Svinicki 1996; Thrupp 1999) has shown that different kinds of teaching styles can be equally effective for different groups of learners, so that being aware of the contextual needs can be crucial.

The contextualisation of staff learning may also need to take account of the very specialised roles that members of staff have. Whether the role be teacher, lecturer, head of subject department, librarian, teaching assistant, clerical officer, etc., some of the learning may need to give the role holder greater insight into those skills and knowledge specific to the role. Thus, Balshaw and Farrell (2002), in describing the training necessary for assistants supporting children with severe learning difficulties, refer to the uniqueness of the role and how important it is in training to differentiate it from the teacher's or care worker's, however closely they need to work as a team. Similarly, Best (2000), in a large-scale survey of deputy headteachers' perceptions of their training, found that a substantial majority most valued the training aimed specifically at deputy headship, compared with more generic training about leadership and management.

One of the significant points of ensuring that role-focused learning exists as part of overall staff learning is that it contributes to the value which the role holder perceives as being placed on the work done. So Burton's (1994) study of the role of the reprographics supervisor, and Foreman-Peck and Middlewood's (2002) interviews with teaching assistants, all showed that these people felt training in their role had raised their esteem in the eyes of others. This in itself no doubt contributed to the subsequent value placed on the training by these employees.

Recognising how professional development occurs

The different means by which the learning of members of staff can occur can be divided into four broad categories, as shown in Figure 13.1.

- Studying and analysing one's work includes reflecting in both single-loop and double-loop terms upon one's own practice, and

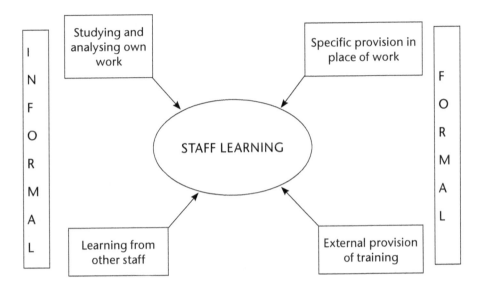

Figure 13.1 Different means by which staff learn

perhaps sometimes undertaking a systematic analysis of a process undertaken, as advocated by Brighouse (1991) who speculates why this microanalysis is so little used in education compared with training in medicine, sports or the arts.

- Learning from other staff includes all everyday opportunities to talk with other colleagues, both more and less experienced than oneself. It also includes informal observations both in one's own school or college and when visiting, for whatever reason, other organisations.

- Specific provision will be all the processes and structures provided by the school or college, ranging from being mentored, appraised or formally observed to being given the opportunity to participate in decision-making or understudying a particular post for a period. This is in addition to seminars, workshops, conferences or structured visits which may be provided.

- External provision. Despite the emphasis on site-based provision in some countries, it is still important for staff to meet and discuss with staff from other schools or colleges, so that an insular attitude is avoided and the widest possible pool of ideas is accessed.

The role of leaders and managers

If leaders and managers wish to enable staff learning to flourish, and the organisation to develop as a learning community, the evidence suggests that the following can contribute significantly to the huge importance of leaders in this.

Being role models as learners

This should be on at least two levels. First, leaders and managers need to be personally committed to their own individual learning. If they are to lead their schools and colleges into future and unknown environments, they need the continuous development of themselves as people who are constantly reassessing their own behaviour, emotions and reasoning in the light of new experiences, both their own and others'. Lifelong learning should be a reality for them personally.

This begins with self-awareness, because 'leaders who know themselves are far more likely to be able to get to know others in a non-defensive, non-aggressive way' (Beatty 2008, p. 150). As change develops in the organisation and the community, the self-aware leader also becomes aware of what is happening within themselves and this enables them to 'capture the energy of people' (Slater 2008, p. 67). Much of this is arguing for emotionally intelligent leaders who are self-motivating and empathetic (Lambert 2003).

Secondly, leaders and managers display their own learning role by encouraging behaviours in the organisation which demonstrate learning and discourage non-learning (Honey 1993). This encouragement and discouragement needs to be explicit and overt so that people understand that this is how they and their organisation learn and develop. A simple example is of the person who brings a problem to the leader or manager. Learning behaviour here is in the response: 'What are you proposing to do about this?' or 'What are the options for dealing with this?' The non-learning response is 'Okay, I'll deal with it for you'.

Having awareness and analysis of the specific

As discussed earlier, the CPD needs to be seen as relevant to the organisation's specific context. For this to happen, leaders need to be able to 'analyse that context comprehensively and respond knowledgeably to the local context' (Zhang and Brundrett (2011, p. 157). Draper and McMichael (2000) note that there was a need to become integrated with the specific organisational context so that leaders could assess the attitudes and skills of colleagues, gain their support and thereby plan the changes needed. This relating of learning to the local context is true for staff at all levels and with many support staff located in the locality as community members, the need for the leadership of learning to be fitted within this context is important (Zhang and Brundrett 2011; Emira 2011).

Recognising the importance of all staff as individual learners

The potential for each person employed at the school or college to develop as a learner needs to be recognised through:

- ensuring that every single person, regardless of role, has some opportunities for personal professional development. This may involve extensive use of needs identification, mentoring, 'buddying', in-house networking, and of course appropriate use and allocation of finance and resources where necessary.

- differentiating between the developmental needs of people according to, for example, age, experience, stage of career progression, as well as capability and ambition. Since the 'first step of every learning experience is to understand where you are now' (Middlewood et al. 2005, p. 64), everyone needs to be helped in reflecting on their current stage to enable them to go forward.

Being aware of the different learning styles of people

There are a number of different models of learning that enable people to discover the most effective mode of learning for themselves. Regardless of which models are used, leaders need to give staff the opportunities to find out which style of learning is most appropriate to them, using diagnostic tools such as the visual, auditory, kinaesthetic (VAK)/emotional quotient (EQ) 'test', an analysis, a brain hemisphere diagnosis or a neuro-linguistic programming (NLP) analysis.

Actively encouraging learning by all staff

It is not sufficient for leaders to recognise the importance of learning and to be certain that every individual is capable of it, but they will also need to take positive action to encourage people to take steps – especially first steps – to do something about it! As noted earlier, some adults lack confidence in their ability to learn new skills or knowledge and some fear failure in a new venture. This might be especially true of some support staff, but there is ample evidence to show that support staff in particular roles have made a huge contribution to their organisations through their own learning, whether special needs assistant (Middlewood et al. 1998), school caretaker (Middlewood et al. 2005), office staff (Middlewood and Parker 2009) or TAs (Emira 2011; Attwood and Bland 2012). Leaders of learning schools or colleges will probably also want to explore ways in which teachers or lecturers who are temporary or come in to substitute for absent staff are given opportunities for new learning. As we noted in Chapter 10, effective CPD is an important element in retaining quality staff.

In many countries, schools often have to take on a new national initiative which involves the learning of new skills. Information technology developments have obviously been key examples of this across most developed and several developing countries. The imparting of particular skills is important 'training', but the leader of a learning organisation will perhaps strive to look beyond this training to analyse whether the new initiative offers new challenges which require double-loop as opposed to single-loop thinking (Argyris and Schön 1974). For example, the use of a new piece of technology in classrooms may not just mean learning how to use a new piece of equipment. As Woollard (2012, p. 47) explains, for teachers whose skills and experiences have developed over years, 'in virtual world teaching, there are new dexterities to be learned and traditional dexterities to be re-learned'.

Building an emphasis on learning into all leadership and management processes

The final section of this book has dealt with various processes which leaders and managers need to handle effectively – recruitment, selection, induction, performance management, etc. The 'learning' school or college will stress the importance of learning through all these stages. At the recruitment stage, many schools and colleges stress the opportunities provided for staff development (for example by on-site programmes), so they can attract people who are committed to their own learning. At selection interviews, candidates can be asked about what they have learned over a recent period. In appraising performance, an emphasis on the individual's learning (and the pupil's or student's) since the last review can be made overt. Observations of a teacher or teaching assistant at work need to focus on learning. All such practices need to be seen to be organic; a natural and routine part of the way the educational organisation operates. Initially, the encouragement of this may need to be overt as mentioned above, so that in daily leadership and management behaviour people become aware that this is a place of learning.

This learning of course includes learning for leadership and management as well. Leadership development and the various models of leadership are dealt with extensively elsewhere in this volume but it is worth noting that research into effective learning organisations strongly suggests that distributed leadership is seen as prevalent and often a key factor in their effectiveness (Dinham et al. 2008; McCharen et al. 2011). It has been proposed in fact that an indicator of successful learning organisations in the future may be 'the numbers of those inspired to become leaders themselves' (Slater 2008, p. 67).

Encouraging a collaborative approach to learning

In developing a learning community, the sharing of learning is perhaps one of the most important features to be encouraged. This can involve specific plans to enable and encourage shared learning and 'support between at least two teacher colleagues on a sustained basis' (Cordingley et al. 2004, p. 2). Those plans may include ensuring there is sufficient time for collaboration and looking for particular people who are willing to share, preferably enthusiastically (King 2011). In a project in disadvantaged schools in the Republic of Ireland, teachers who had previously collaborated found that their own practices were improved, and their enthusiasm influenced others who had previously been unwilling to be involved. Significantly, this collaboration was not simply some people copying from others, but challenging and adapting processes and practices to meet the needs of their own particular classes. This, according to King (2011, p. 152), showed 'evidence of deep learning which is a prerequisite of sustaining practices,' and was referred to earlier.

The form of leadership needed to encourage collaboration is essentially an enabling one, so that the sharing is primarily voluntary rather than forced or contrived. Such a form empowers people, based on trust, to embark on collaborative CPD which meets both their personal and professional needs.

Developing a culture of enquiry and reflection

The notion of an organisational culture was fully explored in Chapter 4, but it follows from an emphasis on collaboration that the aim for the leader is to develop a set of shared values which focus on learning. Beatty (2008, p. 154) suggests that it is 'learning with others' that enables a community of dynamic enquiry and collaborative reflection to thrive.

A learning school or college will necessarily be constantly questioning and challenging its own practices and processes in order to improve them. For this improvement to be valid, it needs to be based on an authentic enquiry or research. Sometimes, this research can be carried out by a person external to the organisation, but there is in several countries a considerable growth and interest in the organisation carrying out its own investigations. This is done sometimes by the provision of Masters level programmes based in the schools or colleges themselves (Middlewood et al. 1998) or by staff accessing these universities' programmes (Taysum 2010). It is critical that all research carried out in and for the organisation is of a high standard, using professional methodologies. One principal of a college with a high incidence of in-house research wrote that 'by becoming a research-engaged school, it has benefited enormously in that we have established a culture where all those working in the school have the opportunity and the means to question, evaluate and enrich the quality of the service that is being provided' (Parker 2011, p. 83).

Such a culture should include the notion and practice of 'student voice'. If it is really to be all pervading and a true sharing of values, the omission of those people in the organisation who are ultimately the receivers of the impact of staff learning makes no sense. A number of schools and colleges involve students in their in-house research, the majority at secondary and post-compulsory level, but with a growing number of primary schools. The strongest argument for this in terms of developing a learning community is that the students or pupils, when given an opportunity to engage in debates about learning (based on their research) very readily become partners in the process rather than mere recipients. When professional practice is located 'in authentic student voice', it is able to be 'constantly redefined in terms of what it means to be a teacher today' (Kidd 2012, p. 127).

A culture of shared values about learning must also include celebrating success in learning and leaders will find the means of acknowledging and celebrating learning achievement in all kinds of ways. Ultimately, as Holyoke et al. (2012, p. 439) suggest: 'It is the cultural norms that define the effectiveness of the learning', and several of these norms are found in the 'unique nature of education as compared to business and industry' (McCharen et al. 2011, p. 689).

Assessing the effectiveness of staff learning and CPD

The need for leaders and managers to understand whether policies and practice in staff learning are being effective cannot be ignored, and this issue is one that has been found to be complex, precisely because it is about people. Although models for evaluation of the effectiveness of staff development programmes have been proposed (for example, Middlewood 1997), and research carried out into the impact of CPD on groups of staff or course members, it is the long-term impact of staff learning on the school or college that is both crucial and harder to assess. The following are suggested as possible indicators of progress made towards establishing a more effective learning school or college over a period of time:

- Are meetings given over to debate about learning rather than operational issues?
- Are more staff using libraries and resources centres?
- Are more staff offering to lead discussions?
- Are staff acknowledging the role of other agents in the learning role, for example parents?
- Are staff willing to identify and acknowledge mistakes (their own and others') as learning experiences?
- Are the barriers to creativity in learning and teaching being recognised?
- Are the learning capabilities of *all* staff being recognised and acted upon?
- Are different learning styles for staff being recognised in their learning?
- Are all staff having opportunities to formalise their learning achievements, if they wish to do so, and what proportion are doing so?
- Are more staff involved in research projects?
- Are more staff using self-evaluation exercises or reviews?
- Are more staff involved in working collaboratively, especially across subject areas?
- Are more celebrations of learning success occurring?
- Is more in-house research taking place?

Conclusion

In a number of countries, CPD is becoming more and more the responsibility of the autonomous school or college. This can be seen as an opportunity for leaders to try to develop the learning organisation as a reality. However, progress towards becoming a learning school or college is likely to be uneven and even turbulent. Disagreements are fundamental to a culture of critical reflection and debate, and changes of staff at all levels will inevitably occur. Hopkins et al. (1994) stress the importance of 'living with ambiguity' for staff as they progress in their own development and that of the organisation. What is certain is that staff learning 'cannot be an optional luxury' (Hargreaves 1997, p. 101). It has to be made integral to the organisation's way of facing new challenges in a complex, rapidly changing world. Only a learning organisation can face those challenges with real confidence.

References

Argyris, C. and Schön, D. (1974) *Theory in Practice: Increasing professional effectiveness*, San Francisco, Jossey-Bass.

Attwood, T. and Bland, K. (2012) 'Deployment and impact of higher level teaching assistants: how do small-scale studies fit into the bigger picture?', *Management in Education*, 26 (2), 82–88.

Ball, S. (2003) 'Performance and fabrication in the educational economy: towards the performative society,' in Gleeson, D. and Husbands, G. (eds), *The Performing School*, London, Routledge.

Balshaw, M. and Farrell, P. (2002) *Teaching Assistants*, London, David Fulton.

Beatty, B. (2008) 'Theories of Learning', in Lumby, J., Crow, G. and Pashiardis, P. (eds), *International handbook on the preparation and development of school leaders*, London, Routledge.

Best, R. (2000) 'The training and support needs of deputy headteachers', *Professional Development Today*, 4 (1), 39–50.

Blandford, S. (2000) *Managing Professional Development in Schools*, London, Routledge.

Brighouse, T. (1991) *What Makes a Good School?* Stafford, Network Educational Press.

Brookfield, S. (2005) *The power of critical theory: Liberating adult learning and teaching*, San Francisco, Jossey-Bass.

Burton, T. (1994) 'The photocopy lady: the role of the reprographics supervisor', in Crawford, M., Kydd, L. and Parker, S. (eds), *Educational Management in Action: A Collection of Case Studies*, London, Paul Chapman Publishing.

Bush, T. and Glover, D. (2003) 'Leadership development for early headship', *School Leadership and Management*, 25 (3), 217–239.

Cardno, C. (2012) *Managing effective relationships in education*, London, Sage.

Chisholm, L. and Vally, S. (1996) *The Culture of Learning and Teaching in Gauteng Schools*, Witterand Education Policy Unit.

Coleman, M. (2003) 'Developing a culture of learning and teaching', in Coleman, M., Graham-Jolly, M. and Middlewood, D. (eds), *Managing the Curriculum in South African Schools*, London, Commonwealth Secretariat.

Cordingley, P., Bell, M. and Thomason, S. (2004) *Continuing professional development: the evidence base.* Centre for Use of Research and Evidence in Education (CUREE).

Cummings, C., Dyson, A., Mujis, D., Papps, I., Raffo, C., Tiplady, L. and Todd, L. (2007) *Evaluation of the Full-Service Schools Initiative: Final Report*, London, DfES.

Dalin, P. (1994) *How Schools Improve*, London, Cassell.

Day, C. (1999) *Developing Teachers: The Challenges of Lifelong Learning*, London, Falmer Press.

Dinham, S., Aubusson, P. and Brady, L. (2008) 'Distributed leadership as a factor in and outcome of teacher action learning', *International Electronic Journal for Leaders in Learning*, available at http://people.ucalgary.ca/~huartson/iejll/volume12/dinham.htm_ (accessed November 2012).

Draper, I. and McMichael, M. (2000) 'Secondary School Identities and Career Decision-making,' *Scottish Educational Review*, 32 (2), 155–167.

Dryfoos, J., Quinn, J. and Barkin, C. (2005) *New Community Schools in Action*, Oxford, Oxford University Press.

Earley, P. and Bubb, S. (2004) *Leading and Managing Continuing Professional Development*, London, Paul Chapman Publishing.

Emira, M. (2011) 'I am more than a TA!' *Management in Education*, 25 (4), 163–174.

Foreman-Peck, L. and Middlewood, D. (2002) *Formative Evaluation of the Foundation Degree for Teaching Assistants*, Northampton, University College Northampton.

Freed, J. (2001) 'Why become a learning organisation?' *About Campus*, 5 (6), 16–21.

Gardner, H. (1983) *Frames of Mind: The Theory of Multiple Intelligences*, New York, Basic Books.

Golman, D. (1996) *Emotional Intelligence*, London, Bloomsbury.

Hargreaves, A. (1997) 'From reform to renewal: a new deal for a new age', in Hargreaves, A. and Evans, R. (eds), *Beyond Educational Reform*, Buckingham, Open University Press.

Holyoke, L., Sturko, P., Wood, N. and Wu, L. (2012) 'Are academic departments perceived as learning organisations?' *Educational Management Administration and Leadership*, 40 (4), 436–448.

Honey, P. (1993) *Creating a Learning Organisation*, Maidenhead, Peter Honey Publications.

Hopkins, D., Ainscow, M. and West, M. (1994) *School Improvement in an Era of Change*, London, Cassell.

Jansen, J. and Middlewood, D. (2003) 'From Policy to Action: Issues of Curriculum Management at School Level', in Coleman, M., Graham-Jolly, G. and Middlewood, D. (eds), 'Managing the Curriculum in South African Schools', London, Commonwealth Secretariat.

Kidd, L. (2012) 'Relational agency and pre-service trainee teachers: using student voice to frame teacher education pedagogy', *Management in Education*, 26 (3), 120–129.

King, F. (2011) 'The role of leaders in developing and sustaining teachers' professional learning', *Management in Education*, 25 (4), 149–155.

Knowles, M. (1980) *The modern practice of adult education*, NY, Cambridge Books.

Lambert, L. (2003) *Leadership capacity for lasting school improvement*, Alexandria VA, Association for Supervision and Curriculum Development.

Law, S. and Glover, D. (2000) *Educational Leadership and Learning*, Buckingham, Open University Press.

McCharen, B., Song, J. and Martens, J. (2011) 'School Innovation: the mutual impacts of organisational learning and creativity', *Educational Management Administration and Leadership*, 39 (6), 676–694.

Merriam, S. (2001) *The New Update on Adult Learning Theory*, San Francisco, CA, Jossey-Bass.

Middlewood, D. (1997) 'Managing staff development', in Bush, T. and Middlewood, D. (eds), *Managing People in Education*, London, Paul Chapman Publishing.

Middlewood, D. (2001) 'The future of managing teacher performance and its appraisal', in Middlewood, D. and Cardno, C. (eds), *Managing Teacher Appraisal and Performance: A Comparative Approach*, London, RoutledgeFalmer.

Middlewood, D. (2003) 'Teacher professionalism and development', in Coleman, M., Graham-Jolly, M. and Middlewood, D. (eds), *Managing the Curriculum in South African Schools*, London, Commonwealth Secretariat.

Middlewood, D. and Parker, R. (2009) *Leading and Managing Extended Schools*, London, Sage.

Middlewood, D., Coleman, M. and Lumby, J. (1998) *Practitioner Research in Education: Making a Difference*, London, Paul Chapman Publishing.

Middlewood, D. Parker, R. and Beere, J. (2005) *Creating a Learning School*, London, Paul Chapman Publishing.

Neil, P. and Morgan, C. (2003) *Continuing Professional Development for Teachers: From Induction to Senior Management*, London, Kogan Page.

Parker, R. (2011) 'The impact on school culture,' in Middlewood, D., Parker, R. and Piper-Gale, J. (eds), *Learning Through Research*, Leicester, Beauchamp College.

Piggot-Irvine, E. (2010) 'One school's approach to overcoming resistance and improving appraisal: organisational learning in action', *Educational Management Administration and Leadership*, 38 (2), 229–245.

Purdon, A. (2004) 'Perceptions of the educational elite on the purpose of a national framework for continuing professional development for teachers in Scotland', *Journal of Education for Teaching*, 30 (2), 131–149.

Revans, R. (1982) *The origins and growth of action learning*, Bromley, Chartwell-Bratt.

Ribbins, P. (2008) 'A life and career-based framework for the study of leaders in education', in Lumby, J., Crow, G. and Pashiardis, P. (eds), *International handbook on the preparation and development of school leaders*, London, Routledge.

Sammons, P., Power, S., Elliot, K., Robertson, P., Campbell, C. and Whitty, G. (2003) *New community schools in Scotland: final report, national evaluation*, London, Institute of Education, University of London.

Slater, L. (2008) 'Pathways to building leadership capacity', *Educational Management Administration and Leadership*, 36 (1), 55–69.

Stoll, L., Fink, D. and Earl, L. (2003) *It's About Learning (and It's About Time)*, London, RoutledgeFalmer.

Strain, M. (2007) 'Some ethical and cultural implications of the leadership "turn" in education: on the distinction between performance and performativity', *Educational Management Administration and Leadership*, 37 (1), 67–84.

Sugimine, H. (1998) 'Primary schooling in Japan', in Moyles, J. and Hargreaves, L. (eds), *The Primary Curriculum: Learning from International Perspectives*, London, Routledge.

Svinicki, M. (1996) *When teachers become learners*, Centre for Teacher Effectiveness, University of Texas.

Taysum, A. (2010) *Evidence informed leadership in education*, London, Continuum.

Thrupp, M. (1999) *Schools making a difference. Let's be realistic!*, Buckingham, Open University Press.

Woollard, J. (2012) 'When teaching a class of daemons, dragons and trainee teachers – learning the pedagogy of the virtual classroom', *Management in Education*, 26 (2), 45–51.

Zhang, W. and Brundrett, M. (2011) 'School leaders' perspectives on leadership learning: the case for informal and experiential learning', *Management in Education*, 24, (4), 154–158.

14

Succession planning and leadership development

Introduction

Succession planning has become increasingly important because of the shortage of headship applicants in England, and in many other countries (Bush 2008; Thomson 2009; Thompson 2010). Thomson (2009, p. 32) says that 'succession planning is a major plank in any cogent strategy to address the risks inherent in the "supply problem"'. Leadership development is a central part of any succession planning strategy. This chapter discusses succession planning and links it to leadership development, drawing on evidence from several countries.

What do we mean by succession planning?

Hargreaves and Fink (2006) say that 'effective succession means having a plan and making plans to create positive and coordinated flows of leadership, across many years and numerous people'. It also identifies four 'succession challenges' that need to be addressed as part of a co-ordinated strategy. These are the retirement boom, negative perceptions of the job, a drawn out apprenticeship and significant regional variations.

These challenges apply in several countries. The post-war 'baby boom' affected many nations, perhaps particularly those in Europe, and the 'drawn out apprenticeship' is a factor in some education systems. Cyprus and Malta, for example, both tend to appoint highly experienced teachers as heads. '[In Cyprus], the average age of principals on first appointment is around 55' (Pashiardis 2003, p. 36).

Thomson (2009, p. 31) identifies seven elements of the head teacher 'supply problem'. She points to a lack of applicants and a particular shortage in specific locations. These shortages are caused by concerns about the nature of the headship role, notably the heavy workload and perceived low pay. Linked to the low number of applications, particularly from women and ethnic minorities, is a lack of quality which often leads to the need to re-advertise the vacancy. These negative perceptions also impact on leader retention (see Chapter 10).

In centralised systems, the bureaucracy is involved in defining criteria for leadership succession and in selecting candidates for preparation and/ or preferment. Because England does not have a centralised system, it is not possible to adopt this approach. The English NCSL says that succession planning 'is not a problem that can be handled by government or any single agency acting alone. It is a system-wide challenge' (NCSL 2007, p. 5). This view is reflected in the 'local solutions' strategy adopted by NCSL as a central element of its succession planning programme.

In decentralised systems, people interested in leadership positions may be able to 'self nominate' by applying for available posts. The main limitation of this approach is that insufficient well-qualified candidates may submit themselves for scrutiny. Because career development is the prerogative of the applicant, rather than the employer, it is not possible to adopt a planned approach. In England, for example, the governing body of each school appoints its headteacher while, in South Africa, the responsibility is shared between the school governing body and the provincial education department (Bush 2008; Bush et al. 2011).

Thomson (2009, pp. 36–37) says that relying on potential leaders to identify themselves is a 'risky assumption'. They may not do so for a range of reasons, including family responsibilities, or because, as BME teachers, they do not wish to be culturally isolated, or because they work for a workaholic head and do not wish to emulate this approach.

The second strategy, typically used by centralised systems, is a planned approach, leading to central decisions about who should be considered for promotion. This approach reduces the 'chance' element, and provides the potential for smooth leadership succession, but may be criticised because it does not facilitate equal opportunities (Bush 2008). The Singapore government, for example, identifies suitable teachers for promotion, as Chong et al. (2003, p. 167) indicate:

In the Singapore context, [leadership succession] has not been left to chance. The Ministry of Education has drawn up a framework where promising teachers are selected for various leadership or managerial positions in the school.

One of the problems of such an approach is that it tends to reproduce the qualities of the existing group of principals. This reproductive stance has been described as 'cloning' (Thomson 2009) and 'ascriptive' (Gronn and Ribbins 2003). These terms both refer to the personal characteristics of individuals, leading to the appointment of a leadership cohort from a narrow social base. These personal characteristics may be related to gender, ethnicity, age and social class. Such features combine to create an 'identity' and may lead certain leaders not to pursue promotion to the principalship because their identity does not 'fit' the perceived requirements in the relevant context. In Cyprus, for example, age is the main factor influencing appointments but most new principals are also male (Pashiardis and Ribbins 2003). This issue also makes the notion of 'talent spotting', one aspect of the NCSL succession planning initiative, highly problematic. Only talent fitting the desired profile is likely to be 'spotted'. Bush et al. (2007) note that BME leaders often decided not to seek promotion, because they were told by their existing principals that they were not 'ready' for headship.

Succession planning in England

The NCSL has developed its own succession strategy to alleviate the problem and provide a secure supply of qualified heads. The NCSL approach involved the provision of earmarked funding to local authorities (LAs) to enable them to find their own 'local solutions' to the problem. The NCSL also appointed 23 National Succession Consultants (NSCs) to work alongside LAs as they formulated their own customised responses to this problem. This part of the chapter draws on the evaluation[1] of the programme (Bush et al. 2009b; Bush 2011).

The scale and nature of the succession problem

The NCSL (NCSL 2007, p. 6) shows that the 'retirement boom' means a need for a 15–20% increase in the number of school leaders 'to maintain a healthy supply of good quality candidates for headship'. It also points to particular challenges in inner London, faith schools, notably in the Catholic sector, and small schools.

The authors' survey and case study data showed that primary schools are experiencing greater difficulties than the secondary sector, although the problems in both sectors are easing. There were four main themes:

- Recruitment to primary schools is more difficult than to secondary schools. The final survey shows 58 per cent of LA respondents reporting 'problems' in making appointments for primary headships, but only 28.4 per cent doing so for secondary schools.

- Faith schools, especially in the Catholic sector, present particular problems. In one diocese in northern England, participants report that it takes two or three advertisements to create a viable short list.

- Small rural schools are a particular challenge because of the demands on teaching heads and the low salary differentials.

- There are concerns about closure or reorganisation in some areas. Potential heads do not apply to such schools because of the uncertainty over their future.

Recruitment

As noted earlier, there are significant recruitment problems for many English primary schools, notably in rural areas, and in faith schools. Seven of the 12 case studies have clearly articulated arrangements to enhance recruitment to headships and other leadership positions within their LAs. These are often seen as part of a 'grow your own' strategy, and may involve 'talent identification' (Thomson 2009). For example, one case study LA has established a 'Primary Greenhouse Network', linked to an intention to expand the 'pipe' of new heads. This is targeted at 'lead learners' with leadership potential.

Leadership development

The notion of 'growing your own' leaders often links to wider provision for leadership development. Thompson (2010, p. 98) says that 'leadership development should not be left to chance, but should be part of a planned effort at all levels from the broader organisation through to the leader. This [is a] call to grow your own leaders'. Similarly, Davies and Davies (2011, p. 73) point to the need for 'talent development' in education. One recent example of talent development is the Fast Track programme introduced by the UK government. Jones (2010, p. 162) states that this was a 'highly valued learning experience' but he adds that it 'cannot relieve all concerns about the next generation of school leaders' (ibid.).

Providing sufficient and suitable opportunities for leadership development is a significant strand in the NCSL's succession planning programme. Effective leadership is increasingly regarded as a vital component of successful organisations. The research shows that new principals experience great difficulty in adapting to the demands of the role (Bush and Oduro 2006; Daresh and Male 2000). The process of professional and organisational socialisation is often uncomfortable as leaders adapt to the requirements of their new post. Developing the knowledge, attributes and skills required to lead effectively requires systematic preparation. Recognition of the importance of specific training and development has grown as the pressures on school principals have intensified. The greater complexity of school contexts, allied to the trend towards site-based management in many countries, has heightened the need for preparation. There is also an acceptance of the moral basis for specific training and a growing body of evidence showing that preparation makes a difference to the quality of leadership and to school and pupil outcomes (Bush 2008; Bush and Oduro 2006; Lumby et al. 2008).

Nine of the 12 English case studies in the succession planning evaluation (Bush 2011; Bush et al. 2009b) have introduced arrangements to develop their leaders. These include clearly targeted activities for all levels of leadership, including programmes for aspiring leaders, specific training for BME teachers, targeted support for National Professional Qualification for Headship (NPQH) graduates, a deputy heads' support group, a middle leaders' conference, and robust mentoring programmes at all levels. One case study adopts a 'personalised' approach, including induction and mentoring for new heads, courses for 'aspiring' and 'future' leaders, and a deputy heads' network, including an annual residential conference. Another LA has opened its own Leadership College to co-ordinate development activities.

New models of leadership

The NCSL (2007, p. 10) discusses new models of headship which are 'emerging to cope with the demands of modern school leadership'. These include federations, co-headships and executive headships. Thomson (2009, pp. 41–42) notes this trend but cautions that it is 'far too soon to ascertain whether this is an effective supply solution'. Davies and Davies (2011, p. 151) advocate inter-school collaboration to enhance talent development, especially for smaller schools, and also point to the emergence of more formal arrangements, such as soft and hard federations.

Four of the 12 English case studies have engaged with one or more of these new models (Bush 2011). One London LA, for example, has used federations to address recruitment problems. Where schools experience problems, or receive a critical inspection report from Ofsted, a federation is often used as a strategy, linking a successful school with the school requiring support. One such federation appears to have been successful, with key stage 2 results improving dramatically and a positive Ofsted report. However, the key question is whether the gains are inherent in the federation model or simply a product of visionary leadership.

The prospect of schools being 'federated' has acted as a disincentive for some potential heads. In one case study, for example, the network leader reports that 'it is difficult to recruit to small schools for the fear of imminent closure or fear of absorption into a federation' (Bush 2011).

Federations may be regarded as an example of inter-school networking although the process is much more formal, and is often prescribed by the local authority, rather than being voluntary, as suggested in the literature (for example, Townsend 2010).

Diversity issues

The NCSL believes that a diverse leadership workforce – one that draws from all the talents and experiences of people from different backgrounds – is a stronger and more effective workforce (NCSL, 2009, p. 1). However, this view is not reflected in the appointment of significant numbers of BME leaders in England (Bush et al. 2007) and elsewhere:

> Schools in Western countries are overwhelmingly run by white administrators. This is the result of racist institutional practices which allow limited numbers of people ascribed with 'minority heritage' to become teachers. (Thomson 2009, p. 21)

To help address this problem, the NCSL appointed three diversity consultants and also provided targeted funding to those LAs actively seeking to diversify their leadership workforce.

The survey of LA partners (Bush et al. 2009b) asked them to assess the implementation of diversity policy within their LAs. Contrary to the intentions of the NCSL, the responses indicated that there has been limited progress in matching ethnic representation to that of the population. Only 4 of the 12 case studies appear to be giving a high priority to this issue. These are all diverse urban LAs. These positive strategies are underpinned partly by an equal opportunities perspective and partly by a wish to recruit more BME leaders to help in addressing the wider problem.

The other eight case studies give little attention to this issue. BME leadership is a low priority, and this is justified by reference to predominantly white communities and by a view that simply filling vacancies is more important than being concerned with ethnic balance. However, evidence from earlier studies also shows that heads are reluctant to assess BME teachers favourably when considering possible promotions (Bush et al. 2007; Thomson 2009).

The importance of leadership development

There is great interest in educational leadership in the early part of the twenty-first century. This is because of the widespread belief that the quality of leadership makes a significant difference to school and student outcomes. In many parts of the world, including both developed and developing countries, there is increasing recognition that schools require effective leaders and managers if they are to provide the best possible education for their students and learners. Pashiardis (2001) argues that educational leaders should be 'torchbearers' for educational change and Leithwood et al. (2006, p. 4) show that 'school leadership is second only to classroom teaching as an influence on pupil learning'.

While the argument that leadership *does* make a difference is increasingly, if not universally, accepted, there is ongoing debate about what preparation is required to develop appropriate leadership behaviours. This relates to conceptions of the principal's role, 'preparation for what?' (Crow et al. 2008, p. 3). In many countries, school leaders begin their professional careers as teachers and progress to headship via a range of leadership tasks and roles, often described as 'middle management'.

Principals may continue to teach following their appointment, particularly in small primary schools. This leads to a widespread view that teaching is their main activity (Roeder and Schkutek 2003, p. 105). This underpins the view that a teaching qualification and teaching experience are the only necessary requirements for school leadership. Bush (2008) notes that principals in Africa and much of Europe are often appointed on the basis of a successful record as teachers with the implicit assumption that this provides a sufficient starting point for school leadership. However, the increasing literature on leadership development in the twenty-first century (for example, Bush 2008; Hallinger 2003; Huber 2004; Lumby et al. 2008; Watson 2003) portends a sea change in attitudes accompanied by a more limited but still tangible shift in policy and practice. These authors and editors point to a growing realisation that headship is a specialist occupation that requires specific preparation.

The journey from classroom teacher to school principal usually involves the gradual accumulation of leadership responsibilities, linked to a reduction in the teaching role. Middle leaders, for example, typically receive some 'non-contact' time to compensate them for their work outside the classroom. Although the extra time is widely regarded as inadequate (Bush 2010; Bush and Glover 2008), it provides a modest recognition that leadership is a different role, with discrete demands.

Many second-tier leaders (variously described as deputy or vice-principals, assistant, associate or deputy heads) often have substantial non-contact time, which may be 50 per cent or more, depending on school size and the availability of financial and human resources. Most principals are either full-time leaders, or have only a limited classroom teaching role, suggesting a substantial shift over time from teacher to leader (Bush 2010). Ideally, each of these stages should be accompanied by specific preparation and development but, in practice, the main or exclusive focus in most countries is on preparing principals. This links to what Gronn (2002) describes as the 'heroic' model of leadership where the principal is held accountable for school outcomes, neglecting the reality that effective schools require many successful leaders, not just a competent principal.

Towards customised leadership development

In some countries, the need for customised leadership preparation is becoming evident. What may be presented as 'generic' components of leadership have been dismissed by Leithwood et al. (1999, p. 4) as 'never more than the "basic skills" of leadership' because 'outstanding leadership is exquisitely sensitive to the context in which it is exercised'. Southworth (2005, p. 77) adds that 'where you are affects what you do as a leader'.

It is a small step from acknowledging context-specific leadership to advocating the desirability of customised development opportunities for school leaders. Heck (2003) uses the twin concepts of professional and organisational socialisation as a lens to examine the impact of preparation. Professional socialisation includes formal preparation, where it occurs, and the early phases of professional practice. Organisational socialisation involves the process of becoming familiar with the specific context where leadership is practised. This distinction is helpful in thinking about how leadership preparation and development should be planned. Where leaders are preparing to take a more senior position, such as principal, they are engaged in a process of professional socialisation. Because future leaders rarely know where they will be appointed, context-specific preparation is not possible, although developing skills of situational analysis is both possible and desirable. In-service leadership development, however, needs to include a significant element of school-specific learning. This leads to a consideration of the nature of leadership preparation and development.

The curriculum for leadership development

Bolam (1999, p. 196) argues that leadership development can be grouped into four modes:

- knowledge for understanding

- knowledge for action

- improvement of practice

- development of a reflexive mode.

Content-led programmes, particularly those provided by universities, may be regarded as predominantly aiming at 'knowledge for understanding'. Each programme has a 'curriculum' that gives an indication of the topics to be included. Bush and Jackson (2002, p. 421) conclude that there is an 'international curriculum' for school principal preparation:

> Most courses focus on leadership, including vision, mission and transformational leadership, give prominence to issues of learning and teaching, often described as instructional leadership, and incorporate consideration of the main task areas of administration or management, such as human resources and professional development, finance, curriculum and external relations.

In the USA the content is linked to the Standards for School Leaders, developed by the Interstate School Leaders Licensure Consortium (ISLLC). Bjork and Murphy (2005, p. 14) claim that such programmes 'tend to place greater emphasis on the application of knowledge to improve practice than on theoretical issues' (p. 15). In Singapore, there has been a national programme for school principals since 1984. The most recent version of this course, Leaders in Education, introduced in 2001, stresses 'delivery' rather than curriculum content (Chong et al., p. 170). This example illustrates a widespread shift in emphasis in the twenty-first century, from content to process, from 'what' is included in development programmes to 'how' they are designed and delivered.

Leadership development processes

Bolam's (1999) categories of 'knowledge for action', and 'improvement for practice' (see above) suggest a focus on process rather than content. Instead of the adoption of a prescribed curriculum, leaders are developed through a range of action modes and support mechanisms, often customised to the specific needs of leaders through what is increasingly referred to as 'personalised' learning (Simkins 2012). Such individualisation is justified because school leaders are adults, and senior professionals, who expect to be involved in determining their own leadership learning.

Personalised learning can be achieved in several ways, including facilitation, mentoring, coaching, networking, and portfolios (see Chapter 11 for a discussion of mentoring and coaching). Bush et al.'s (2007) overview of NCSL evaluations shows that networking is the most favoured mode of leadership learning. It is likely to be more effective when it is structured and has a clear purpose. Its main advantage is that it is 'live learning' and provides strong potential for ideas transfer. Visits with a clear purpose may also lead to powerful leadership learning. Visiting similar contexts (for example, other small primary schools) appears to be particularly valuable.

Internships can be seen as a specific form of networking and Crow (2001) argues that this may help with professional socialisation. Huber (2008, p. 171) claims that school-based internships may be regarded as 'the authentic workplace' to assure 'adequate complexity and authenticity leading to the learning processes required'. He notes that interns often shadow leaders, then partially take over leadership tasks and carry out projects independently. Rusch (2008, p. 228) comments that internships have replaced the traditional requirement for school leaders to demonstrate mastery of leadership knowledge. Heck (2003, p. 247) adds that internships helped aspiring principals to develop 'a clear understanding of their roles and responsibilities'.

The impact of leadership and management development

There is widespread belief in the efficacy of development programmes, leading to the introduction and growth of such interventions in many countries (Bush 2008; Hallinger 2003; Huber 2004; Lumby et al. 2008; Watson 2003). Governments are investing substantial sums on leadership and management development because they believe that it will produce better leaders and more effective education systems. Individuals are also contributing their time, and often their own resources, to their own professional development because they think that it will enhance their career prospects and make them better leaders. However, the empirical evidence for such assumptions is modest (Bush 2008; Leithwood and Levin 2008).

Leadership development programmes are often subject to evaluation but the approaches usually employed are subject to two main limitations:

1   They rely mainly or exclusively on *self-reported evidence*. Participants are asked about their experience of the activity and, more rarely, about its impact on their schools. This is a weak approach because it is not subject to corroboration, for example by colleagues, and because it is inevitably subjective.

2   The evaluation is usually *short-term*. Participants' views are often sought during and/or at the end of the development activity. It is widely recognised that the impact of interventions, such as a leadership programme, takes time. It is unlikely that significant changes in leadership practice will have occurred during the training period (Bush 2008, p. 114).

Even where these two pitfalls are avoided, there is still the problem of attributing beneficial effects to the development activity when there are likely to be many other contemporaneous events that could also contribute to change. However, addressing the two limitations set out above would produce more credible, if not totally reliable, findings.

The weaknesses of self-reporting can be addressed through adopting role set analysis. The perceptions of programme participants can be triangulated (Bush 2012) by seeking views from close colleagues at the school or workplace. This enables candidates' claims to be corroborated or challenged by the perceptions of those who should be aware of changes in practice. The authors adopted this approach in three impact studies, two for the NCSL (Bush and Glover 2005; Bush et al. 2006) and one in South Africa (Bush et al. 2011).

Leadership development and succession planning in South Africa

The South African DBE has introduced a new threshold qualification[2] for aspiring school principals as part of its wider strategy to improve educational standards. This links to concerns about the disappointing learner outcomes in national tests, and the belief that raising leadership quality would lead to enhanced learner performance.

The scale and nature of the succession problem

Unlike in England, the supply of school principals is not a problem, and turnover is low. The main issue relates to the *quality* of school leadership and a principal's qualification is seen as one way of improving leadership performance.

Recruitment

As noted above, there are few problems with the supply of principals in South Africa. The main issues here relate to the perceived quality of school principals, especially in township and deep rural schools. As a consequence, there is no specific recruitment initiative in South Africa, partly because principals remain in post for many years, leading to an attrition rate as low as five per cent (Bush et al. 2009; Bush et al. 2011).

Leadership development

The main focus of the South African initiative is to enhance the quality of existing and prospective principals through a new course: the ACE: School Leadership. From 2007, the course was tested nationally with candidates, including serving principals, as well as members of SMTs. The ACE is being delivered by universities, through a common framework agreed with the DBE. The course rubric stresses its applied nature: 'Its primary purpose is to ascertain how much of the course learning has been internalised, made meaning of and applied in practice in the school.'

This part of the chapter reports the evaluation[3] of the ACE programme (Bush et al. 2009; Bush et al. 2011). The research examined all aspects of the course, including:

- contact sessions
- teaching materials
- mentoring
- networking.

Contact sessions

Five universities were responsible for delivering the ACE course with the first pilot cohort. The size of the learner group ranged from 25 to 200. The research shows that there is a link between class size and levels of interactivity. Despite the aspirations of most lecturers, interaction is very limited in the larger groups, thus working against the philosophy of the programme. Most universities deal with the problem of scale by also providing smaller group facilitation activities. These sometimes lead to successful, interactive sessions, as observed in three provinces. However, they may simply be used for administrative purposes, as observed with one Mpumalanga group, or result in 'no proper group work', as in the Eastern Cape (Bush et al. 2009; Bush et al. 2011).

Teaching materials

The national teaching materials were intended to be used by all providers, except in Gauteng, where different arrangements applied.

The impact survey shows very positive findings with 80 per cent saying that the materials are 'of great help' and only 2 per cent responding that they are 'of limited help'. In many cases, this was candidates' first engagement with leadership and management ideas, so they could not adopt a comparative perspective. Some of the case study candidates were more critical, saying that the materials are too long or too 'bulky', and require too many activities.

Most lecturers were content with the modules, saying that they are valuable because they are practice based. However, it is clear that the HEIs have chosen to use them in different ways. Some supplement these modules with their own resources and others make only limited use of the national programme, preferring to use it for reference, while leading with their own materials. The varied use of the materials raises questions about the extent to which the ACE can be regarded as a genuinely national programme (Bush et al. 2011).

Mentoring

The intention of the ACE programme is to go beyond knowledge acquisition to achieve measurable changes in candidates' leadership and management practice. Mentoring and networking are the main approaches chosen to facilitate knowledge transfer and enhanced practice.

Mentoring is a distinctive and central feature of the ACE programme. The matching process between mentor and mentee is critical to its effectiveness. This also links to the selection procedure. Some universities employ people who have worked with the HEI on other similar programmes. These are often retired principals, whose professional experience is seen as directly relevant to their role. In some provinces, the mentors are representative of the student population in terms of race, gender and their experience of similar school contexts, providing the potential for appropriate matching of mentors and mentees. Elsewhere, however, mentors are predominantly male, overwhelmingly white and with leadership experience in well-resourced city schools, not in the township and rural schools where the great majority of candidates are employed.

In most provinces, there is a two-stage 'mentoring' process:

- group 'facilitation' as part of, or separate from, the formal teaching sessions at the university

- visits to candidates' schools to provide on-site support.

Mentors are responsible for a number of candidates, ranging from 9 to 38. The facilitation sessions take place in groups and do not match the generally accepted definition of mentoring, which assumes a one-to-one relationship. Where mentors were able to visit schools, as in most provinces, the candidates often praised the help and support they received, but researchers' observations suggest that candidates are 'over-dependent' on the mentors, who adopt 'a tightly focused teacher–student relationship', which is not likely to lead to innovative leadership practice.

Networking

The principles underpinning the ACE include an emphasis on school managers working and learning together in networks or clusters. Most of the provinces have some form of network activity, usually initiated by the mentors or the candidates themselves. However, the evidence from the case studies is that groups in most provinces meet rarely and that the sessions are often informal and voluntary, with variable attendance levels. Where networks functioned, the prime focus was on working together to complete assignments, not to share experience in order to improve their schools. This does not suggest sustainable groups, and there is little evidence of the networks continuing following the completion of the course (Bush et al. 2011).

Diversity issues

South Africa's schools' system was stratified on racial criteria until the dismantling of apartheid structures following the 1996 South African Schools Act. Many city schools are now multi-racial but most township and rural schools remain mono-racial, and some are also mono-ethnic. Bush and Moloi's (2007) study of 'cross-boundary' leaders shows the problems experienced by black leaders appointed to previously whites-only schools. Many were subject to racism and they were often excluded from the decision-making process, even when appointed to senior management positions.

Conclusion

Problems in maintaining a sufficient supply of good quality candidates for headship have been reported in several countries (Bush 2008; NCSL 2007; Thomson 2009; Thompson 2010). Rhodes et al. (2009, p. 450) refer to the 'diminished interest' in assuming the demands of headship. These difficulties have been variously attributed to demographic considerations as leaders from the 'baby boom' era approach retirement, to negative perceptions of headship, and to inadequate salary differentials (NCSL 2007; Rhodes et al. 2009; Thomson 2009).

The NCSL's succession planning programme has enjoyed a significant measure of success. Between 2007 and 2009, problems in appointing to secondary school headships diminished and there were also fewer difficulties in primary schools. These improvements result from LAs implementing 'local solutions' such as talent identification (talent ID), leadership development programmes and, in some places, new models of leadership. Problems remain for many small primary schools, and for those in the Catholic sector.

Succession planning in a distributed system is a major challenge. While the NCSL (2007) advocates a systematic approach, this is much easier to achieve in centralised countries. In Singapore, for example, the Ministry of Education identifies suitable teachers for promotion and is able to implement its strategies through a centrally-determined appointments process (Chong et al. 2003). In decentralised systems, the approach has to be more subtle. The National College has largely succeeded in creating an appropriate climate for leadership succession through targeted funding and the support of the NSC. It remains to be seen if the momentum can be maintained (Bush 2011).

The challenges facing the South African education system are much more profound. Most schools serve deprived township or rural communities, with high levels of poverty, unemployment, child-headed families, drug and alcohol abuse, and, in secondary schools, teenage pregnancy. This provides an unpromising context for learner achievement. However, the South African government is right to judge that enhancing leadership quality would contribute to raising standards, providing it is linked with strategies to improve classroom teaching and to address the wider social context, which inevitably inhibits learning (Bush et al. 2009b, Bush et al. 2011).

The generally accepted belief that effective leadership is vital for successful schooling is increasingly being supported by evidence of its beneficial effects (Hallinger 2003; Leithwood et al. 2006; Leithwood and Levin 2008). Where there is failure, inadequate leadership and management is often a major contributory factor.

Given the importance of educational leadership, Bush (2008, p. 125) argues that the development of effective leaders should not be left to chance. It should be a deliberate process designed to produce the best possible leadership and management for schools and colleges. As the NCSL (2007, p. 17) succinctly argues, 'leadership must grow by design not by default', an implicit recognition that school leadership is a different role from teaching and requires separate and specialised preparation. The trend towards systematic preparation and development of school and college leaders, while by no means universal, has advanced to the point where the argument is widely accepted. However, there is continuing and ongoing debate about the nature of such provision.

In the past decade, there has been a global trend towards more systematic provision of leadership and management development, particularly for school principals. Hallinger (2003, p. 3) notes that, in 1980, 'no nation in the world had in place a clear system of national requirements, agreed upon frameworks of knowledge, and standards of preparation for school leaders'. In the twenty-first century, many countries are giving this a high priority, recognising its potential for school improvement.

This trend is encapsulated most powerfully by the English NCSL but it can also be seen in France, Singapore and South Africa. Candidates undertake 'centralised' training before becoming principals and receive national accreditation on successful completion of the activity. Much of the development work is work based, recognising that leadership practice takes place in schools. Increasingly, current or former principals are involved in designing, leading and delivering leadership programmes, showing that 'craft' knowledge is increasingly respected. The case for systematic, specialised training for principals is persuasive and increasingly accepted (Bush 2008).

Notes

1 The views expressed in this chapter are those of the authors, not the NCSL.
2 New principals are expected to take this qualification within three years of appointment.
3 The views expressed here are those of the author, not those of the DBE or the Zenex Foundation, which funded the research.

References

Bjork, L. and Murphy, J. (2005) *School Management Training Country Report: The United States of America*, HEAD Country Report, Oslo, BI Norwegian School of Management.

Bolam, R. (1999) 'Educational administration, leadership and management: towards a research agenda,' in Bush, T., Bell, L., Bolam, R., Glatter, R. and Ribbins, P. (eds), *Educational Management: Redefining Theory, Policy and Practice*, London, Paul Chapman Publishing.

Bush, T. (2008) *Leadership and Management Development in Education*, London, Sage.

Bush, T. (2010) 'Leadership development', in Bush, T., Bell, L. and Middlewood, D. (eds), *The Principles of Educational Leadership and Management, Second Edition*, London, Sage.

Bush, T. (2011) 'Succession planning in England: New leaders and new forms of leadership', *School Leadership and Management*, 31 (3), 181–198.

Bush, T. (2012) 'Authenticity in research – reliability, validity and triangulation', in Briggs, A. and Coleman, M. (eds), *Research Methods in Educational Leadership and Management, Third Edition*, London, Sage.

Bush, T. and Glover, D. (2005) 'Leadership development for early headship: The New Visions experience', *School Leadership and Management*, 25 (3), 217–239.

Bush, T. and Glover, D. (2008) *Managing Teaching and Learning: A Concept Paper*, Johannesburg, Matthew Goniwe School of Leadership and Governance.

Bush, T. and Jackson, D. (2002) 'Preparation for school leadership: international perspectives', *Educational Management and Administration*, 30 (4), 417–429.

Bush, T. and Oduro, G. (2006) 'New principals in Africa: preparation, induction and practice', *Journal of Educational Administration*, 44 (4), 359–375.

Bush, T. and Moloi, K.C. (2007) 'Race, racism and discrimination in school leadership: evidence from England and South Africa', *International Studies in Educational Administration*, 35 (1), 41–59.

Bush, T., Briggs, A.R.J. and Middlewood, D. (2006) 'The impact of school leadership development: evidence from the "New Visions" programme for early headship', *Journal of In-Service Education*, 32 (2), 185–200.

Bush, T., Glover, D. and Harris, A. (2007) *Review of School Leadership Development*, Nottingham, NCSL.

Bush, T., Kiggundu, E. and Moorosi, P. (2011) 'Preparing new principals in South Africa: The ACE: School Leadership programme', *South African Journal of Education*, 31 (1), 31–43.

Bush, T., Allen, T., Glover, D., Middlewood, D. and Sood, K. (2007) *Diversity and the National Professional Qualification for Headship*, Nottingham, NCSL.

Bush, T., Duku, N., Glover, D., Kola, S., Msila, V. and Moorosi, P. (2009a) *The Zenex ACE: School Leadership Research: Final Report*, Pretoria, Department of Education.

Bush, T., Allen, T., Glover, D., Middlewood, R., Parker, R. and Smith, R. (2009b) *Succession Planning Programme Evaluation: Final Report*, Nottingham, NCSL.

Chong, K.C., Stott, K. and Low, G.T. (2003) 'Developing Singapore school leaders for a learning nation', in Hallinger, P. (ed.), *Reshaping the Landscape of School Leadership Development: A Global Perspective*, Lisse, Swets and Zeitlinger.

Crow, G.M. (2001) *School leader preparation: a short review of the knowledge base*, NCSL Research Archive.

Crow, G., Lumby, J. and Pashiardis, P. (2008) 'Introduction: Why a handbook on the preparation and development of school leaders?', in Lumby, J., Crow, G. and Pashiardis, P. (eds), *Preparation and Development of School Leaders*, New York, Routledge.

Daresh, J. and Male, T. (2000) 'Crossing the boundary into leadership: experiences of newly appointed British headteachers and American principals,' *Educational Management and Administration*, 28 (1), 89–101.

Davies, B. and Davies, B. (2011) *Talent Management in Education*, London, Sage.

Gronn, P. (2002) 'Distributed leadership as a unit of analysis', *The Leadership Quarterly*, 73 (2), 1–10.

Gronn, P. and Ribbins, P. (2003) 'The making of secondary school principals on selected small islands', *International Studies in Educational Administration*, 31 (2), 76–94.

Hallinger, P. (2003) *Reshaping the Landscape of School Leadership Development: A Global Perspective*, Lisse, Swets and Zeitlinger.

Hargreaves, A. and Fink, D. (2006) *Sustainable Leadership*, San Francisco, Jossey Bass.

Heck, R. (2003) 'Examining the impact of professional preparation on beginning school administrators', in Hallinger, P. (ed.), *Reshaping the Landscape of School Leadership Development: A Global Perspective*, Lisse, Swets and Zeitlinger.

Huber, S. (2004) 'Context of research', in Huber, S. (ed.), *Preparing School Leaders for the 21st Century: An International Comparison of Development Programs in 15 Countries*, London, RoutledgeFalmer.

Huber, S. (2008) 'School development and school leader development: New learning opportunities for school leaders and their schools', in Lumby, J., Crow, G. and Pashiardis, P. (eds), *Preparation and Development of School Leaders*, New York, Routledge.

Jones, J. (2010) 'Leadership lessons from the Fast Track programme for teachers in England', *Educational Management, Administration and Leadership*, 38 (2), 149–163.

Leithwood, K. and Levin, B. (2008) 'Understanding and assessing the impact of leadership development', in Lumby, J., Crow, G. and Pashiardis, P. (eds), *Preparation and Development of School Leaders*, New York, Routledge.

Leithwood, K., Jantzi, D. and Steinbach, R. (1999) *Changing Leadership for Changing Times*, Buckingham, Open University Press.

Leithwood, K., Day, C., Sammons, P., Harris, A. and Hopkins, D. (2006) *Seven Strong Claims about Successful School Leadership*, London, Department for Education and Skills.

Lumby, J., Crow, G. and Pashiardis, P. (2008) *Preparation and Development of School Leaders*, New York, Routledge.

National College for School Leadership (2007) *Leadership Succession: An Overview*, Nottingham, NCSL.

National College for School Leadership (2009) *Diversity Project update*, Nottingham, NCSL.

Pashiardis, P. (2001) 'Secondary principals in Cyprus: The views of the principal versus the views of the teachers – A case study', *International Studies in Educational Administration*, 29 (3), 11–23.

Pashiardis, P. (2003) 'The selection, appointment and development of principals of schools in Cyprus', in L. Watson (ed.), *Selecting and Developing Heads of Schools: Twenty-Three European Perspectives*, Sheffield, European Forum of Educational Administration.

Pashiardis, P. and Ribbins, P. (2003) 'On Cyprus: The making of secondary school principals', *International Studies in Educational Administration*, 31 (2), 13–34.

Rhodes, C., Brundrett, M. and Nevill, A. (2009) 'Just the ticket? The National Professional Qualification and the transition to headship in the East Midlands of England', *Educational Review*, 61 (4), 449–468.

Roeder, W. and Schkutek, H. (2003) 'The selection, training and further education of headteachers in Germany', in Watson, L. (ed.), *Selecting and Developing Heads of Schools: 23 European Perspectives*, Sheffield, European Forum on Educational Administration.

Rusch, E. (2008) 'Curriculum and pedagogy', in Lumby, J., Crow, G. and Pashiardis, P. (eds), *Preparation and Development of School Leaders*, New York, Routledge.

Simkins, T. (2012) 'Understanding school leadership and management development in England: Retrospect and prospect', *Educational Management, Administration and Leadership*, 40 (5), 621–640.

Southworth, G. (2005) 'Learning-centred leadership', in Davies, B. (ed.), *The Essentials of School Leadership*, London, Paul Chapman Publishing.

Thomson, P. (2009) *School Leadership: Heads on the Block?*, London, Routledge.

Thompson, K. (2010) 'How strategic is the school-based planning for leadership succession?', *International Studies in Educational Administration*, 38 (1), 98–113.

Townsend, A. (2010) *Educational action research networks as participant interventions*, unpublished Ph.D thesis, Coventry, University of Warwick.

Watson, L. (2003) *Selecting and Developing Heads of Schools: 23 European Perspectives*, Sheffield, European Forum on Educational Administration.

Author Index

Subject Index

Third Edition

Leading and Managing People in Education

Tony Bush and David Middlewood

'Educational Leadership for Social Justice' Series

Titles in the series:

Lumby with Coleman (2007) *Leadership and Diversity: Challenging Theory and Practice in Education*

Bush (2008) *Leadership and Management Development*

Middlewood and Parker (2008) *Leading and Managing Extended Schools: Ensuring Every Child Matters*